BULL TERRIERS
TODAY

David Harris

HOWELL
BOOK
HOUSE

New York

Copyright © 1998 by
Ringpress Books PO Box 8, Lydney,
Gloucestershire GL15 6YD, United Kingdom.

HOWELL BOOK HOUSE
A Simon & Schuster / Macmillan Company
1633 Broadway
New York, NY 10019

MACMILLAN is a registered trademark of Macmillan, Inc.

Library of Congress Cataloging-in-Publication Data
available on request

ISBN 0–87605–076–3

Manufactured in Singapore

10 9 8 7 6 5 4 3 2 1

CONTENTS

4

To Anna
To Bess and her heirs
Partners through life's ups and downs
For the fun and the joy

ACKNOWLEDGEMENTS

This book owes much to the congeniality and responsiveness of the Bull Terrier community worldwide. I received a wealth of information and photographs, far more than I could possibly use in a single volume. My thanks and appreciation go to everyone who responded to my requests. Special thanks to the breeders in the UK and North America whose kennels are featured and also to the contributors to the chapter covering the breed around the world, namely Steve and Judy Isaacs and Jamie and Shirley Watkiss (Australia), Lotte Berg and Marianne Duchwaider (Denmark), Tuija Wegelius (Finland), Georg Scherzer (Germany), Frank and Diane Denson and Heidi Holland (New Zealand), Alice van Kempen (Netherlands), Grete Pedersen (Norway), Colin Bohler (South Africa) and Ruth Hagglund (Sweden). I greatly appreciate the help of veterinarian Dr. Carl Pew with the chapter on health care and of my wife, Anna Burke Harris, with those covering whelping and rearing.

Again special thanks to Bill and Barbara Burrows, now enjoying retirement, for permission to reproduce a number of their classic Thomas Fall photographs, to Alice van Kemper for an assortment of superb photographs of Bull Terriers simply being Bull Terriers and Viv Rainsbury for bringing the breed alive in her delightful drawings.

DAVID HARRIS

*F*OREWORD

Dr David Harris, noted breeder, judge and author of the widely acclaimed coloured Bull Terrier chronicle *Full Circle,* has again taken pen in hand. The result is a thoroughly educational and entertaining book with a delightfully fresh approach. It is guaranteed to capture the interest of newcomers and dedicated fanciers alike. David's background, expertise, and undying passion for Bull Terriers lend a style and flair to his writing that sustains your interest throughout. He has never been one to mince words or deny you his opinion, and these characteristics give the book life and set it apart.

David leads you through an extensive assortment of topics beginning with a profile of the breed, its origins and development, choosing and training a puppy, health issues, breeding principles,

whelping and raising puppies as well as training and showing. His illustrated depiction of the Standard comes alive through photographs as well as drawings, while his kennel chapters take you around the world for an in-depth look at some of the best this breed has to offer, supported by a spectacular collection of photographs.

Bull Terrier breeders and owners everywhere are fortunate to have access to a talent such as David's and we are indebted to him for his commitment to share his remarkable knowledge. The fancy has long awaited an explicit, highly informative, "fresh approach" book that deals with these ageless topics and this David has delivered in grand style with *Bull Terriers Today.* It is truly a book for all lovers of the breed.

Norma Smith
Magor Bull Terriers

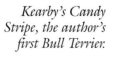

Kearby's Candy Stripe, the author's first Bull Terrier.

*I*NTRODUCTION

Looking back I marvel at the innocence with which Anna and I brought Bess, our first Bull Terrier, home. We had both grown up with dogs and were used to having them under foot. Yes, we wanted a dog to join us as an integral part of the family, but little did we realize the degree to which Bess and her heirs would impact our lives. There was ne'er a thought of showing, much less of breeding. But Bess worked her magic. We discovered the joys of Bull Terriers, including that wonderful camaraderie among owners, and were drawn fully into their world. Bess and company had snared us hook, line and sinker.

So when asked by Ringpress Books – through the offices of Andrew Brace – to write this book, I had no hesitation in accepting the challenge, combining as it does my passion for the breed, penchant for research and enjoyment of writing. Besides, Bull Terriers are such remarkable characters, as indeed are many of their breeders and owners, that there is a veritable treasure trove of material from which to select. The breed has a wonderful heritage, with anecdotes and myths galore, plus many great dogs and larger-than-life people. Yet set against tradition there is much that

changes; I view the breed as one in constant transition. Breeders are as committed today to creating an ever more dramatic downface to that hallmark Bull Terrier head, as they were in 1915 when the term downface was first introduced into the standard. And there are other changes going on too, though perhaps less obvious to the casual observer.

Hopefully, more constant is their unique multi-faceted personality, making Bull Terriers – in the admittedly biased view of their owners – the best possible friends and companions for the individual or the family. I have never resolved to my satisfaction whether over time Bull Terriers grow more like their owners, or their owners more like them. Or perhaps it's simply a matter that soul-mates attract and draw out the best – and sometimes the worst – in each other. Readers must solve this quandary for themselves.

The Bull Terrier community has always been closely knit, with leading breeders cognizant of what is happening around the world. Top breeder-judges are much in demand abroad as well as in their homelands, while Bull Terrier trophy shows are magnets for all aficionados.

There is no breed that enjoys life more than the Bull Terrier.

Photo: van Kempen.

International news and results now flash around the world with the electronic speed of the Internet, progressively breaking down the conventional barriers between countries, breeders and gene pools. Indeed, only the antiquated British quarantine laws stand in the way of near unrestricted travel for dogs as well as their owners. And surely the days of these last controls are numbered. It is with this in mind that I have reviewed not only major kennels throughout the UK and North America, but also the progress of the breed around the world, from Europe to South Africa and on to Australia and New Zealand.

Bull Terriers are wonderful dogs. I commend them wholeheartedly. However, they aren't suited to everyone and certainly not to every situation. Hopefully I have conveyed this point and also prepared newcomers for the vicissitudes as well as the many delights of owning, or arguably being owned by, one or more of them. No dogs enjoy life and have more fun than do Bull Terriers. Life without them is simply unthinkable.

David Harris, May 1997

1 PROFILE OF THE BULL TERRIER

BULL-AND-TERRIERS

The Bull Terrier was the first of several distinctive dog breeds developed from the Bulldog-terrier crosses so popular with the sporting fraternity in the UK during the 19th century. The breed shares a common heritage with the Staffordshire Bull Terrier, the direct descendants of those original crosses, and three other breeds created in America – the Pit Bull Terrier, the Staffordshire Terrier and the Boston Terrier.

Modern Bull Terriers are medium-sized dogs, but in those early days smaller specimens, often under 16 lbs (7 kg) in weight, were equally popular. These smaller dogs are now classified as a separate breed,

the Miniature Bull Terrier.

Strength and substance came from the Bulldog, while, from its terrier ancestors, the Bull Terrier inherited grace, speed and activity. The breed's character combines the courage, determination and stubbornness of the Bulldog with the terrier's quick wit and love of games and mischief. The Bull Terrier head is the breed's most distinctive attribute – long and egg-shaped, with a wicked or varminty expression.

THE PURE WHITE DOG

The breed is a product of the affluence of mid-Victorian society and the burgeoning interest of the middle classes in dog shows

Two Bull-and-Terriers, oil painting, British school, circa 1830.

Courtesy of the Remer Collection.

LEFT: James Hinks of Birmingham, the founder of the breed.

ABOVE: Hinks' Madman, the first great show dog.

and owning 'pet' or 'prize' dogs. In response to these demands, James Hinks, a dog and animal dealer of Birmingham, in the English Midlands, created a pure white dog, cleaner in lines and longer in head than contemporary Bull-and-Terriers. In 1862 he introduced the celebrated Puss to the public at a show in London, where she not only took a first prize but also came out on top in a fight with one of the older-style dogs. A couple of years later, James Hinks brought out the famous Madman, the first in a long line of dogs to bear that illustrious name. Madman became a top show dog and leading sire, doing much to establish and popularize these new 'white cavaliers'. They soon captured the public's imagination, becoming London's dog of fashion and an early example of conspicuous consumption. The old multi-coloured Bull-and-Terriers were ousted from the show ring and, indeed, from the public eye.

Little is known about the pedigrees of these early Bull Terriers. In 1868 Victor, a dog of unknown pedigree, appeared from the Black Country – the industrial area near

Birmingham better known for its Staffordshires. With his clean head and superior type, Victor assumed Madman's mantle as the leading sire and became a model for breeders. His son, Young Victor, was considered by many to be an even better specimen. Young Victor, however, was sometimes left out of the ribbons because of a brindle or brown patch on his head. Such was the resentment against any markings on the Bull Terrier's pure white coat that Young Victor (the 'mark-eye' dog) was poisoned after taking first prize at a show in Hull in 1875. The first champion in the breed was Nelson, a miniature owned by Sewallis Shirley – chairman of the newly formed Kennel Club (KC). In 1876 Tarquin, an all-white son of Young Victor, became the first full-sized Bull Terrier champion. This was the heyday of the new breed's popularity.

THE MODERN BULL TERRIER
The type established by James Hinks has changed and arguably improved considerably through the intervening years. Most breeds have been refined and

enhanced for show purposes since Victorian times, though few to the same extent as the Bull Terrier. The head has been completely refashioned with a dramatic 'downface'; upright ears have replaced the original cropped ears; even Hinks' spotless white coat is now a rarity, the modern Breed Standard permitting markings on the head and (quite unthinkable at the turn of the century) coats of other hues – brindle, black brindle, red, fawn and tricolour. Nevertheless, the breed has retained its unique character and continues to win the hearts of discerning dog owners around the world.

CHARACTER AND PERSONALITY
Distinctive as the Bull Terrier may be in appearance, it is ultimately personality that sets the breed apart and maintains its hold on discriminating owners. Most of us find that, having once owned a Bull Terrier, we are hooked for life. For many years I wrote a breed column called 'Never a Dull Moment', a title that aptly portrays our daily routine in a house full of Bull Terriers.

Their personality is multi-faceted. They can be the sweetest and most affectionate of creatures, yet, the next moment, do something quite disgraceful. Neither are they in the least bit hesitant to put us in our place if we should offend them. They delight in playing games, having fun and, in particular, acting out their roles as canine clowns for family and visitors. They possess charm in abundance, yet even this can be misdirected, such as when they attach themselves to a visitor whom they sense is afraid of them. They possess an advanced sense of curiosity and rooting around in a lady's purse, for example, will keep them out of other mischief for quite some time. Bull Terriers can also be wilful, obstinate and totally single-minded; being chastised on numerous occasions will not necessarily

Ch. Charlwood Victor Wild: Key stud dog at the turn of the century.

distract a Bull Terrier from achieving its disreputable goal several days later, by which time we have forgotten about it. All of this mischief, however, is carried out with child-like innocence, to amuse and delight us, never with a sense of malevolence. So genuine is their love and affection that it is difficult to remain annoyed with them for long.

There is no doubt in the minds of all self-respecting Bull Terriers that they are full members of their families, not appendages to be locked away in a kennel when not wanted. They demand and thrive on attention. As far as they are concerned, they want to be involved in everything. They are happy to help us – actively – read the paper, take a shower, make the bed, vacuum the carpets or cook dinner. Bull Terriers are also dedicated couch potatoes, ready to help us to take a snooze at a moment's notice. Sleeping on top of, against, or at least in contact with, a member of their family is much to be preferred. Indeed the desire to be in contact with their people is a strong breed characteristic.

Juvenile Bull Terriers have been likened to three-year-old children, a not-unreasonable comparison. At times they can be simply adorable; on the other hand there are also times when they are completely incorrigible – trouble looking for a place to happen is the expression that comes to mind. We simply have to survive Bull Terrier adolescence. The effort is well worthwhile since, like fine red wine, Bull Terriers just get better and better as they get older. This is not to imply that they become inactive and lose their sense of mischief; they do not. My eleven-year-old male still thinks nothing of charging around the house, at top speed, doing figures of eight just for fun.

Like other members of the bull-and-terrier family, Bull Terriers adore kids – they are complete family dogs. With proper early training, they are ideal companions for children of all ages from babies to teenagers. They have an innate sense of how to behave with youngsters of different ages, whether it is helping a toddler learn how to walk, being dressed up and wheeled around in a pram by a little girl, or roughhousing with older boys. And yes, they are excellent guardians of the kids, as they are of all members of their family. Their behaviour is this regard is instinctive, not a matter of training. By nature and by choice, Bull Terriers love everyone. If, however, they sense fear on the part of a family member, or a threat from a stranger, their attitude changes completely; they are all business.

How intelligent are Bull Terriers? To their devotees, they are very clever, not to say extremely smart. However, at the risk of giving a politically incorrect answer, I would suggest that, as a breed, they are probably no more or less intelligent than most other dogs and, as individuals, they run the gamut. More to the point is how they apply their intelligence. Being so people-oriented and such dedicated sybarites, they focus much mental energy on doing things to amuse and attract the attention of their family and friends on the one hand. and to cater for their love of luxury and self-indulgence on the other. Training their people, and bringing them around to their way of thinking, is a lifelong task for all Bull Terriers worthy of the name.

The oft-quoted statement that James Hinks developed the Bull Terrier as a better fighting dog is a myth. Yes, they came from stock in which gameness was of prime importance, but Hinks made his living from selling animals to the public and what he created was a distinctive canine, highly attractive to the public at large. Real fighting dogs are bred for one purpose and one purpose only, and that purpose is to fight. For the past 135 years Bull Terriers have been bred as show dogs and as pets. Are today's Bull Terriers aggressive towards other dogs? In my experience the vast majority are not, or at least they do not start out that way. Of course, individuals do vary considerably and, no doubt, a few Bull Terriers are quite aggressive. This is a most undesirable trait and responsible breeders make every effort to eliminate it from their lines. Unfortunately, at some point or other, almost every Bull Terrier, leashed or not, is subject to an attack from a loose dog. Initially, most of them are confused by such belligerence and do not respond immediately in kind. But, if exposed two or three times to such unprovoked aggression, the Bull Terrier's pride asserts itself and his fine physique usually assures him of coming out on top. Even though the Bull Terrier did not initiate the altercation, he will probably be blamed for it. For this reason

Bull Terriers should *never* be encouraged to be aggressive towards dogs or other animals. Over the years, mine have lived happily with horses, cows, pigs, chickens and Siamese cats and, unless provoked, they have been quite civilized with strange dogs.

However, even though male Bull Terriers may be quite friendly with, or at least tolerant of, other males under most circumstances, this does not apply to living with another male dog. Sooner or later, and this may take a year or so, the two dogs will get into an argument as to which one is dominant. The tiff may begin over a toy or a bone or perhaps a local bitch on heat, but start it will and, from that point on, the two will have to be permanently separated. Examples of a male Bull Terrier living happily with another male are simply exceptions that prove the rule. A final word: Bull Terriers should never, never be aggressive towards people – it is not in their nature.

Individual Bull Terriers, of course, vary greatly in temperament as do family lines. Some are constantly busy, while others prefer to spend much of their time on the couch. To a certain degree, their characters follow those of the breeds from which they were developed. Heavyweights have more in common with Bulldogs, being far less busy and more easy-going than the lighter-weight terrier-types, though they give away nothing in terms of stubbornness. A few Bull Terriers fall into what I describe as a 'houndy' category; these tend to be very sweet and, to me, rather dull in comparison to typical middle-of-the-road dogs. Regardless of these variations, however, all Bull Terriers share a love of people, especially family, and a sense of fun.

A COMPANION PAR EXCELLENCE
Their many sterling qualities make Bull Terriers wonderful companions for

There is never a dull moment when you live with a Bull Terrier.
Photo: van Kempen.

individuals and families alike. Yet addictive as these qualities may be, they are not ideal dogs for everyone or for every situation. Bull Terriers can be the most demanding of dogs; they want and need to be involved with what their folks are doing. Locking them away in a crate or kennel can lead to boredom, which is their worst enemy, bringing out, as it does, the breed's most undesirable traits. Bored Bull Terriers can become destructive and bark incessantly, though by nature they are not noisy. They may begin to lick and chew their paws or take up other unsavoury habits.

Firm discipline, coupled with love and understanding, are keys to bringing out the

Comfort comes high on the list of priorities.   *Photo courtesy: Gasiorowski.*

best in Bull Terriers. The Breed Standard requires them to be amenable to discipline. The implication here that must not be missed is that they do need appropriate discipline; without it these energetic and rumbustious dogs can, all too easily, get out of hand. Bull Terriers see their families as a pack and need to understand where and how they fit into it; until this happens neither canines nor humans will be content or comfortable with the situation.

Having emphasized the negatives, I can declare without reservation that Bull Terriers are the most delightful and loving of pals – friends through thick and thin and ever-ready for a game, to entertain or just to keep us company.

2 CREATION OF THE BREED

Hinks of Birmingham,
Hinks of Brum,
Found the Bull Terrier
A tattered old bum;
Made him a right 'un,
Made him a white 'un,
Made him a dog for a gentleman's chum.

S. N. Jewot *(California)*

SOCIAL CHANGE

With the exception of a few companions to the aristocracy like the King Charles Spaniel, dogs had been developed as working animals; they had jobs to do, whether hunting, retrieving, herding sheep, killing vermin, as guards or carrying out a myriad of other tasks. In Victorian England, however, they took on a new role – one destined to become their primary function in the 20th century – that of pet or prize animals. Their changing role was driven by the rise of a large and prosperous middle class, who sought dogs that would convey status and bring prestige to their owners. In his devastating social commentary, *The Theory of the Leisure Classes,* Thorstein Veblen wrote: "The commercial value of...pet dogs...rests on

their high cost of production, and their value to their owners lies chiefly in their utility as items of conspicuous consumption."

No doubt the Victorians would have been quite horrified at such a notion. Today we would argue cogently for the dog as our best friend, the exception to the rule that money cannot buy love, and point to the enrichment of our lives that canine companionship brings. Nevertheless, conspicuous consumption was the underlying socio-economic impetus that gave rise to many new breeds, the Bull Terrier among them, and to the modern sport of pure-bred dogs, along with clubs, shows, literature and the accompanying infrastructure.

The growing public interest in dogs was reflected, in the mid-19th century, by the rise of exhibitions at which pets competed for prizes awarded on the basis of appearance or, for want of a better term, beauty. The first recorded exhibition of fancy pets took place at Charlie Aistrop's pub in London in 1851. These early dog shows were called 'leads', as they were staged prior to pit events at which bull-and-terriers fought each other or were required to dispatch large numbers of rats in short order. The popularity of these informal events led to the introduction of properly organised shows, the first two of which were held in 1859 at Newcastle and at Birmingham. The next Birmingham show in 1860 saw James Hinks win prizes with a white Bulldog and an English White Terrier. Leeds, in 1861, was the first show to put on classes for Bull Terriers; the records reveal that two were entered, Violet and Grip. They were owned by a Mr Mastkick, but we know nothing of their size, colour or conformation.

HINKS' PURE WHITE DOGS
This, then, was the social environment into which James Hinks launched his new all-white strain of bull-and-terriers. Writing many years later, his son, James Hinks Jr., described his father's creation of what was destined to become a new breed:

"Around the end of the 1850s a great change came about. My father who had previously owned some of the gamest of the old stock which he had been experimenting with and crossing with the White English Terrier and Dalmatian, bred a strain of all-white dogs, which he called Bull Terriers, by which name they became duly recognized.

"These dogs were refined and their Bulldog appearance being further bred out,

they were longer and cleaner in head, longer in foreface, free from lippiness and throatiness and necks were longer; they became more active; in short, they became the old fighting dog civilized, with all of his rough edges smoothed down without being softened; alert, active, plucky, muscular, and a real gentleman. Naturally, this change brought the Bull Terrier many admirers, and the milk-white dog became the fashion."

James Hinks made his living as a dog dealer and was known for his honesty, a rare commodity among dealers in that day and age. With the introduction of Puss in 1862 he was able to offer the public a more elegant version of the old stock and one certainly much more attractive as a fancy pet. The success of Hinks' dogs, both in the show ring and in lining their master's pocket, was recorded by a contemporary canine chronicler, 'Stonehenge' (a pseudonym for J.J. Walsh). In 1867 Stonehenge wrote: "Mr Hinks, of Birmingham, the breeder of Puss, Madman, Tartar and other celebrated Bull Terriers, has shown white dogs equal to anything we have ever seen." A few years later Stonehenge added that Hinks had held undisputed sway in the breed with his kennel of white dogs, in which a Madman always existed; an apparently identical animal who varied almost every year, as he

Champion Como. Oil painting, English school, 19th century.

Courtesy of the Remer Collection.

Tarquin, the first full-sized Champion.

was enticed away by high bids from lovers of the breed.

Naturally James Hinks did not develop the Bull Terrier entirely on his own; among his close collaborators were fellow dog-dealer Charles Boyce, who bred Champion Tarquin, and noted judge Carleton Davidson. Another friend and supporter was Bill George of London, one of the great figures in dogs at that time. Many of the leading breeders in the 1860s – men like Joe Willock, who bred Ch. Nelson, J.F. Godfree, and W.G. Mayhew – were close neighbours of Hinks in central Brum (the local idiom for Birmingham). However, such was the popularity of Hinks' creation that he and his fellow Brummies were soon in competition with breeders and exhibitors throughout the country. Another effect of the new breed's prominence was to drive the older style bull-and-terriers from the show ring. At first their presence was tolerated, but, by 1878, Stonehenge noted that the colour of the Bull Terrier "for show purposes must be pure white, though there are many well-shaped dogs of other colours. This is, however, purely a fancy breed, and as such there is not the slightest reason why an arbitrary rule should not be made, as it was without doubt in this case, and it is useless to show a dog of any other colour."

EARLY PEDIGREES AND WINNERS

Very little is known about the pedigrees of these early Bull Terriers. James Hinks played his cards very close to his chest and we have no records of how he bred Puss, Madman and company. His son's narrative was written in 1930, nearly seventy years later, and long after Hinks' death in 1878. Speculation continues as to whether Hinks crossed English White Terriers, now extinct but much like a Manchester Terrier in size and conformation, with white bull-and-terriers or whether an accidental mating between an English Terrier and one of his white Bulldogs resulted in the cross. We shall never know. His grandson, Carleton Hinks, confirmed that "he dipped slightly into the Dalmatian for this breed's movement, soundness and arched neck." This is generally acknowledged within the breed. It has also been suggested that other breeds were used, not necessarily by Hinks, during the development of the Bull Terrier, for example the Spanish Pointer, which may account for the straight tail and the tendency of some Bull Terriers to point.

The other problem in tracing these pedigrees is the repeated use of names like

Puss and Madman, with, in many cases, no way of differentiating the dogs. The KC was formed in 1873 and issued its first stud book the following year, covering the period 1859 to 1873. No less than twelve Madmans, eight Nelsons and five Pusses were registered in this first book. Names like Madman, Victor, Rebel and Puss usually indicated full-sized dogs, while others like Nelson and Dick were popular for small ones. Hinks' original dogs were referred to as 'Old' Puss and 'Old' Madman. When 'Young' Victor appeared, his sire took on the name 'Old' Victor, even though he was registered as just Victor. Sometimes the name of the dog's breeder or owner was added, as, for example, with Puss (number 2819 in the 1874 stud book), who was by Mayhew's Victor (by 'Old' Victor) out of Steel's Puss. It would be a number of years before the KC required unique names for registered dogs, and so confusion and doubts continued to cloud the pedigrees of even the leading Bull Terriers. To make matters worse, many breeders did not bother to register bitches and so nothing was recorded as to their pedigrees.

During the 1870s there was a changing of the guard as older breeders retired. James Hinks disposed of most of his dogs to R.J. Hartley of Cheshire, while J.F. Godfree sold his entire kennel, including Tarquin, to Vero Shaw, the well-known Bulldog fancier. Hartley campaigned his Violet and Magnet with great success, Magnet completing her championship in 1881. Then in 1882 came Ch. Quick, a small specimen bred, according to the stud book, by none other than J. Hinks. The two leading Bull Terriers of this decade were, without question, J.R. Pratt's Ch. Maggie May (by Hinks' Old Prince ex Kit by Dick, the last two being unregistered) and Dutch (a son of Old Victor and usually referred to as Old Dutch), owned by James Hinks' older son,

Fred. Maggie May produced a remarkable five UK champions, several sired by Dutch, and a further two in America. Though the dominant sire of his day, Dutch was never shown "as he was all wrong in front." Another leading breeder and exhibitor of this period was Bill George's son, Alf. Many Bull Terriers went abroad, with Fred Hinks and Alf George noted as the leading exporters. A number of champions and top winners went to America, including, at more than eight years of age, the illustrious Maggie May. For her new owner, Frank Dole, Maggie May produced the legendary Am. Ch. Starlight, unbeatable in her day and still able to win even when she had hardly a front tooth left, taking first in Winners at New York in 1899, when nearly twelve years old.

The closing years of the century saw a new cadre of fanciers, who were to address so successfully the many challenges facing the Bull Terrier in the early 1900s: the popular Fred North, active in the breed for more than 50 years, made up his his first champion, Streatham Monarch, in 1891; Harry Monk (Bloomsbury), a great character and veritable wizard at training and handling, did more than anyone else to refashion the breed in the years prior to World War I; the much-loved Tom Gannaway owned and bred a number of key dogs and later devoted his time to handling; W.J. Pegg made up his first two champions, Woodcote Pride and Wonder, during the 1890s; W. Ely's Hampstead dogs are behind all of today's winners; Billie Tuck began showing his famous Gladiator dogs in 1898 and remained active in the breed till 1947; Mrs Olive Milner began exhibiting in 1895 and six years later became the first lady to judge the breed.

TYPE AND SIZE
The type and points of these early Bull

Terriers soon settled into a consistent pattern. For general appearance, terms like symmetry, agility, grace and elegance were used to embellish the requirement for strength and determination. The head, which over time became a more distinctive feature than coat colour, was described as long, flat, wedge-shaped, without a stop between the eyes and without cheek muscles. Already this description of the head distances the Bull Terrier from the other bull-and-terrier breeds, all of which emphasize a short head and well-defined stop. Another distinguishing feature, the Bull Terrier's eyes, were small, black and variously described as oblong or almond-shaped; ears were always cropped. Other points included the long, slightly arched neck, short back, straight front legs, cat-like feet, deep, well-ribbed chest, and long, muscular hind legs with short hocks. The coat was characterised as short, harsh to the touch and, of course, all-white in colour. The first formal set of points or Breed Standard was published by the newly-formed Bull Terrier Club (BTC) in 1887.

The dogs' sizes varied greatly, this first Standard noting weight as 15 to 50 lbs (6.8 to 22.7 kg). At shows, Bull Terrier classes were usually divided by weight, for example under and over 15 lbs. Early on, the small dogs were very popular, but their numbers gradually dwindled and by the 1890s very few were shown. Interest then turned to what we would describe today as toy dogs, some as small as 3 lbs. These were hardly typical of the breed and did not survive World War I, after which the 'miniatures' were struck off the KC's list of recognised breeds. Efforts to revive these small dogs succeeded with the formation, in 1939, of the Miniature Bull Terrier Club and the granting of a separate KC register for them.

EAR CROPPING BAN

Many of the terrier breeds, including, of course, Bull Terriers, were shown with cropped ears. Opposition to this practice had been growing steadily. Following an impassioned speech against cropping by the Prince of Wales (later Edward VII), the KC ruled that dogs born after July 1889 were ineligible to win prizes at shows if their ears were cropped. This ruling, however, was not enforced. Then, in 1895, the Royal Society for the Prevention of Cruelty to Animals, better known as the RSPCA, successfully prosecuted three individuals for cropping the ears of an Irish Terrier. At this point the KC determined that no dog born after March 31st 1895 could, if cropped, win a prize at any show held under Kennel Club rules. This time the ban was enforced.

The impact on Bull Terriers, as well as other cropped breeds, was little short of devastating. Their popularity plummeted – the dashing appearance of these white cavaliers being quite ruined by the large, thick ears that had been developed for cropping purposes. The BTC responded by changing the Standard to accept erect, semi-erect or rose ears, with an unwritten understanding that the goal was to develop an erect or tulip ear. There was no such ban in America, where cropping is still permitted to this day. It was not removed from the American Bull Terrier Standard until 1956! So, while the breed reached a low point in the UK, its cropped cousins continued to flourish in North America at the end of the 19th entury.

3 DEVELOPMENT OF THE BREED

THE BREED RE-FASHIONED

Many challenges faced UK breeders during the early years of the new century. The popularity of Bull Terriers was at a low point, primarily because of the ban on ear cropping, but the prevalence of deafness certainly did not help their image. Dogs known to be deaf were still exhibited – some like Mascotte Cheeky becoming champions. Deafness was rife among English White Terriers and was a major factor in their demise, the last specimens being registered with the KC in 1904. With the heritable nature of deafness recognised, the BTC, in 1909, took firm action against the showing of deaf Bull Terriers and later required members to sign a pledge not to breed from or sell such dogs.

But, like a phoenix rising from the ashes, the Bull Terrier was being rejuvenated and re-fashioned at the hands of gifted and dedicated breeders. The driving forces for these changes were threefold: namely, the development of the upright ear, the downface, and the coloured coat – the latter two quite radical departures from James Hinks' vision.

Gains in the ear department were steady and progressive, though perfecting the upright ear took many years. Harry Monk was credited as doing more than anyone else to improve ears. The first prick-eared champion is believed to be Fred North's White Noel, who gained his title in 1911. The heritage of those 19th century ears persists even to this day, with quite a few Bull Terrier puppies needing assistance in getting their ears up.

It is difficult to pinpoint why and exactly when the move towards a downfaced head took root. The first mention appeared in a 1903 critique of Harry Monk's Bloomsbury Charlwood, whom W. Pegg described as having a downfaced head, the best of the year. What generated this interest in a downward curvature of the skull and muzzle in a breed requiring a flat head we simply do not know. It was incorporated in a revised Breed Standard in 1915, and has since become sine qua non for the show Bull Terrier.

Coloured patches on the coats of these white cavaliers were anathema to the BTC and its members. Marks on the head were now tolerated, but a coloured version of the Bull Terrier was unthinkable; it was like saying Staffordshires and Bull Terriers were one and the same breed. So when, in the words of Tom Gannaway, "a certain gentleman with a decided and determined kink for the emancipation of the brindle or coloured Bull Terrier" took to backcrossing white Bull Terriers with the old-style coloureds, the stage was set for a conflict that would preoccupy breeders for decades to come.

DOWNFACE AND THE EGG-SHAPED HEAD

The chief architect of the re-fashioned breed was Harry Monk. Raymond Oppenheimer compared Harry's contribution as "the improver of the modern Bull Terrier" with that of James Hinks as the originator, and afforded Monk "the credit of assembling the breed for the first time into a coherent whole". Harry purchased Bloomsbury Charlwood as an outcross. Born in 1902, this dog, as noted above, excelled in head and also possessed upright ears. He was sired by a grandson of Tom Gannaway's first Bull Terrier, Ch. Charlwood Victor Wild (a pivotal dog from whom all modern Bull Terriers are descended) out of a daughter of Ch. Woodcote Wonder. Bred back into Harry Monk's own line, Bloomsbury Charlwood produced a grandson in Bloomsbury Czar, who became the key sire of his day.

Billie Tuck was more dedicated than perhaps anyone else to producing the downfaced head and, in 1918, by doubling up on Czar, he bred the famous Lord Gladiator. Though having an incredible head for his day, Lord Gladiator was rather unsound. Indeed, Billie "always maintained that a good body could be obtained from any street mongrel." Lord Gladiator and his grandson, Ch. Crookes Great Boy, soon monopolised the top line of the pedigrees of nearly all of the leading Bull Terriers and, such is the obsession of most breed historians with this tail male, that readers

might imagine these were the only dogs of consequence. Nothing could be further from the truth. Yes, Billie Tuck did lock in the new style of head – egg-shaped and downfaced – and for this he must go down as a major figure in re-fashioning the breed. But it was W. Ely's Hampstead dogs that dominated most of the other lines of those pedigrees.

After W. Ely discovered Hampstead Heathen tied to a barrel, the dog was purchased by his friend and associate Tom Gannaway (by then using the Lillington affix). Heathen's cross was a big brown patch on his rump. That apart, however, Tom considered him the best of his sex alive. Sired by Bloomsbury Charlwood (thus the progenitor of both major lines), Heathen confirmed Tom's faith in him by siring three champions, plus the important stud Robert the Devil. The Hampstead and Lillington dogs enjoyed considerable success from about 1910 through to the early 1920s, providing the type, quality and soundness necessary for progressing the whole dog.

Born in 1921, Ch. Crookes Great Boy marked another milestone in the breed, proving himself a great stud dog and maintaining control of the tail male for his grandsire Lord Gladiator. Bred by Fred Lee, he was sired by Am. Ch. Gwent Graphite (Lord Gladiator ex a grand-daughter of Cheery of Blighty) out of Dinah Morris (Cheery of Blighty ex Kitty Lillington). Noted for his outstanding head, Cheery was a great-grandson of Hampstead Heathen, while Kitty also went back to Heathen through Robert the Devil. And so the great race to perfect the modern head was joined in full – in the UK, that is.

Meanwhile Hinks' model, or rather a refined version of it, continued to rule the roost in North America. Ears were still cropped and heads remained flat.

Contemporary writers noted the greater strength and depth of the breed in America at the beginning of the century. Also, while English fanciers focused on the downface and upright ears, their counterparts across the Atlantic began to favour a dog somewhat taller on the leg and narrower in chest. Such was the case with Humphrey Elliot's acclaimed Am. Ch. Haymarket Faultless, when in 1918 he became the first and only Bull Terrier to take Best in Show (BIS) at the Westminster Kennel Club Show. Dogs like Faultless excelled in balance and construction, and were the very antithesis of Lord Gladiator.

COLOURED BULL TERRIERS

Returning from India, where he was used to the gameness of coloured bull-and-terriers, Edward (Ted) Lyon found white Bull Terriers soft and lacking in the spirit he expected of them. With remarkable dedication and in the face of derision from the establishment, he set about – according to Theo Marples – "bringing the coloured Bull-terrier, and in particular the brindles, up to the level and type of the whites, which, for half a century, have held undisputed sway in the general public esteem and on the show bench." Ted Lyon (Sher) began his crusade about 1907. Essentially, he wanted to produce a show version of the coloureds, his focus being on "a brindle coat, a dark eye and a game temperament". He was aided in these efforts by Walter Tumner (Doncas). It is to these two gentlemen, and to Ted Lyon in particular, that we owe this infusion of colour and especially of brindle into the breed. By backcrossing white stock with coloured bull-and-terriers (Staffordshires), they systematically set about their daunting task. Head type was, of course, their most elusive challenge. It would be many years before downfaces and erect ears were obtained, and eliminating the Staffordshire's eye proved the most difficult task of all, with 'button' eyes being associated with all but the very best coloureds through to modern times.

The coloureds achieved their first milestone when, in 1919, the dark brindle Bing Boy won the first of his two Challenge Certificates (CCs). Bing Boy was by Ch. Oaksfield Gladiator, sire of Lord Gladiator, out of the brindle and white Stoat (of unknown pedigree). This first CC was awarded by Count Vivien Hollender, one of the many larger-than-life characters attracted to Bull Terriers, a long-time supporter of coloureds and never one to avoid controversy. And controversy there was, with a protest being lodged by the BTC. These, and subsequent protests against the coloureds, were unsuccessful, which simply added fuel to the fire of those who saw the coloureds as a threat to the integrity of their white breed. It would be 1931 before the first coloured champion – Bill Dockerill's Lady Winifred – was

Bing Boy, the first coloured Bull Terrier to win a Challenge Certificate.

Photo: Rouch.

*Ch. Romany
Rhinestone.*

Photo: Fall.

crowned, with none other than Count
Hollender awarding her qualifying CC. The
first coloured male to gain his title was
Boko's Brock in 1935. Both Winifred and
Brock were brindle and white.

A stalwart of the coloureds during the
1920s and 30s was Mrs Violet Ellis, who
kept her dogs in the public eye and often
guaranteed classes for the coloureds. She
had lost the brindle factor, most of her dogs
being reds. Perhaps her best-known was the
sensationally-headed Hunting Blondi, who
won his second CC in 1931 but died
shortly afterwards. The most illustrious
coloured kennel was that of Miss 'D'
Montague Johnstone. D purchased her first
Bull Terrier, the brindle Sher Fustian, from
Ted Lyon in 1927 and vowed to breed a
coloured champion within ten years. She
did so with her red Ch. Romany
Rhinestone, born in 1936. At the close of
World War Two, Meg Williams joined D as
a partner, and together they continued to
breed the world-famous Romany coloureds
until 1980. D, for her early efforts, and
both women for their post-war successes,
rank among the truly great breeders of Bull
Terriers. In 1938, the super-headed
Rhinestone was mated to R.H. Justice's
lovely brindle Jane of Petworth. From this
litter came two Ch. bitches – Stronghold
Jeanette and Lollipop – who were destined
to carry the coloureds forward and who are

behind every winning Bull Terrier today.
With the advantage of hindsight, it is clear
that this infusion of colour and the
persistence of the pioneers in gaining
acceptance of the coloured coat were
critical, arguably indispensable, to the long-
term health and vitality of the breed.

THE WHITE STUD BOOK
In 1932 *Our Dogs* published a monograph
on the coloureds by Tom Hogarth, Scottish
veterinarian and devotee of Bull Terriers.
Chapters contributed by leading geneticists
confirmed that white Bull Terriers breed
true – in other words white to white begets
white. Dr Fraser Darling noted that "the
White Bull Terrier as we know him is not a
true white...but a coloured animal
inheriting a factor which inhibits the
outward expression of the colour except in
the nose and eyes and those little flecks or
ticks of colour which appear on the body of
almost every Bull Terrier. Any whites which
arise from coloured-and-white parents
could be confidently expected to breed true
for white." Yet this scientific evidence was
largely ignored and the path ahead for the
coloureds remained a rocky one, with every
effort being made to segregate them from a
breed that its admirers believed fervently
must remain all-white. The BTC required
its members "to undertake not to breed
from 'brindle-bred whites' as the foundation

of a white strain." In practice, most members who bred coloureds bucketed such puppies.

But the tide was turning and, inevitably, a colour-bred white (CBW), Rebel of Blighty, gained his championship and was then exported to America in 1936. This caused an outcry from the British canine establishment, which soon set up a white stud book, entries to which were restricted to dogs with four generations of pure white breeding. Opposition to the coloureds and CBWs in America was even more vehement. The Bull Terrier Club of America (BTCA) and its members considered themselves the guardians of pure white dogs and continued to do everything in their power to segregate the coloureds and maintain the purity of the whites.

THE 1920s AND 1930s
During the 1920s, the re-fashioned Bull Terrier was on a roll, with numbers increasing as breeders strove to outdo each other. The new downfaced type was at a premium, with soundness often taking a back seat. In 1925 annual registrations exceeded one thousand for the first time, a far cry from the dark days of the cropping ban.

The tail male line was dominated by the progeny of Great Boy, in particular his sons Ch. Devil of Dore and Galalaw General, both of whom were doubled up on Lord Gladiator. Meanwhile, Great Boy's illustrious daughter Ch. White Rose Girl was sweeping all before her in the show ring; in the words of Harry Monk "the only fault I can see in her is that she does not belong to me." In the Midlands the name of James Hinks appeared again among the ranks of breeders, in the guise of the founder's son, James Jr. He and his own son, Carleton, were to maintain their family's involvement with the breed for

many years to come. James' first Champions were the bitch White Surprise and the key sire Hades Cavalier (double Hampstead Hell Fire), whom he purchased from W. Ely. Mated together, they produced champions White Wonder and Wonder's Double, both of whom were exported. Another successful Birmingham breeder was Jimmy Thompson, whose Dauntless Beauty produced three champions; the most important of these, to a son of Devil of Dore, was Ch. Shure Thing. To a daughter of White Wonder, Shure Thing sired Ch. Beshelson Bayshuck. In turn, Bayshuck was mated to Ch. Debonair of Brum (by Hades Cavalier) and produced the key stud dog Rubislaw, owned by Jimmy Thompson. Incidentally, Debonair, who gained her title in 1926, was the first champion to carry the Hinks family's Brum affix.

A number of the top breeders at this time were ladies. Mrs Gladys Adlam (Brendon), dubbed 'Granny Adie' many years later by Raymond Oppenheimer, entered the breed about 1907 and remained involved until her death in 1969. Her great bitch, Ch. Rhoma, went back to Hampstead and Lillington lines. In 1930 Rhoma's daughter, Ch. Brendon Becky, won the first Regent Trophy, an annual award donated by Dr Geoffrey Vevers (Regent) for the best Bull Terrier first shown that year. Rhoma's sire Silver Key was believed to have been deaf. The foundation bitch of Mrs Dolly Robbs' successful Cylva kennels was Silver Key's sister, Ch. Silver Belle, who was ultra-typey and weighed in at only 30 lbs. Mated to Galalaw General, Silver Belle produced Ch. Cylva General, sire to a Cheery of Blighty grand-daughter of Geoffrey Vevers' Regent Pluto.

The stage was now set for the spectacular advances of the 1930s. Pride of place during the first part of the decade must go to Harry Potter and his Gardenia dogs. The great-headed Ch. Gardenia, who was by a son of Regent Pluto out of a daughter of this same dog, won the 1932 Regent Trophy. Gardenia's brother, Ch. Gardenia Guardsman, won the trophy in 1934, with a son and daughter of Guardsman carrying off the trophy the next two years.

BRIGADIER, VINDICATOR AND McGUFFIN

In 1937 the celebrated Ch. Raydium Brigadier swept all before him and easily won the trophy. Doubled up on Guardsman, with a line going back to Gardenia for good measure, Brigadier was

perhaps the outstanding member of a family that excelled in heads, quality and breed type. Brigadier was a corky dog tending to the terrier end of the spectrum; soundness and movement were not his forte. He was bred by Mrs A. Clark and owned by Gladys Adlam.

The second key dog to come down from Pluto was Ch. Velhurst Vindicator, bred and owned by Eva Weatherill's sister, Peggy Phillips. He was line-bred to Velhurst Viking, a son of Pluto, with one line going back to Rubislaw. Vindicator was a heavyweight dog of superb quality and conformation, possessing a classical head – all attributes that were to be of the utmost

TOP RIGHT: Ch. Raydium Brigadier.

Photo: Fall.

BOTTOM RIGHT: Ch. Velhurst Vindicator.

ABOVE:.Ch. Ormandy's Mr. McGuffin.

Photo: Fall.

importance to the future of the breed. Rubislaw epitomized the type of Bull Terrier bred in the Midlands and North of England, much tougher and sounder than his southern counterparts, but lacking their quality of head and coat. When his champion brothers Ringfire of Blighty (1931 trophy winner) and Aberdonian were exported, it was left to Rubislaw to uphold the honour of his line. This he did with unparalleled success, becoming the leading sire of his day and producing many wonderful bitches, including the 1933 trophy winner Ch. Isis Io, and the full sisters Chs. Queen High of Brum and Cedran White Queen. Unfortunately, these fabulous Rubislaw daughters were not reproducing their virtues, despite being bred to leading dogs like those bred by Harry Potter. It was Raymond Oppenheimer who unlocked the secret when he took the unprecedented step of doubling up on Rubislaw, a dog not noted for his evenness of temperament. He sent White Queen, whom he co-owned, to Rubislaw's only champion son, Krackton Kavalier; the result was the first of Raymond's many supreme dogs – Ch. Ormandy's Mr. McGuffin, winner of the 1939 trophy and noted for his terrific substance, bone, quarters and the smallest, blackest eyes. The complementary virtues of Brigadier, Vindicator and McGuffin were to carry the breed to new heights following the dark days of World War II.

FULL CIRCLE

When shows started again after the war, Raymond Oppenheimer led the way with Champions The Knave of Ormandy and an even better sister, Ormandy's Dancing Time, whom Raymond described as "further ahead of her contemporary bitches possibly than any before or since". They were by Vindicator out of a McGuffin

daughter. Meanwhile, 'D' Montague Johnstone had bred the top winning male, the black brindle Ch. Romany Reliance, whose head was unquestionably the best yet. Remarkably, the coloureds had surpassed the whites in head, if not in make and shape. Reliance's dam Romany Rivet was doubled up on Stronghold Jeanette; he also had lines back to the three great white dogs Brigadier, Vindicator and McGuffin.

Inevitably, the first of the great CBWs arrived on the scene, when in 1949 the supremely shapely Ch. The Sphinx made his sensational debut. The Sphinx was sired by a litter brother of the Knave and Dancing Time out of a colour-bred bitch, who was doubled up on Brigadier. He was bred by Charlie Gibbons, who all those years ago had bred White Rose Girl – not a bad record. The appearance of The Sphinx was too much for Raymond Oppenheimer, who like other members, was restricted by the BTC's pledge not to use coloureds or CBWs for their pure white lines. Breeders of coloured Bull Terriers and non-members were free to take advantage of the best of the pure white stock and so were racing ahead. Meanwhile, Raymond was noticing loss of pigmentation and other weaknesses among the pure whites. Matters came to a head in 1950, when Raymond and a few supporters, including his forward-looking friend Granny Adie, were able – by the narrowest majority – to delete the outdated pledge from the club's membership forms. Events had turned full circle, with no distinction between coloured and CBWs on the one side and the so-called pure white stock on the other. Members were free to use any Bull Terrier, regardless of colour or coloured heritage. The white stud book continued for a few years, then fell into disuse. The genetics of coat colour had finally won out over generations of prejudice in the UK, the home of the breed.

This was not true in America, however. There, the battle had raged with far greater intensity – supporters of the pure white dogs digging in and fighting for every inch of ground. Initially they insisted that coloureds should be registered as a separate breed. These efforts were finally rejected in 1942 when the American Kennel Club (AKC) determined that coloureds and whites should be separate varieties of the same breed. The AKC also insisted that the BTCA, as the parent club, must take both varieties under its wing. This the club refused to do until 1949, by which time animosity had cooled sufficiently for a motion to be passed accepting ownership of the Standards for both varieties. Nevertheless, to this day, coloureds and whites, even if they are littermates, compete separately for their championships and meet only in the Group ring or when the two Best of Variety (BOV) winners meet for Best of Breed (BOB) at an independent Specialty show. America is the only country in which Bull Terriers of all colours do not compete together as a single breed, without division.

Back in the UK, the 1950s saw the emergence of two commanding stud dogs, Champions Ormandy Souperlative Snowflash and Beech House Snow Vision, who paved the way for the quality and superior type we see today in the show ring. Raymond Oppenheimer and Eva Weatherill's Snowflash was the last of the pure white stock with several lines back to each of the great trio of Brigadier, Vindicator and McGuffin. Snow Vision, bred by north-countryman John Swales, was colour-bred on both sides, being sired by The Sphinx out of a daughter of Reliance. Today's Bull Terriers all trace back many times over to Snowflash and Snow Vision, and hence back through the decades to Great Boy, Bloomsbury Charlwood and Charlwood Victor Wild.

4 CHOOSING A BULL TERRIER

He is worth the money
for his shadow on the wall.
Harry Monk *(Bloomsbury)*

THE BIG DECISION

So, having done your homework – read books, talked to breeders and owners and generally got to know the breed – you have decided on a Bull Terrier. You will be having one of those funny-looking critters (as some of your friends will no doubt comment) to share his or her ten or twelve-plus years with you and your family. This is a major commitment and one that demands discussion and consensus within the family. It is certainly not something to rush into, although, having written those words, I recognise it is exactly what most of us do.

Now you have several choices. Dog or bitch? Coloured or white? Puppy or adult? These are all questions it is wise to discuss with folk who really know and understand the breed. Such people do not include the local pet store owners, or that couple around the corner who mated their pet bitch and are now desperate to sell the pups. You should seek the counsel of a responsible, committed breeder, who can guide your decisions and prepare you for the new family member.

DOG OR BITCH?

Within the typical set of breed characteristics, individual dogs run the gamut from easy-going to very demanding, from couch potato to high-energy, from diabolical to dull. Some authors comment that there is little difference in character and temperament between dogs and bitches. Perhaps this is true for those who are used to Bull Terriers. However, for novices – those not used to the bull-and-terrier breeds – there can be a world of difference. For the uninitiated, I recommend starting off with a bitch every time. Females are smaller, more tractable and less likely to get out of control if not subjected to appropriate discipline. The male of the species is far more likely to try to take over the family – his 'pack'; he needs to understand his place in the hierarchy. A consideration in the male or female decision is whether you already have another dog in the household. Adult male Bull Terriers do not get on with other males. They may be fine as youngsters, but sooner or later there

A bitch puppy: This may be the best choice for the novice owner.

Photo courtesy: The Geist family.

The male Bull Terrier is a more challenging companion.

Photo: Scott.

will be a dispute and they will have to be separated. Regard any examples you hear of males living together happily as exceptions that prove the rule. If you already own a male, get a Bull Terrier bitch, and vice versa.

COLOUR

Colour is a matter of aesthetics and of personal preference. I prefer coloureds, in particular brindles and black brindles. Many owners, however, still associate Bull Terriers with James Hinks' original pure white dogs; others demand a white with the eye patch made famous in America by Spuds MacKenzie.

PUPPY OR OLDER DOG?

Purchasing a puppy enables you and your family to mould the newcomer to your own household norms. You get the fun of raising the pup along with the burden of Bull Terrier adolescence. An alternative that should not be discounted without due consideration is to take on an older dog. Breed welfare and rescue services have a surprising number of dogs in need of homes. Such dogs usually end up in welfare through no fault of their own – divorce rates are high, families move and cannot take their Bull Terrier with them; some owners do not see their dog as a lifetime responsibility. Taking on an older dog has

Black brindle: Nl. Ch. Asphasia vom Kindertreff.

Photo: van Kempen

many rewards; he or she should be quite civilised and should offer many years of companionship. Welfare dogs are invariably spayed or neutered before being placed in their new homes. Do not expect to secure one without your being thoroughly checked out; the welfare organisations want to ensure your home is a suitable one. It is a good idea to give a home to a rescue dog on a trial basis, if this can be arranged. Two or three weeks of living with the dog is sufficient to cement the bonds and establish a lifelong relationship. But, occasionally, a dog does not fit into the new home, in which case he or she can be returned to the welfare people without ill will.

Taking on an adult Bull Terrier is probably not a good idea if you have other animals around. A puppy can be trained to live amicably with most other animals. In England, our dogs lived happily as part of a menagerie comprising a Siamese cat, horses, Jersey cows, pigs and chickens. Bull Terriers raised with cats will accept them as pals, a member of their pack; however, an adult dog who has never been around cats and has developed a penchant for chasing will probably not settle down with a resident cat in a new home – certainly not without a great deal of effort. In these circumstances it is better to go with a puppy.

Brindle: Fin. Ch. Warmasters Christmas Cracker.

Photo: Heikkinen-Lehkonen.

*Red: Am. Ch.
Brummagem
Sterling's Bonfire.*

PREPARING YOUR HOME

You must be prepared for your pup or adult dog before actually acquiring him. A properly fenced yard or garden is essential – to keep the Bull Terrier in and other dogs out. Make sure this is in place beforehand. Also decide where the pup will sleep; the kitchen, if warm, is a good place, giving the pup ready access to the exterior of your home.

Note, however, that any Bull Terrier worth his or her salt will aspire to sleep in your or the kids' bedroom, preferably on the bed. All of our dogs have their own individual crates, hidey-holes in which they feel safe and secure from life's vicissitudes.

Some new owners are not happy with the idea of using a crate and feel it is cruel to lock a dog in one, even for a short period. At one time I too was of this opinion, but I now preach as one of the converted; our dogs love their crates and make a dash for them if they hear their biscuit-tin opened. Properly used, the crate is an invaluable tool for house-training your pup and also for transportation purposes. Remember, if you start out with a crate of puppy size, you will need to purchase a bigger one later. Old blankets make good bedding material, though purpose-made products are much longer-lasting.

*White with eye patch:
Ch. Terjo's
Masquerade.*

White without markings: Ch Swagon's Roll of Caliber, 1996 Regent Trophy winner.

FINDING A BREEDER

I would argue that, for the novice, choosing the right breeder is the key step to securing the right puppy. A knowledgeable breeder, besides doing his or her best to answer your long list of questions, can guide you through the decision-making process. You will be able to meet the dam of the litter and perhaps the sire and some close relatives, which will give you a much better idea of what to expect when the pups mature. No responsible breeder wants to place a pup in a home that is not a good match. If you have a house full of noisy, active teenagers, you do not want a quiet, retiring pup; equally, if you prefer a more tranquil existence you may not want that hell-raiser, who may have looked quite angelic after having exhausted himself prior to your arrival. Here the breeder, who has had the opportunity to assess the litter from birth, can help you to select the one best suited to your personality and lifestyle. Of course, this is always assuming that in the meantime a particular puppy has not already picked you.

CHOOSING A PUPPY

You need to focus on finding a healthy, happy, typical puppy; do not select one that fails to meet these primary requirements. *Never* buy a pup because you feel sorry for him; this may be a highly effective sales technique for pet stores, but it is not a good way to select the best puppy for you and your family. Take the breeder's advice. Often what differentiates pet and show puppies in a litter is the quality of their heads, or rather how the breeder anticipates they will turn out. Assuming you are looking for a pet puppy, you might well be able to obtain one who excels behind the collar, despite having a rather plain head.

Bull Terriers are a lot of dog packed into a medium-sized frame, so, even as puppies, they should never appear skimpy or thin-boned. You should look for a strong, plump pup, with sturdy bone, a straight front with strong pasterns, broad chest, short back, a good wide rump and well-bent hind legs. In all, the pup should appear four-square. Heads can and do change a lot, particularly in profile, but, regardless of age, a long, strong muzzle and a deep, wide underjaw are desirable. Tiny, dark eyes, set high and obliquely, are essential to that typically diabolical expression, so avoid pups with button eyes if expression is important to you.

Pups are usually ready to go to their new

White with head markings: Dan. Ch. Firebrand Kim.

owners at eight weeks of age or thereabouts. However, canine behaviourists refer to the eighth and ninth weeks as the fear-imprinting stage and advise that stress should be kept to a minimum during this period. This does not mean that you should not take on a puppy at this stage, but you do need to be aware that he may be sensitive to anything out of the ordinary. However, pups soon outgrow this and are back to being little Bull Terrors! Some breeders like to run pups for several months to aid their decision as to which ones to keep themselves. You may therefore be offered an older pup. My advice is to bring the pup home as soon as he is available and you are ready for him – preferably at about eight weeks and certainly by 12 weeks of age. The earlier the pup settles into your household the better.

THE SHOW PUPPY
In the above discussion I have made the assumption that you want a typical, healthy Bull Terrier as a family pet and have no intention of showing and breeding. However, if this is your goal, then I recommend further study of the breed and lots of patience. You should study and digest the Bull Terrier Standard, attend

shows, ask questions, visit the kennels of breeders with a track record of consistently breeding good stock and ask more questions. Please do not assume that the pup you bought purely as a companion will turn into a champion. Yes, it does occur, and perhaps you have a better chance of this happening than of winning the lottery, but not much better.

Picking puppies – in other words trying to predict what they will be like as adults – is an art and is best left to the experts, who, incidentally, quite often fail to get it right. A potential flier can turn into a dud for show purposes. As Gladys Adlam used to say "they change so, my dear!". Many things can and do go wrong; bites often go undershot or heads may not come on as expected. With the best will in the world, even top breeders cannot guarantee how a particular puppy will turn out. Frustrating as it may be, the bottom line is 'caveat emptor' – buyer beware!

But all is not lost. Successful breeders can tell you a lot about the general quality and potential of their pups. They can ensure that you have a puppy with good conformation and promise as a show dog. Because there are no guarantees, it is better to choose a female. Even if she does not turn out to be a top winner, she may well make an excellent brood bitch and, bred to the right dog, produce really outstanding pups. If a male does not quite make it in the show ring, he will have little or no value for breeding purposes – the vast majority of bitches are mated to a few outstanding dogs. Some breeders keep the most promising pups for themselves, while others are willing to part with really good ones either outright or often in co-ownership. With the trend towards smaller kennels, breeders often keep just a few dogs themselves and try to place other pups of show and breeding potential in co-ownership. Such an arrangement provides an excellent opportunity for the novice to take home a top-class pup. Obviously, it is important for there to be clear agreement on the terms of such an arrangement, preferably by means of a written contract. Occasionally, I hear of a breeder placing quite unreasonable terms on the co-owner. But this is the exception and, at their best, such contracts work to the advantage of both parties. Sometimes such arrangements develop into long-term relationships, with the newcomer becoming a junior partner, an associate of the breeder in maintaining and progressing the latter's line. In America there is a growing trend toward such partnerships. Remember, it is worth waiting for a good specimen; do not jump at the first so-called show puppy you are offered. Also remember that there are no guarantees when it comes to show dogs.

THE BREEDER'S RESPONSIBILITIES

The customer always comes first. Right? No, actually that is wrong. The primary concern of a caring breeder is matching the right puppy to the right family, with equal responsibility to both. The breeder wants to provide you with a suitable puppy that is sound and healthy, both physically and mentally. In return, the breeder wants an assurance that you are ready to take on a new family member and provide a loving home for the puppy's natural life. A responsible breeder, who is not satisfied on these counts, does not have to – and hopefully will not – sell you a puppy.

On purchasing the pup you should receive all of the paperwork – pedigree, registration certificate (if it has been returned by the national kennel club; remember only the breeder can register the pup), inoculation certificate, rearing and feeding instructions and, ideally, small quantities of the pup's food to carry you through the first few meals. Reputable breeders stand behind their stock. They should give what I would term a limited warranty on the pup's health for a specified period, especially covering any inherited problems or diseases. It cannot be an all-inclusive guarantee and should not be expected to cover conditions resulting from a subsequent injury or infectious disease for which you as the owner are obviously the accountable party. Most importantly, the breeder should continue to give advice and help and to answer those desperate telephone calls that Bull Terrier puppies, by their very nature, can so readily generate. My wife and I always tell our new puppy owners to call us any time if concerned or in doubt.

Like the vast majority of breeders, we also love to hear about the pup's progress and to receive photographs. You can imagine our emotions when, out of the blue, we received a letter from a family in Coventry, England – with whom we had lost contact after moving to America – telling us that the pup we sold them was now 19 years old and rather frail, but still enjoyed her daily walk. It is typical of the Bull Terrier fraternity that many owners become firm friends with the breeder of their first puppy.

DIET AND HEALTH

Even if you later decide to alter the pup's diet, it is important to continue to feed according to the breeder's instructions. There are enough changes going on in the pup's life without making diet another of them. Indeed, if this is your first Bull Terrier, it is advisable to follow the breeder's regimen in all respects. During this key formative stage, the pup is entirely dependent on you and your family and it is not the time for experimentation. The sooner you establish a routine for the pup the better: regular meal times, consistent house-training and discipline, time for play and lots of undisturbed sleep are all essential.

Also take the pup to your veterinarian for a general check-up. The pup should be brimming with good health, but it is reassuring for both you and the breeder to get an independent opinion. You can also schedule the pup's vaccinations and wormings and get advice regarding infectious diseases that are doing the rounds locally. If a health concern does arise, do not delay, contact the breeder immediately. In the unlikely event that the problem is a serious hereditary one, this is the time to discuss returning the pup. Again, in fairness to the puppy and to the breeder, do not procrastinate; get on the phone immediately. However, the odds are that your pup will continue to thrive and that your reports back to the breeder will be positive ones. Soon you will not be able to imagine what life was like without a Bull Terrier.

Bull Terriers thrive on love and affection.

Photo: van Kempen.

5 CARING FOR YOUR BULL TERRIER

GENERAL PRINCIPLES

Dogs are creatures of habit and do best on a routine of eating, exercising, playing and sleeping at regular hours. This is particularly important for your new puppy, and there is no better time to start than day one. Indeed, every aspect of socializing your puppy is so much easier if begun in the correct way. Bull Terriers can be the most stubborn of dogs and, with their elephant-like memories, once they have picked up a bad habit, it is amazingly difficult to set them back on the path of righteousness. For example, given an old shoe to play with, your puppy will decide that any and all shoes, even your expensive designer pair, are equally good for chewing. You may spend a lifetime trying to persuade your Bull Terrier otherwise. Similarly, if allowed to soil your home during the first few weeks, the pup will be so much more difficult to house-train than if training is begun immediately and maintained conscientiously. This advice may sound obvious and simplistic, but disregard it at your peril. Your puppy will be constantly trying you out and, once he has got away with something two or three times, you will be in trouble. The initial test of wills is

decided during the first night the puppy is with you. How will you respond to those pitiful cries from a lonely pup trying to attract your attention? I suggest stuffing cheese in your ears!

Bull Terriers demand and thrive on love and attention. They feel their purpose in life is to be with you or the kids. Given the choice, they will spend nearly all of their time helping you with whatever you are doing, whether it is preparing food (ensuring no tidbits reach the floor), assisting with gardening or just taking a nap – the only problem with this is that their definition of help may not agree with yours. However, such help is vastly preferable to the alternative, as a puppy left on his own for long periods will be bored, miserable and much more likely to be destructive and generally to get into bad habits.

Serious training – for obedience or for show purposes – should be delayed until the pup is around six months of age or older. In practice, however, training begins the moment you bring the pup home. What goes on during those formative early months – the initial day-to-day tutoring and teaching your puppy the basics, like house rules, how to walk with collar and lead, a few social skills, and, most importantly, who is boss – is arguably much more important than any formal training classes the pup may attend as a teenager.

If you are a paragon of consistency, patience and persistence, you will breeze through this trial. If not, join the rest of us; do the best you can, enjoy your successes (without taking your failures too seriously) and hopefully have some fun – along with the pup. I have the advantage of a pack of Bull Terriers to help me with a new pup. They do a much better job than I of accustoming the pup to life here at Brummagem. Remember, if you have a problem with your pup, the fault will rest with you rather than the pup, 99 out of 100 times. Problems can nearly always be traced back to what you did not do right, or perhaps what you did not do at all and should have done. So, when things go wrong, do not blame the pup.

FIRST SIX MONTHS
HOUSE-TRAINING

The sooner you start house-training in earnest, and the more persistent you are, the better. Take the pup outside whenever he wakes up, after every meal, before bedtime, indeed any time the pup appears to even think about it. Stay outside with the pup, especially at night. Make it fun, with lots of praise when the duties are completed. We place newspapers near the door just in case we do not let the pup out quickly enough. And remember, unless caught in the act, puppies have no idea why they are being scolded. Crates can be an invaluable aid to house-training. The pup will not want to soil the bedding and so will soon learn to signal that he needs to go out *now*.

FEEDING

There are as many variations on puppy-

The Bull Terrier puppy has a great sense of curiosity.

Photo: van Kemprn

feeding regimes as there are breeders. Initially, you should follow the advice of the pup's breeder; later you can decide on how best to feed your pup. Here I would emphasize the importance of the quality of the food and hence its nutritional value. The key nutrients should be present in appropriate quantities; remember you can feed too much of a good thing. Basically, dogs need proteins (containing the essential amino acids), carbohydrates (starch, sugar and fibre, though dogs' diets often contain too much starch and not enough fibre), fats (to provide fatty acids), minerals (many of them in trace quantities only), vitamins and, of course, water.

It seems simple then – just feed one of those complete manufactured dog foods!

37

Unfortunately, it is not that simple. Indeed, I am no advocate of cereal-based commercial dog foods, complete, balanced or otherwise. They may be convenient and, of course, lucrative to manufacturers and suppliers, but they are not the best way of feeding dogs. I belong to the growing cadre of breeders who have found that the closer to a natural diet dogs are fed, the healthier they are. For purely practical reasons, most of us still use some kibble, but we also feed raw natural foods like meaty bones, vegetables (shredded to aid digestion), fruit, eggs and unpasteurized yoghurt.

The importance of feeding your pup a really good diet is summed up by my wife's comment that what you do not put into them as pups you cannot put into them later. We continue to feed four meals a day, two of cottage cheese, egg yolks and goats' milk and two of raw lean beef and kibble moistened with hot water; we add yoghurt every few days. We prefer to use a kibble of medium protein and fat content, rather than puppy kibble, because we are feeding a lot of protein through the eggs and beef, as well as ample fat, and we do not want to give the pup too much. We use only stainless steel bowls – plastic ones are far too chewable. We place the bowl on a block so that the pup can eat without having to straddle the bowl with its front legs. By five to six months, most puppies are down to two meals a day, of their own volition. By this time we have replaced the beef with cooked chicken; we prefer not to feed chicken raw and so we compromise by pressure-cooking the whole chicken, bones and all. For treats, we feed dog biscuits (again quality, not cheap generic ones), cheese and whole carrots, which the pup enjoys chewing on. When teething begins in earnest we provide the pup with a beef marrowbone, having carefully checked that there are no dangerous bone splinters.

Finally, you must ensure that clean, fresh water is readily available at all times, though for house-training purposes you may want to restrict intake before bedtime.

LEAD TRAINING
The first task is to accustom your pup to wearing a collar. Use a light leather or nylon collar and, initially, put it on for only a few minutes a day while you play with the pup; it is preferable to do this when the pup is not too full of beans. Next, attach a thin lead and let the pup trail it around for a few minutes; take up the lead while talking to and playing with the pup. Some puppies learn to walk on a lead, or something approximating to it, quite quickly. With those who do not, persistence and cajoling will win through – eventually. Both conformation and obedience shows require the dog to walk on the handler's left side, so it is better to train your pup to walk on your left from day one.

By 14 to 16 weeks of age, you should be ready to teach your pup some additional commands. I am assuming the pup already understands "Good", "No" (the command I seem to have to use all too frequently with Bull Terrier puppies) and "Come", probably as much by the tone of your voice as the words themselves. Incidentally, always use the pup's name before each command. With the pup on the lead you can add "Sit" and "Stay" to your joint vocabulary. To teach the first of these commands, push down on the pup's rump while saying "Sit"; once the pup is sitting down, provide a treat and praise. Initially the pup will probably jump and cavort around immediately after each Sit, but as the novelty wears off the Sits can be lengthened progressively. Next, while in the Sit position, the pup can be taught to "Stay", which is essentially a prolonged Sit. It is against a Bull Terrier's nature to stay while you go, so this is not easy. You must be persistent and reward the pup only for staying, not for wandering off to sniff the nearest shrub or for dashing to you before being called. It is helpful to have the assistance of a second person, who can return the pup to the Sit and Stay position as needed, while you teach the pup to Stay at a distance.

Bull Terriers love being talked to, especially when they are being praised, so be lavish with your praise. Also use bribery, in the form of treats, or indeed anything that will keep the pup's attention. I still have reservations about teaching a show pup to sit – for the very good reason that my first Bull Terrier used to sit down in the ring at the slightest provocation. No doubt she did not understand what was expected of her and the fault was entirely mine. Do not let this deter you, but do bear in mind the importance of ensuring the pup really understands each command and, if in doubt, get expert advice.

The key to all of this puppy training is to have fun. It is all too easy to make your own life, and the puppy's, a misery when things do not go right or do not happen as soon as you would like. So lighten up! Remember the pup's attention span is limited and, probably, so is your patience. A few minutes spent regularly is much more effective than longer sessions periodically. Sometimes a pup will decide there is a dragon behind a particular bush or become frightened or over-excited in certain situations. Avoid such triggers – a pup who is frightened or excited will not be able to learn, and the trigger can wait till the pup is older and more confident. If the pup runs away from you, do not give chase; it is better to run in the opposite direction. And never, never chastise the pup when he or she does return (though this is exactly what you would love to do); instead give praise and a treat. On the other hand, Bull Terrier

puppies must not be allowed to get into bad habits, such as nipping at your hands or clothes. A sharp tap on the nose together with your harshest "No" is needed. I have also been known to lift the pup off the ground and have an eyeball-to-eyeball discussion, something the pup soon learns I keep for really bad "No" behaviour. Punishment should be quick and immediate; never prolong it or hold a grudge, as this will simply serve to confuse the pup. Whenever possible, try to create positive situations, so you can lavish praise on your pup and, of course, have fun.

SOCIALIZATION
The pup should soon settle down and become comfortable with the environment in your home. The exception may be the vacuum cleaner. Most of my dogs love to be vacuumed; however, occasionally a pup has taken a lifelong dislike to this noisy and clearly dangerous device. Anyway, it is soon time to familiarize the pup with all of those strange noises, scents and happenings in that big world out there – traffic, crowds of people, noisy kids, other dogs and so on. Whenever you are introducing your pup to something new, be highly supportive and do everything possible to make it a positive experience; the pup may appear confident at home but can be really apprehensive in this strange situation.

Bull Terriers love to ride in the car. Begin with short trips – not after meals when the pup might be sick – and gradually extend the duration. If initially your pup appears worried about meeting strangers, it is better to let him do so from the security of your arms. I usually take one of my older dogs along to teach the pup how to respond, in other words to show the youngster the ropes. Common sense dictates how fast to proceed. Also, do not be surprised if your pup takes pretty much everything in his

ABOVE (LEFT): Your puppy will soon feel comfortable in the home environment.
RIGHT: Learning by experience is all part of growing up.   *Photo: van Kempen.*

stride. Most of mine have been far too enthusiastic about all of these new experiences rather than timid, which is why some breeders call this the "No" stage. If, for example, your pup becomes too excited when meeting a child or perhaps another dog, do not force the issue; it is a lose-lose situation. Go back home and practise in a more controlled environment.

A word here about puppies and kids. Never leave a pup alone with a small child, as things may rapidly get out of control; both need to learn how to deal properly with the other and, until this happens, close supervision is essential. This also goes for the child picking up and possibly dropping the pup. Having said this, I would not hesitate to let any of my own adult Bull Terriers play with a child, even a baby; as adults, they seem to possess an inbuilt sense of how to adjust to youngsters of all ages.

Your goal should be to emerge from the first six months with a puppy who understands the basic rules and is amenable to discipline. The pup should be able to

deal in a reasonably civilized manner with most situations. However, unless you are a gifted trainer, do not expect too much of your puppy when it comes to the social graces.

GROOMING

A Bull Terrier, puppy or adult, in good health requires minimal grooming. Regular brushing, followed perhaps by a rub-down with a dry towel, should maintain the customary texture and gloss of the coat. This is preferable to frequent baths, which tend to remove the natural oils. I have yet to own a Bull Terrier who did not love taking a bath – it is such fun that mine jump straight into the tub. Remember that the pH (acidity-alkalinity) of a dog's skin is different from that of humans, and so you should use a shampoo formulated for canines. Special shampoos are available to help brighten white coats and these are fine if not used too often.

Trimming nails is usually not too difficult when the pup is small. Many older Bull

Terriers, however, are none too fond of having it done and, as a result, their owners prefer to forget about it too. Putting off the evil day only makes matters worse, so getting into a routine of trimming nails regularly is well worthwhile. Make the procedure as quick and uneventful as possible, and be sure to lavish praise and rewards on the pup for being good about it. I recommend sharp guillotine-type nail clippers. Make sure you cut only the end part of the nail, avoiding the quick. If you cut into the quick, blood will flow freely. This is not as bad as it looks and will soon stop with the aid of an ice cube or some styptic powder. Some owners prefer to file the nails rather than cut them. Filing takes much longer, but is certainly less traumatic. As an aside, regular exercise on a hard surface such as paving stones will help to keep the nails trim, so that they need clipping less frequently.

Routine brushing of teeth I would also place under the heading of maintenance. Start once teething is completed, and you will familiarize the pup with the process for later in life, when regular brushing and periodic scraping to remove plaque become essential. I use a soft human toothbrush with either canine toothpaste or bicarbonate of soda.

EARS

As an unfortunate legacy of the cropped ears of the 19th century, quite a few Bull Terriers need assistance in getting their ears up. Some pups have them up by five or six weeks, usually those who will be relatively small as adults. Those who have them at half-mast or better by, say, three months need at most minimal assistance. Others, however, definitely require help. This last group are characterized by having larger, thicker ears that are more open at the base; the more cupped the ear at the base, the

more easily it comes up. Even ears that are up or nearly up may come down again during the stress of teething at around four months, but they will usually come right back up afterwards.

Most breeders recommend taping the ears up if they are still down at 12 or 13 weeks of age. There are numerous variations on when and how best to do this; no doubt your pup's breeder will have specific recommendations. Here is a typical procedure. You will need a packet of the thinnest available self-adhesive chiropodist's felt, a roll of nylon first-aid tape (ordinary tape pulls off the hair when removed, though it will soon grow back), surgical alcohol and cotton wool, plus an assistant to hold the pup. Clean the wax out of the inside of the ears with cotton wool and alcohol. Cut two pieces of the felt, roughly the same shape as, but only about two-thirds the size of, the ear flap. Remove the backing and stick a piece of felt inside each ear flap. Then hold one ear in the upright position and tape it around the base; repeat with the other ear. Next, holding both ears in the desired positions, tape over and around the existing tape to form a bridge that joins and holds them in that position; note the ears should be upright and separated, not leaning over so that they touch. Leave the tape on for about five days. Check the ears daily to ensure there are no infections, scratches or irritation. If they do not stay up when the tape is removed, wait a couple of days, then keep repeating the process until they do. Some breeders do not bother to use felt, while others use a double layer of felt with a matchstick sandwiched between them. Do whatever works best for you.

All well and good, you say, but how do you stop the pup from removing the tape or scratching it till the ears bleed? Good question! For starters, tire out your pup before taping up the ears for the first time. Then use every means of distraction at your disposal. Whenever the pup starts to scratch, present a favoured toy or a marrowbone, or simply play with the pup. You must be just as persistent as your puppy.

SPAYING AND NEUTERING

Any puppy purchased purely as a pet – with no intention of it being bred from – should be spayed or neutered. There are many sound reasons for doing so, from canine over-population to the nuisance of a bitch on heat or that of an over-sexed male. Not least is the expectation of a longer life. Traditionally, bitches were spayed after their first season and males neutered at around 12 months of age. Today, however, many vets are recommending that the operation take place much earlier, long before sexual maturity. While there are no clinical reasons for not doing so, I do not support their recommendation. My argument is summarized by the adage that "green apples do not have much flavour." I want the full flavour of a mature Bull Terrier, not the limitations of an overgrown puppy. So, do spay or neuter, but delay until after the dog's adolescence.

TOYS

Anything and everything left within reach is viewed by your pup as a toy and thus fair game for being chewed and then swallowed. Many objects that would be perfectly safe with other breeds, can end up in a Bull Terrier's stomach with potentially deadly results. Electrical wires are another potential hazard. Over the years, my pups have consumed vast quantities of wood pulp from chair stretchers as well as sticks they found outside, all without apparent ill effect. True, some pups are not as bad as others, but most have to be supervised

carefully through the worst of their teething – roughly between four and five months.

Take it from me that your pup will chew whatever is available, and so my advice is to keep him supplied with a variety of carefully chosen toys that are relatively Bull Terrier-proof. Very hard rubber balls (never hollow ones) and bones, especially made for dogs, are excellent for pups and adults alike. Large nylon bones are pretty safe. Rawhide chews are not suitable; even pups can chew and suck on them until the rawhide becomes soft and can be torn off and swallowed – be warned. Marrowbones are another staple, as are the calcified bones that can be purchased at pet shops. Beyond that, I recommend improvising: for example tearing up a cardboard box can occupy a pup for a very long time. I also supply plenty of carrots and large dog biscuits – for chewing on rather than nutritional purposes. And always check for missing objects or parts thereof, as they may be inside the pup.

SIX TO TWELVE MONTHS

Adolescence can be a most trying period with a growing Bull Terrier showing boundless energy combined with a 'ready-to-try-anything' outlook on life. Also sexual hormones make their presence felt, with males starting to feel their urges. A balanced regimen of a healthy diet, ample exercise and attention, and lots of things to occupy them is imperative. Boredom continues to be a nemesis, especially in the case of pups left for hours on their own without an appropriate outlet for their energy and inquisitiveness. Bad habits can appear overnight and need to be dealt with immediately – any delay permits the habit to take root and makes resolution much more difficult. Obsessive-compulsive disorders like tail-chasing are heritable traits; puppies with the correct Bull Terrier

Adolescence can be a trying time.

Photo: van Kempen.

temperament do not spin and chase their tails. However, those prone to such traits may well develop them when boredom sets in. Even those with a typical temperament may start to suck on their paws or become particularly destructive if left to their own devices for hours on end. As an aside, we always leave a radio on for the dogs while we are out, preferably tuned into a talk show; this is not the answer to loneliness, but it helps.

Our adolescents receive two meals a day, breakfast plus an evening meal. We also give them meaty marrowbones, which provide exercise as well as nutrition. This is where the gifted stockman comes into his own, knowing instinctively by weight, coat condition and muscle tone that the quantity of food and the balance of the diet are just right. Stuffing a young Bull Terrier full of lots of the highest-protein food you can find is not the answer and, indeed, it can push a youngster too hard. Do not let the pup become overweight, as this places too much strain on developing bones and musculature.

The other side of the equation is a proper exercise, which I would suggest all too few dogs get, in an age when there never seems to be enough time. An adolescent needs time to be able to scamper around the yard and play, some free running plus regular controlled exercise on a lead. I am lucky in having several acres of land, in which my dogs can play. They can dig holes, a natural terrier characteristic; the word terrier derives from the Latin *terra*, meaning earth. They can also chase birds and other 'critters', and each other if you have more than one Bull Terrier. However, a typical small city garden is not adequate for this purpose. Finding places where the pup can safely run off the leash, chase a ball and generally whoop it up is increasingly difficult. This places even greater emphasis on controlled exercise, or road work as I call it. Disciplined road work is essential to the proper conditioning of your adolescent – building up muscle tone, tightening feet and burning off some of that excess energy. This does not mean strolling up and down the road or to the local bar; it means walking off some of your own excess calories too. In days of yore, it was not unusual to see an owner riding a bicycle with a Bull Terrier trotting happily alongside, but times do change. There are no hard and fast rules as to how much exercise a Bull Terrier should have; it depends on the dog and the circumstances. Take it for granted, however, that your pup will not get sufficient exercise just running around the back garden.

When out and about, you and your adolescent Bull Terrier become ambassadors for the breed. Bull Terriers readily attract attention. Discipline and continued training are essential to ensure your pup is looked upon favourably by neighbours and the public at large. Most people will ask you about your dog out of genuine interest. A few, however, will ask about the Bull Terrier's fighting ability; play this down, explaining that the pup is purely a family pet not a fighting dog. *Never* encourage your pup to be aggressive.

FURTHER TRAINING

Some owners – not us, of course – are inclined to treat their Bull Terriers more like people than dogs. Yes, the pup is a member of your family, but he is a dog and naturally thinks and responds like a dog. Dogs lack the reasoning powers we associate with the human mind. However, they do possess remarkable instincts, intuition and memories, which together can be harnessed for training purposes. Above all, they are creatures of habit and so our challenge in training a dog is to instil appropriate behaviour to the point at which it becomes habit. We do this largely by repetition, so that the dog associates a particular command with a certain action, "Come" for example, and is rewarded for doing so. The flip side of this is the difficulty of undoing a habit, once learnt.

Successful trainers establish a rapport with each dog in their charge, essentially putting him or herself inside the dog's mind. Other attributes of such a trainer include consistency, fairness and firmness; he or she is able to achieve goals without

raising his voice or losing his temper, adjusting to the demands of the individual dog. Timing and the use of the lead are also key factors.

If, like me, you do not fit this mould closely, it is advisable to seek help from one of the skilled people who offer basic training classes for dogs. Not all trainers like Bull Terriers, and some employ techniques to which the breed does not respond well. You should check with other Bull Terrier breeders and first visit the class, without your pup, to ascertain its suitability. The trainer's appreciation of the breed's idiosyncracies and ability to make classes fun to attend (rather than a drudgery) are the qualities you should be looking for.

Experts recommend that more formal training of pups is delayed until around six months, while some prefer eight months. More important than a fixed age is identifying the point when you and the pup are ready for additional training; you need to able to devote time on a regular basis and the pup should have been socialized to the stage at which he is comfortable attending a class – a frightened puppy will not be able to learn effectively. Whether you plan on going to a class or taking on the task yourself, I suggest you prepare by reading one or more of the excellent dog training texts available. Also note that, while attending a class, your pup will be around other dogs of assorted sizes, varieties and dispositions, a valuable social experience the pup will miss if you do the training yourself.

To "Sit", "Stay", and the other commands with which your pup is already familiar, you should add "Heel" and "Down". Heeling is especially important for puppies who take their owners for walks rather than the other way around. This is the time to use a choke or training collar, made of steel links pounded flat. Ensure the collar is on the correct way around – there is a wrong way – and attach a light but strong nylon lead, about six feet or two metres in length. It is now a matter of teaching your pup to walk to heel on your left side. Experts differ on exactly how to teach heeling, but these are the basic steps. Start off with your left foot, give the "Heel" command, preceded of course by the pup's name, and give the lead a jerk to get the pup moving with you. Use further sharp jerks to keep the pup close to your left side. Then practise right and left turns at varying speeds. You should also practise the command "Sit" when you stop. Remember to keep the lessons short and always to make them positive experiences with lots of praise. Taught properly, these lessons should serve to cement the relationship between you and your pup.

ADULTS
GRADUATION
Fortunately adolescence soon passes – it just seems like forever at the time – and somewhere between one and two years of age most Bull Terriers settle down to become relatively civilized members of the household. In my view, from then on they simply get better, not that they ever lose

their sense of fun and mischief. They often appear to be telepathic, intuitively knowing what you are thinking and, of course, ready to assist at the drop of a hat. In the same vein, they instinctively adjust to kids of all ages and are wonderful nursemaids, whether dressed up and being wheeled around in a pram, wrestling with a teenager or helping a baby make those first few tottering steps. An adult Bull Terrier should be absolutely 100 per cent reliable with family, friends and, indeed, the public at large. It is not in a Bull Terrier's nature to be aggressive towards people and they should never be taught or encouraged to be so. They will defend their family should the need arise, quite naturally and without need of schooling.

Your graduate Bull Terrier will continue to mature, essentially to fill out in body, for a year or so and should then settle down to live a long, healthy life. Many remain active and fun-loving through into old age, while others become couch potatoes. Disposition, of course, is a major factor here, but do not discount the effect of your family's lifestyle and also the regimen of feeding and exercise that you provide for your dog.

There is a tendency among pet owners to

The adult Bull Terrier should be totally reliable with friends and family – and with the public at large.

Photo courtesy: Pew.

overfeed – in terms both of protein and of overall amount – and to under-exercise young dogs. Initially, they may appear to be doing well. They burn off the excess calories as youthful energy, while their kidneys work hard to process the surfeit of protein; unfortunately neither of these processes augur well for the future. A distinctly overweight dog is not a healthy one, and remember that some Bull Terriers are prone to early kidney failure. If in doubt, seek advice from the breeder or an experienced Bull Terrier owner. We cut our dogs back to a maintenance diet far sooner than suggested by the food manufacturers. This means our usual diet of cottage cheese, eggs and chicken, but with the addition of a medium-to-low-protein kibble and with shredded vegetables as a regular substitute. We continue to feed meaty marrowbones on a regular basis.

Ideally, daily exercise on the lead should continue, only decreasing in pace and duration as old age approaches. Try to balance regular road work with play time in the yard and some free running. Other than the wear and tear to be expected of an active canine – the occasional cut, abrasion or split toenail – your dog should remain fit and healthy for many years to come. Regular grooming, as for the adolescent, does not take up much time. Do not procrastinate about keeping those nails trim; the same goes for brushing your dog's teeth and, later in life, also scraping off any plaque.

FIGHTING

Most Bull Terriers are relatively easy-going and non-aggressive with other dogs – at least until they find cause to act differently. I can say in all honesty that, with one exception, all of my dogs have been friendly with strange dogs at first. Then the inevitable happens, an unprovoked attack by a dog running loose while mine is on a leash. The first time or two my dog may not respond in kind, but after that...beware! No self-respecting Bull Terrier is going to stand for this, and so you had better be prepared for a real fight. You should do everything possible to avoid such situations. Prevention is far better than cure; in fact there really is no cure. Every disagreement with another dog makes another fight more likely. And, believe me, even if your dog did not start the fight, he will be blamed for it. It goes without saying that you should never ever encourage your Bull Terrier to be aggressive with other dogs.

In case your dog does become involved in a fight, you should know how to separate the protagonists. The first rule is not to get bitten yourself; keep your hands away from those snapping jaws. Wait till one dog has taken hold of the other, or perhaps both are biting and holding each other. Your next move depends on the circumstances. If your dog is biting and holding on to the other one, and the latter appears anxious to escape, then you should take hold of your dog's collar and twist it with all of your strength. The purpose is to cut off your dog's air supply – momentarily – so that he has to release his hold on the other dog to take a breath. When that gasp for air comes, immediately yank your dog away; hopefully, the other dog will take off at top speed. If, however, both are intent on turning it into a serious contest, you should try to enlist the help of a bystander. If the other dog is wearing a collar, the helper can choke off this dog while you do the same with yours. If no help is available, you must improvise. Perhaps you can drag the dogs to a gate and, during a momentary lull, close the gate between them. Alternatively, if you get a lead or rope around the other dog's neck, tie it to a nearby rail or lamp-post, then separate and remove your dog from the scene. Shouting, kicking the dogs and general hysteria will have no impact on the combatants, so you must try to remain as calm as possible, letting go your emotions only after the event. Also, there is no point in chastising your dog. Avoiding confrontations in the first place is the only solution.

MULTI-DOG HOUSEHOLDS
Keeping a Bull Terrier with other dogs demands experience and understanding of how canines interact. Some breeds are sufficiently easy-going for several to live together in longterm harmony; for others, Bull Terriers among them, such arrangements are much more demanding and potentially problematical. I am not suggesting that it should not be attempted or cannot be implemented successfully, but you need to know what you are doing. My wife and I will not sell a puppy into a household with one or more other dogs unless the potential owners have experience with Bull Terriers or a similar breed. It is not that the puppy is necessarily going to get into disputes with the other dogs. But,

unless a clear pack order is established and maintained, with the owner as 'alpha', the pack leader, and the dogs having a clear understanding of the pecking order, one day the Bull Terrier is likely to get into an argument with another dog over a treat, a toy or perhaps just something that one has found in the garden. Thereafter the two may never be trustworthy enough to leave together again. It is the sort of tiff that would never occur if the dogs lived in separate homes and merely met and played in the park during their daily constitutionals.

Many strains of Bull Terriers get on really well with other dogs, unless of course provoked by a direct challenge, but others have low tolerance for strange dogs that bark at them or pose a threat. In general, Bull Terriers get on better with larger, easy-going dogs (for example Golden Retrievers) than they do with small, yappy ones. If your Bull Terrier is going to live with another dog, ensure they are of opposite sexes and, as stated earlier, never keep a Bull Terrier male with another male dog. At some point you may be tempted to

If you want to keep two Bull Terriers, choose a male and a female.

Photo: van Kempen.

Am. Ch. Brummagem the Brigand, aged 11.

buy a second Bull Terrier because your first one becomes bored while you are out. Think this notion through carefully. Your dog wants as much of your attention as possible and may resent having to share it with a newcomer. If boredom is a real concern, consider getting a kitten. Unless discouraged, most Bull Terriers become cat-chasers – cats run away and they revel in the chase. This does not mean that they cannot love a cat of their own, a creature that to them bears no relation to those critters they love to chase. Your Bull Terrier will almost certainly welcome a cat as a pal.

OLDER DOGS

I adore old Bull Terriers. They may grow cranky and eccentric, but these traits only add to the richness of life with the breed. They still enjoy the family and expect to be involved with its activities, whether going on a ramble or taking a ride in the car. They will not be up to really long walks, but still need daily exercise and will require this as they will their other rights (bear in mind that you may consider something a privilege that your oldster sees as a right – like the best spot on the couch, a blanket in front of the fire, attention on demand or special culinary treats). In general, extra rest and warmth are important.

Most older dogs retain their love of food, though quantities should be smaller to balance reduced activity, with lower protein and fat content. You do not want your old-timer to be overweight; on the other hand, a little extra padding will help to ward off the effects of any sudden illness or loss of appetite. Obviously, special care and attention is needed to keep your dog as healthy as possible – all of the regular maintenance, plus periodic checks by your vet. Nails may need clipping or filing more frequently, and anal glands may need regular attention. By 11 or 12 years of age, most of my dogs have suffered noticeable loss of vision and hearing, not that this seems to worry them unduly, and sometimes it seems to be selective – such as when they still hear the cookie-tin being opened at a hundred paces!

Unfortunately, these twilight years end all too soon, so make the best of them. It is never easy to lose an old friend, but do not let your dog suffer unnecessarily. Bull Terriers may complain vociferously about having their nails trimmed, yet signal little of their great pain when they are suffering from a terminal illness. When they are ready to depart "they tell you with their eyes." This was the advice I received from 'D' Montague Johnson, and I have found it to be true. So, when the day comes, reward their many years of loyalty and devotion by having them put down, preferably resting on your knee. Then, while they enjoy the happy hunting grounds, consider bringing home another Bull Terrier to fill the void.

THE BREED STANDARD

THE BRITISH BREED STANDARD
(Approved July 1986)

GENERAL APPEARANCE
Strongly-built, muscular, well-balanced and active with a keen, determined intelligent expression.

CHARACTERISTICS
The Bull Terrier is the gladiator of the canine race, full of fire and courageous. A unique feature of the breed is a down-faced, egg-shaped head. Irrespective of size, dogs should look masculine and bitches feminine.

TEMPERAMENT
Of even temperament and amenable to discipline. Although obstinate, is particularly good with people.

HEAD AND SKULL
Head long, strong and deep right to the end of the muzzle, but not coarse. Viewed from front, egg-shaped and completely filled, its surface free from hollows or indentations. Top of skull almost flat from ear to ear. Profile curves gently downwards from top of skull to tip of nose which should be black and bent downwards at tip. Nostrils well-developed and underjaw deep and strong.

MOUTH
Teeth sound, clean, strong, of good size, perfectly regular with a perfect regular and complete scissor bite, i.e. upper teeth closely overlapping lower teeth and set square in the jaws. Lips clean and tight.

EYES
Appearing narrow, obliquely placed and triangular, well-sunken, black or as dark as possible so as to appear almost black, and with a piercing glint. Distance from tip of nose to eyes perceptibly greater than that from eyes to top of skull. Blue or partly blue eyes undesirable.

EARS
Small, thin and placed close together. Dog should be able to hold them stiffly erect, when they point straight upwards.

NECK
Very muscular, long, arched, tapering

from shoulders to head and free from loose skin.

FOREQUARTERS

Shoulders strong and muscular without loading. Shoulder blades wide, flat and held closely to the chest wall and have a very pronounced backwards slope of front edge from bottom to top, forming almost a right angle with upper arm. Elbows held straight, and strong pasterns upright. Forelegs have strongest type of round quality bone, dog should stand solidly on them and they should be perfectly parallel. In mature dogs length of foreleg should be approximately equal to depth of chest.

BODY

Body well-rounded with marked spring of rib and great depth from withers to brisket, so that the latter nearer the ground than the belly. Back short, strong with backline behind the withers level, arching or roaching slightly over broad, well-muscled loins. Underline from brisket to belly forms a graceful upward curve. Chest broad viewed from front.

HINDQUARTERS

Hind legs in parallel when viewed from behind. Thighs muscular and second thighs well-angulated with bone to foot short and strong.

FEET

Round and compact with well-arched toes.

TAIL

Short, set on low and carried horizontally. Thick at root, it tapers to a fine point.

GAIT/MOVEMENT

When moving appears well-knit, smoothly covering ground with free, easy strides and with a typical jaunty air. When trotting, movement parallel, front and back, only converging towards centre line at fast speeds, forelegs reaching out well and hindlegs moving smoothly at hip, flexing well at stifle and hock, with great thrust.

COAT

Short, flat, even and harsh to touch with a fine gloss. Skin fitting dog tightly. A soft-textured undercoat may be present in winter.

COLOUR

For White, pure white coat. Skin pigmentation and markings on head not to be penalised. For Coloured, colour to predominate; all other things being equal, brindle to be preferred. Black brindle, red, fawn and tricolour acceptable. Blue and liver highly undesirable.

SIZE

There are neither weight nor height limits, but there should be the impression of maximum substance for the size of dog consistent with quality and sex.

FAULTS

Any departure from the foregoing points should be considered a fault and the seriousness with which the fault should be regarded should be in exact proportion to its degree.

NOTE

Male animals should have two apparently normal testicles fully descended into the scrotum.

THE AMERICAN BREED
STANDARD
(Approved July 1974)

WHITE
The Bull Terrier must be strongly built,
muscular, symmetrical and active, with a
keen, determined and intelligent
expression, full of fire but of sweet
disposition and amenable to discipline.

HEAD
Should be long, strong and deep right to
the end of the muzzle, but not coarse.
Full face it should be oval in outline and
be filled completely up giving the
impression of fullness with a surface
devoid of hollows or indentations, i.e.
egg shaped. In profile it should curve
gently downwards from the top of the
skull to the tip of the nose. The forehead
should be flat across from ear to ear. The
distance from the tip of the nose to the
eyes should be perceptibly greater than
from the eyes to the top of the skull. The
underjaw should be deep and well-
defined.

LIPS
Should be clean and tight.

TEETH
Should meet in either a level or in a
scissors bite. In the scissors bite the
upper teeth should fit in front of and
closely against the lower teeth, and teeth
should be sound, strong and perfectly
regular.

EARS
Should be small, thin and placed close
together. They should be held stiffly
erect, when they should point upwards.

EYES
Should be well sunken and as dark as
possible, with a piercing glint and they
should be small, triangular and obliquely
placed; set near together and high up on
the dog's head. Blue eyes are a
disqualification.

NOSE
Should be black, with well developed
nostrils bent down at the tip.

NECK
Should be very muscular, long, arched
and clean, tapering from the shoulders
to the head and it should be free from
loose skin.

CHEST
Should be broad when viewed from in
front, and there should be great depth
from withers to brisket, so that the latter
is nearer to the ground than the belly.

BODY
Should be well rounded with marked
spring of rib, the back should be short
and strong. The back ribs deep. Slightly
arched over the loin. The shoulders
should be strong and muscular but
without heaviness. The shoulder blades
should be wide and flat and there should
be a very pronounced backward slope
from the bottom edge of the blade to the
top edge. Behind the shoulders there
should be no slackness or dip at the
withers. The underline from the brisket
to the belly should form a graceful
upward curve.

LEGS
Should be big boned but not to the
point of coarseness; the forelegs should
be of moderate length, perfectly straight,
and the dog must stand firmly upon

them. The elbows must turn neither in nor out, and the pasterns should be strong and upright. The hind legs should be parallel viewed from behind. The thighs very muscular with hocks well let down. Hind pasterns short and upright. The stifle joint should be well-bent with a well-developed second thigh.

FEET
Round and compact with well-arched toes like a cat.

TAIL
Should be short, set on low, fine, and ideally should be carried horizontally. It should be thick where it joins the body, and should taper to a fine point.

COAT
Should be short, flat, harsh to the touch and with a fine gloss. The dog's skin should fit tightly.

COLOR
Is white, though markings on the head are permissible. Any markings elsewhere on the coat are to be severely faulted. Skin pigmentation is not to be penalized.

MOVEMENT
The dog shall move smoothly, covering the ground with free easy strides, fore and hind legs should move parallel each to each when viewed from in front or behind. The forelegs reaching out well and the hind legs moving smoothly at the hip and flexing well at the stifle and hock. The dog should move compactly with a jaunty air that suggests agility and power.

FAULTS
Any departure from the foregoing points shall be considered a fault and the seriousness of the fault shall be in exact proportion to its degree, i.e. a very crooked front is a rather bad fault, and a slightly crooked front is a slight fault.

DISQUALIFICATION
Blue eyes.

COLORED
The Standard for the Colored variety is the same as the White except for the sub-head "Color" which reads: COLOR. Any color other than white, or any color with white markings. Other things being equal, the preferred color is brindle. A dog which is predominantly white shall be disqualified.

DISQUALIFICATIONS
Blue eyes.
Any dog which is predominantly white.

THE ESSENCE OF THE BREED
Each and every breed is distinctive, indeed unique. The blueprint for the Bull Terrier is set out in the Standard. This word picture describes the singular characteristics of the Bull Terrier, as well as those that it has in common with other breeds. So what in a few words is the essence of the Bull Terrier? What are the breed's most significant features?

Typical head and expression: These are the hallmarks of the breed, differentiating the Bull Terrier from all others at a glance. Without a terrific head and expression, an individual might be a very nice dog, but it is not a superior Bull Terrier.

Outstanding bone, musculature and substance: A top-class Bull Terrier personifies the maximum amount of dog within the available space. Dense bone and exceptional muscle tone produce that vital

Points of anatomy

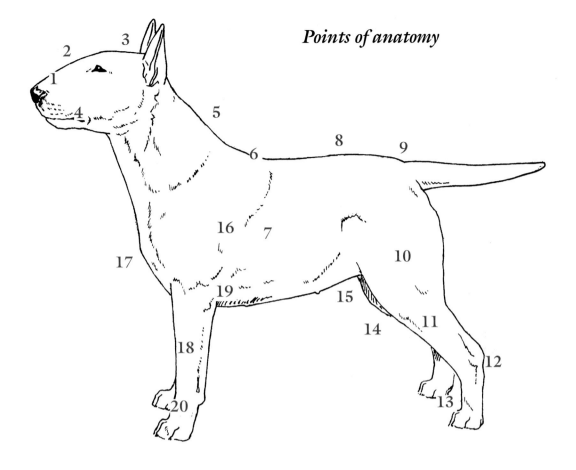

1. Muzzle	8. Loin	15. Tuck up
2. Stop	9. Croup	16. Shoulder
3. Occiput	10. Upper thigh	17. Forechest
4. Flews	11. Second thigh	18. Forearm
5. Neck	12. Hock	19. Elbow
6. Withers	13. Rear pastern	20. Front pastern
7. Ribs	14. Stifle	

impression of substance and power, without detracting from the quality and activity always associated with the breed. A dog that is soft, flabby, coarse or inactive is atypical.

Shapeliness and symmetry: The ideal Bull Terrier is supremely shapely, demonstrating the graceful lines and symmetry called for by the Standard. The profile of the head, the long, arched neck, well-laid shoulders, short back, markedly sprung ribs, tuck-up

and well-angulated hindquarters all contribute to this shapeliness.

Soundness and movement: The breed's distinctive virtues must be packaged without loss of soundness. Correctly constructed, the Bull Terrier moves freely and with a jaunty air. In practice, this is often not a strong point of the breed, but it is nonetheless an important attribute of the ideal Bull Terrier.

Distinctive outgoing temperament: Last

Eng. Am. Ch. Aricon Chief Eye Shy – a truly great Bull Terrier.

but most certainly not least comes the outgoing, loving and lovable character that is another hallmark of the breed. The Standard explains that their exuberance, their joie de vivre, must be amenable to discipline. Bull Terriers love everyone and any indication of aggression towards people is absolutely unacceptable.

VARIATION IN TYPE
Ideally, every Bull Terrier should conform closely to the type defined by the Standard. In practice, however, there are variations in type that trace back to the breeds from which the Bull Terrier originates. So it is not unusual to hear breeders and judges refer to dogs as showing more 'Bulldog', 'terrier' or 'Dalmatian' type. The Bulldog type is typically a heavyweight for its size, excelling in substance, density and bone,

while the terrier type exudes quality and refinement and more often has the desired 'varminty' expression. Dalmatian types are the least common; some fanciers refer to them as 'houndy' in reference to their longer legs, free movement and less compact lines. The point to note here is that these are variations from the exemplary middle-of-the-road dog defined in the Standard.

VIRTUES AND FAULTS
Every dog exhibits both virtues and faults. Over the years the Bull Terrier fraternity has placed greater and greater emphasis on positive virtues, with commensurate downplaying of superficial faults. A lack of such positive virtues is viewed by many within the breed as a major fault in and of itself. Also the Standard makes clear that faults should be judged in accordance with their degree of seriousness.

Fault judging has no place within the breed and this explains why the opinions of breeder-judges are regarded so much more highly than those of all-rounders. Raymond Oppenheimer challenged judges to ask themselves "Which of the animals before me has most to offer the breed?". He believed that neither single faults nor single virtues should be allowed to assume undue significance in the minds of breeders or of judges, the goal being a balanced assessment such that virtues and defects are weighed dispassionately.

INTERPRETATION OF THE STANDARD
The British and American Standards differ in detail, though not in any significant way – other than the separation in America of whites and coloureds into separate varieties. The ensuing discussion follows the British version, with references where appropriate to the transatlantic variations.

54

GENERAL APPEARANCE, CHARACTERISTICS, TEMPERAMENT

These sections give an overview of the Bull Terrier, speaking of its strength, balance and agility and, of course, that piercing expression and unique head. The phrase "gladiator of the canine race" was not added to the Standard until 1915. Certainly, it conveys the correct impression of power, courage and determination. This description, however, fails to portray the fun-loving nature of the breed, its congeniality or quite remarkable sensitivity. Note the requirement for dogs to look masculine and bitches feminine; many breeders abhor a 'bitchy' dog, while being more forgiving of 'doggy' bitches.

The section on temperament, though short, is of paramount importance. With its size and enormous strength, the Bull Terrier must be "amenable to discipline" and, as mentioned above, any aggression towards people is absolutely unacceptable.

HEAD AND SKULL

The modern Bull Terrier head was first described in a new Standard in 1915 with requirement for the head to be "oval, almost egg-shaped, with almost an arc from

Eng. Am. Ch. Catrana Eyeopener of Aricon – stunning expression.

occiput to tip of nose, the more down-faced the better." Today's Standards no longer demand more down-face, yet this is precisely what breeders are still trying to do, indeed succeeding in doing – the use of the adverb "gently" to describe the downward curvature of the profile being largely ignored.

Prior to further discussion, clarification of the terminology used in the Standard and other descriptions of the breed is appropriate. The term "egg-shaped" is self-explanatory, emphasizing the fullness of the head "free of hollows or indentations". In general use, down-face refers to the arc or curvature of the muzzle when viewed from the side; with Bull Terriers the arc extends

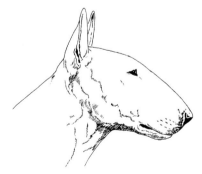

Correct (unexaggerated).

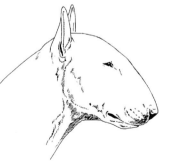

Correct (exaggerated).

Incorrect – weak and snipy, untypical profile.

Am. Ch. Jarrogue's Ms Jennifer Jones – superb head.

from the top of the skull all the way to the nose and, in this sense, the whole head is down-faced. This view, the top line of the head, is usually called the profile. With this unbroken curve, obviously there should be no 'stop' or drop between the skull and muzzle. The Bull Terrier should have a Roman nose; that is, the tip of the muzzle should turn down in a shapely way; old-timers used to say that the nose looked as if it had been hit with a hammer. Another important feature of the Bull Terrier head is the fill, or fill-up, in front of the eyes; there should be no hollows or chiselling, as implied by the egg-shaped requirement. Finally, the bone marking the top of the skull is called the occiput.

The uniqueness of the down-faced, egg-shaped head is noted under 'Characteristics'. The narrative on head and skull states that, viewed from the front, the head should be egg-shaped. This is also an apt description of the head in profile, provided that the egg is a long one – to satisfy the requirement (under the section on eyes) for the distance from the tip of the nose to the eyes to be perceptibly greater than from the eyes to the occiput. The distinctly longer muzzle is a key component of the typical head. The amount of turn-down on the Roman nose has a surprisingly big impact

on the overall appearance of the profile, as can be demonstrated by the improvement resulting from gently pushing down the tip of the nose of an average Bull Terrier. The nose, of course, should be black with well-developed nostrils. Pink areas on the nose of an adult dog, though a cosmetic fault, are worrisome for two reasons; firstly, it seems to be highly heritable, and, more significantly, it indicates a lack of the pigmentation that is vital to the long-term health and vigour of the breed.

The importance of the length, strength and depth of both muzzle and underjaw cannot be over-emphasized. The description "deep right through" is apt. Unfortunately, the Standard makes no mention of width. And, while the muzzle and underjaw should not be wide to the point of coarseness, there should be no hint of snipiness. Heads that sacrifice adequate width, and thereby strength, for a sensational profile are not desirable. Also, the head as a whole must balance and be in proportion to the rest of the dog. Sometimes heads are too small and occasionally too large.

Finally, the head must combine strength and quality. Over-development of the cheek muscles, prominent eyebrows or loose skin lend an element of coarseness, as does any suggestion of lippiness.

MOUTH

Both the muzzle and the underjaw of the Bull Terrier should be long, powerful and of good width, with a full set of large, strong teeth, as befits the breed's image as a gladiator. The teeth should be positioned regularly along the jaws with the incisors (front teeth) meeting in a scissors bite – that is with the upper incisors fitting in front of and closely against the lower ones. The American Standard also permits a pincer bite, that is with the incisors level, without preference being given to either a scissors or pincer bite. Incidentally, the level bite was an option in all of the early Standards. All of this seems quite straightforward, but unfortunately teeth have always been a problem in the breed and never more so than today as the downface becomes more and more exaggerated. Several articles have been written along the lines of 'mouths in disarray' and nowhere are they in greater disarray than in North America. It is not that breeders are not concerned about teeth. It comes down to the pressure of needing a dramatic profile to be successful in the show ring, and then to the balance between virtues and faults. Should an otherwise superior dog lose to an inferior specimen because of an incorrect bite? Some judges

Am. Ch. Brummagem Baracole – a beautiful head without exaggeration.

will not accept such a bite, others are more forgiving, provided the fault is offset by outstanding virtues. Also, as the Standard says, faults should be penalised according to degree: a bite that is slightly wrong is a minor fault; a really bad bite is a very serious fault.

Adult Bull Terriers, like all other canines, are, or should be, equipped with 42 teeth –

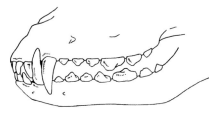

Correct scissor bite.

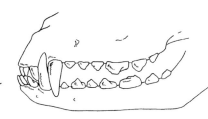

Undershot, canines correct.

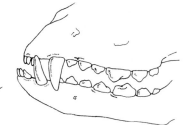

Undershot, canines incorrect.

20 in the upper and 22 in the lower jaw. Each jaw has six incisors (front teeth), two canines (one on each side) and eight pre-molars (four on each side); the lower jaw has six molars or back teeth (three on each side), while the upper jaw has only four molars (two on each side). The most common fault found in the breed is undershot incisors, that is the lower incisors project beyond the upper ones. The opposite, an overshot bite, is relatively uncommon and usually accompanied by a narrow muzzle and jaw, hence the term 'parrot mouth'. A quite new problem is the misplaced lower canine, which, instead of inclining outwards, grows straight up, puncturing the palate. No doubt there have always been cases of missing pre-molars, but this is now becoming much more common.

Naturally, the majority of Bull Terriers have correct bites. However, as breeders strive for ever more dramatic profiles, they are progressively shortening the upper jaw. To compensate, the lower jaw must also become shorter and, not surprisingly, the process of achieving this has resulted in overcrowding and in both misplaced and missing teeth. To maintain full dentition – with, as the Standard states, teeth that are "sound, strong, of good size and perfectly regular" – the underjaw must be long and strong with ample width between the canines. To balance this underjaw, the muzzle must also be long and broad, as well as having the depth to carry the desired downface.

Correct eyes, ears and expression.

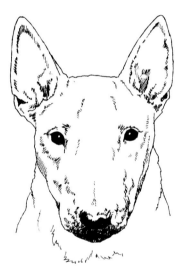

Incorrect - a common-looking head with round eyes and large low-set ears.

EYES
The Bull Terrier's eyes are unlike those of any other breed. They are set obliquely, high up on the head and relatively close together. The opening is triangular, with the outer angle pointing towards the base of the ear. The eyes are sunk well into the skull. The irises should be black or very dark brown; those lighter brown in colour should be faulted. Blue eyes are associated with deafness and therefore highly undesirable; they are a disqualification in America. The desired features combine to give the dog that typical expression that is described variously as piercing, wicked,

varminty or mischievous. To the uninitiated, this expression can give the impression of the devil reincarnate, to their friends a hint that they are ready for fun and games. When members of the public accuse the Bull Terrier of having pink eyes, they are referring to the pink eye rims that often occur on white dogs; pink rims are perfectly natural and not a fault.

Historically, coloured Bull Terriers rarely matched the white variety in eye and expression, tending to throw back to the less deep-set, more open eye of the Staffordshires from which they were bred. Today this is no longer true, at least among the top winning coloureds. The whites usually appear to have the more diabolical expression, in large part because their eyes contrast more sharply with a white background.

EARS
The wording on ears is succinct – "small, thin and close together". The dog should be able to hold them erect, right up on top of the head. Ears are often on the large side and tend to stick out like handles on a jug, neither of which is desirable. On the other hand, ears that are soft or set low on the skull detract from the typical alert expression. Some Bull Terriers are in the habit of laying their ears back flat behind the skull, but can usually be prevailed upon to get them up when in the show ring.

NECK
Again, the wording is clear and concise. That long, muscular, arched neck adds much to the general appearance, indeed elegance, of the Bull Terrier. A short, thick neck, often associated with poorly laid shoulders, disrupts the overall balance and flowing lines of the dog, while a weak neck is completely out of keeping with breed type.

Correct length of neck and lay of shoulders.

Incorrect: Upright shoulders and shorter neck.

FOREQUARTERS
Well-laid shoulders are a key component of the Bull Terrier's conformation. The shoulder blades should be set well back and relatively close together – no more than about two finger-widths apart. The Standard suggests they meet the upper arm at almost a right angle. This is rarely, if ever, attained, an angle of 100 to 110 degrees being much more common. Ideally, the upper arms should be about the same length as the shoulder blades. This positions the elbows and thus the legs well back under the chest, allowing optimal freedom of movement and presenting some

59

Typical Bull Terrier.

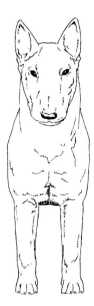

*Incorrect:
'Terrier' front.*

*Incorrect:
'Bulldog' front (also
showing too much bone).*

forechest in front of the legs. A short upper arm resulting in a Fox Terrier-like front is incorrect, restricting as it does forward reach of the legs during movement. The shoulders should be strongly muscled yet clean. Excessive muscling is undesirable, and is associated with the tendency toward a Bulldog front – bunchy shoulders, out at the elbow and 'Queen Anne' front legs.

Despite its broad chest, the Bull Terrier should have a ramrod-straight front, elbows close to the chest, and sturdy, upright pasterns with feet pointing straight ahead. The Standard calls for forelegs with strong, round, quality bone. Quality may not seem like an appropriate term, but this is the impression given by the ideal for the breed – bone that is dense, without in any way appearing coarse, which feels round when handled. There should be no slope to the pasterns, which, with the cat-like feet, places the dog right up on its toes.

Watching a Bull Terrier with a truly superior forehand in action is a joy to behold; such a dog is the epitome of grace, balance and agility and just cannot stand wrongly.

BODY
A short back with a deep chest and marked spring of rib are key characteristics of the ideal Bull Terrier. The chest should reach at least to the elbow. Typically, the depth of chest and length of leg are approximately equal, adding to the symmetry of the dog. The ribs should be carried well back to a short loin. The chest should curve gracefully to the loin; there should also be a discernible waist behind the rib cage when viewed from above. The strength and shortness of the coupling at the loin are essential to the functioning of this heavy yet athletic dog. The slab sides and longer backs found in dogs with hound-like tendencies are most undesirable.

The topline comprises a set of graceful

Am. Ch. Action Hot Item – such type and style.

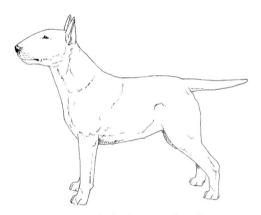

Correct body shape and topline.

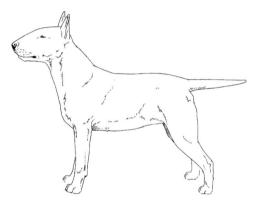

Incorrect: Less depth of brisket and longer in the loin. The topline is too flat.

lines. The arched neck flows into withers set well along the back; only a short section in the middle of the back is level, because the topline rises slightly with the muscling over the loin area and then falls away with the slightly sloping croup to the tail. There should be no dip at the withers – the result of upright shoulders – or any suggestion of slackness in the topline.

HINDQUARTERS

The short description in the Standard belies the complexity of the hindquarters. Behind the collar, the Bull Terrier is sometimes described as a Bulldog on a terrier frame, which points to the importance of properly constructed, well-muscled hindquarters to assure soundness, agility and the necessary driving force when the dog is moving. Correct conformation requires the three sets of bones that make up the hindquarters to be balanced and set at the right angles to each other. First the pelvis should slope down towards the back of the dog at the appropriate angle, which highly respected authority Tom Horner suggests should be about 35 degrees. The upper end of the femur (thigh bone) makes a ball and socket joint with the pelvis – the hip joint. At its lower end, the femur is attached to the shorter tibia and fibula bones, forming the stifle joint, in which the patella (knee cap)

61

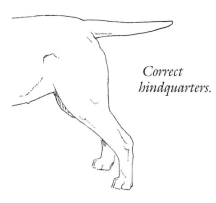

Correct hindquarters.

Incorrect: Straight quarters.

sits in a groove in the femur; if this groove is too shallow, the cap can slip out of the joint – a hereditary condition known as patella luxation. The tibia and fibula then drop down to the hock joint. The hock, or "bone to the foot" as it is called in the Standard, should be short and strong; in the American version the older terminology "well let down" is still used. Long hocks throw the whole assembly out of balance and are most undesirable. The stifle joint should be well-bent, such that, when the dog is standing naturally, the hock is vertical to the ground. The joint can be over-angulated, but more often Bull Terriers are too straight in stifle, throwing back to the shorter thigh bones of the Bulldog. Viewed

from behind the hindquarters should be parallel to each other. Dogs with hock joints closer together than the feet are referred to as cow hocked. Stifle joints that bow outward from each other are indicative of unsound construction; dogs with this conformation typically lack extension and drive when moving. Powerful muscling of the thighs is essential, with the Standard noting the importance of both the (upper) thigh muscles and the development of the so-called second (lower) thigh that covers the tibia and fibula.

FEET
The Standard is brief with regard to feet. The cat-like feet should be well-arched and padded to support this weighty breed. They should be relatively small, which, surprisingly, is not mentioned, with the front feet slightly larger than the rear ones. Open or splayed feet are unsightly and, more significantly, do not serve such an active dog well; badly splayed feet are often accompanied by weak pasterns.

Aust. Ch. Nichmari Sammy Jo – outstanding make and shape.

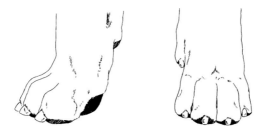

Correct cat feet (viewed in profile and front-on).

TAIL

The tail is attached to a bony plate at the end of the spine called the sacrum. For the tail to be set low and carried horizontally, as required by the Standard, the sacrum must be tilted slightly downwards to the rear. Unfortunately, the majority of Bull Terrier carry their tails above the horizontal in what is termed a 'gay' position, indicating

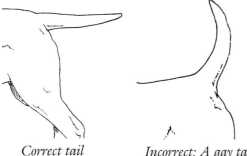

| Correct tail carriage. | Incorrect: A gay tail set on a high croup. |

that the sacrum and therefore the croup do not slope sufficiently. In the worst examples, the sacrum is completely flat and the tail carried vertically as in the Fox Terrier. Gay tails are an anathema to old-timers in the breed, whereas today they are viewed by most fanciers as just a superficial fault. Unfortunately, high tail carriage is more than just a cosmetic fault. It means that the whole rear assembly is set on at the wrong angle, adversely affecting rear movement. Dogs with gay tails simply do not move correctly; the best-moving Bull Terriers invariably have their tails attached to their hindquarters at the optimal angle. However, when excited, most Bull Terriers tend to carry their tails above their toplines. This is characteristic of the breed and should not be faulted, provided the set-on is correct. The short, tapered tail, thick at the root, provides balance and symmetry to the overall picture of the dog.

GAIT AND MOVEMENT

Here, the wording in the American Standard wins the prize for clarity and readability, providing a concise word picture of correct movement. The key words are: "covering the ground with free easy strides", "legs moving parallel", reach in front (and drive behind), that (trademark) "jaunty air", suggesting "agility and power". Unfortunately, too few Bull Terriers come close to the usual interpretation of this ideal and those that do may well not be superior specimens in other respects. The best movers in a general sense are those tending to the Dalmatian type, their narrower chests, rather longer legs and loins aiding length of stride and freedom of movement. However, such dogs tend to fall short of the ideal in terms of power, compactness and jauntiness. This is

Correct jaunty movement.

where those closer to the Bulldog end of the spectrum come into their own; with their broad chests and exceptional musculature they move more like a rhinoceros on a slow charge, a description that has been applied aptly to the movement of Staffordshire Bull Terriers. Terrier tendencies lead to a preciseness and lack of raw power that, again, falls short of optimal movement.

Correct middle-of-the-road Bull Terriers blend the best of the Dalmatian movement with the power, compactness and jauntiness that result from the broader chest and more muscular physique. The legs remain more parallel at higher speeds than they do with Dalmatian types. Reach and extension may be a tad reduced, but there remains that impression of power combined with agility. In other words, correct movement in the Bull Terrier recognizes the Bulldog heritage without sacrificing too much of the free, clean movement expected of taller, narrower, longer dogs.

In practice, many of today's Bull Terriers leave much to be desired in this department. To quote Tom Horner, "movement is the crucial test of

Ch. Caliber Cabin Class – correct construction, ergo excellent movement.

Swed. Dan. Ch. Panzakraft's Swedish Design – exceptional design all-round.

conformation" and few breeders have made conformation a high priority in recent years. Many dogs fail to reach out sufficiently in front or really drive with their hindquarters, pads showing as they move away. Often dogs move with their front and rear feet too close to the centre line, in other words they toe in; such dogs sometimes appear to weave or 'knit and pearl'. Tied shoulders lead to a paddling action in front. Dogs with cow hocks typically lack drive, while this is an even more serious problem with bowed hindquarters. Some dogs move with their legs reasonably parallel, but in fact they are just pottering along, lacking reach and extension. This is why it is important to evaluate movement from the side view as well as from in front and behind. Though not mentioned explicitly in either Standard, the topline should remain firm and horizontal during movement. Finally, some dogs, lacking the requisite angulation fore and aft, get into the habit of pacing – the legs on each side advancing together; this is both ungainly and incorrect. Giving a pull on the lead and moving faster will usually cause the dog to stop pacing and begin to move normally with the legs at opposite corners moving in unison.

COAT

The tight-fitting glossy coat puts the finishing touch to the Bull Terrier's appearance and gives the coloureds that 'smart as paint' look. A healthy coat is indicative of a healthy dog. In winter, particularly in colder climes, dogs may grow an undercoat of softer texture. Sometimes small patches of dark hairs, known as ticks, sully the white undercoat. Such ticking is a fault, albeit a cosmetic one. Fortunately, most dogs lose the ticks when they shed their undercoat in springtime. Dark skin pigmentation must not be confused with ticking; such pigmentation is desirable and definitely not a fault.

COLOUR

For whites this part of the Standard is straightforward. The coat should be pure white, except that markings on the head are permitted and are not to be penalised; coloured patches elsewhere on a white dog are termed mismarks and should be penalised according to size. This is another example of a cosmetic fault and is viewed by most breeders as much less serious than deficiencies that fall into one of the five categories defining the essence of the breed.

For coloureds, the Standard does not define any particular markings; it states simply that colour must predominate. In other words, colour should make up more than 50 per cent of the coat. A few dogs are solid in colour, having minimal white markings, while the majority of coloureds sport a white blaze on the head, white socks, a white collar, white on the belly and a white tip to the tail – the so-called Irish Spotting. At the other end of the spectrum, some dogs have a lot of white on their bodies; in other words they are splash-marked. Despite their meeting the requirement of the Standard to be more than 50 per cent coloured, such dogs have attracted undue criticism. Yes, beautifully marked, Irish Spotted Bull Terriers are more attractive to behold. But specific markings are not imperative to breed type and so should not be a significant factor in judging coloureds. Markings are one of those features that come into play when many other factors – especially those listed under 'The Essence of the Breed' – are found to be equal or very nearly so.

The stated preference for brindle over other colours is another case of all other things being equal – which, of course, they rarely are. In other words, the only time this would become a determining factor is when two dogs are of equal merit in all other respects; then the brindle would win. Blue and liver are considered highly undesirable. These less intense colours occur only rarely and the intention of the Standard is to discourage their being shown or used for breeding purposes.

Markings can create optical illusions, either enhancing or detracting from the appearance of the dog. Particular attention should be paid to those on the head and if necessary the head should be handled to eliminate such potential aberrations.

SIZE
With neither weight nor height restrictions, there is a good deal of latitude allowed in the size of Bull Terriers. What is important, regardless of size, is the requirement for packing the maximum amount of dog into the available space, or, in the words of the Standard, ensuring there is "the impression of the maximum substance consistent with quality and sex".

The majority of bitches fall within the range 45 to 60 lbs (20 to 27 kg), with males typically 55 to 70 lbs (25 to 32 kg). However, bigger or smaller specimens are not uncommon. A bitch weighing in at only about 35 lbs will usually lack the required substance, whereas a 90 lbs male will tend to be coarse and to lose type.

7 SHOWING YOUR BULL TERRIER

THE SPORT

There is tremendous interest in the sporting side of pure-bred dogs the world over. Most serious breeders and exhibitors start out as pet owners, take their dog to a show and then get bitten by the bug. Some thrive on the competitive element, while others really enjoy the social side of the sport. For some it is a casual hobby and attending a show an enjoyable day out for the family. Others, however, literally dedicate their lives to breeding and showing dogs; within Bull Terrierdom a surprising number of devotees have remained active for 40 or even 50 years. The sport spans all social barriers and is increasingly international in scope, with news – from big wins to the latest gossip – flashing around the world via telephone and the Internet.

Worldwide, thousands of competitive events are staged under the auspices of national kennel clubs. For example, in America, more than 10,000 events are held under AKC rules each year. The vast majority of these are conformation shows, in which dogs are examined and placed according to how well they measure up, in the judge's opinion, to the standard of perfection for their breeds. In other words,

Am. Ch. Brummagem Flying Colors, handled by the author, takes BOV at his first show weekend under breeder-judge Marilyn Drewes.

Photo: Mitchell.

dogs are judged not against each other but rather against the ideal as represented by the Breed Standard. The purpose of such competitions is the improvement, over the long term, in breeding stock. Individual breeders can exhibit their stock and compare their progress in producing that elusive perfect specimen against that of their fellow breeders.

When Bull Terrier owners talk about dog events they are almost always referring to conformation shows. However, a few Bull Terriers do compete successfully at obedience trials, which test a dog's ability to perform a set number of exercises. On the other hand, events like field trials for Retrievers, Pointers and Spaniels, and competitions for herding dogs are outside the breed's purview.

Puppies can begin to compete for their conformation Championships at just six months of age, though most are not fully trained or competitive until later. Male Bull Terriers usually reach their peak for show purposes between two and three years of age, though many do much of their winning before then; bitches mature earlier and many, though by no means all, are retired when they have pups. Unlike breeds that mature late and remain competitive for many years, Bull Terriers are typically past their best by their fifth birthday. However, if owner and dog enjoy shows and showing, there is no reason not to continue having fun; older dogs can be entered in the Veterans class.

My advice to novice owners is first to find out about the sport by attending some local shows – leaving your pup at home. If you think you might enjoy becoming involved, join your regional Bull Terrier club, or, if there is not one, join your local all-breed club, and go on from there. You will certainly meet many interesting people and gain new friends, as well as learning what is involved in showing your dog.

DOG SHOWS

Conformation shows range from informal, fun matches, at which only a few dogs compete, to major all-breed Championship events, like Crufts and the Westminster Kennel Club show, that attract thousands of entries and spectators and can last several days. An older term is 'bench' show, so called because each dog is assigned a stall at which it must be 'benched' when not competing. Today, however, the majority of shows are no longer benched. Despite these differences, all shows share the same basic format: dogs are entered in classes, assessed individually by the judge and placed in order of merit; unbeaten dogs then go forward to compete at the next level, with the remainder eliminated.

Formal shows operate under the rules and regulations of the governing kennel club – the KC in the UK, AKC in America and so on. When you enter your dog at such a show you are agreeing to comply with these rules, so be aware of them. At the show, remember you and your Bull Terrier are on display to the general public; you are both ambassadors for the breed and for pure-bred dogs in general.

UK SHOWS

The smallest KC events are sanction and limit shows, which, as the name implies, are limited to members of the show-giving organization. They are ideal for newcomers to the sport, whether two-legged or four. A number of regional Bull Terrier clubs hold limit shows; it was at such an event that my first Bull Terrier and I made our rather hesitant debut. Next in size and standing come open shows, which may be quite large, scheduling classes catering for most breeds or focusing on just one breed. Most open shows put on by Bull Terrier clubs are very popular and highly competitive. The largest and most prestigious events are, of course, the two dozen or so general Championship shows staged annually. Usually the six groups – Gundogs, Hounds, Terriers, Toys, Utility and Working – are scheduled over three days, two groups per day, with the six group winners competing for BIS (Best in Show) on the last day. Some shows like Crufts offer CCs (Challenge Certificates) for all breeds, others do not. Those offering CCs for the breed attract the strongest Bull Terrier entries, typically with Champions and CC winners battling with young and upcoming dogs for top honours. A certain number of CCs are allocated to breed clubs, permitting the Bull Terrier Club (BTC) and several of the regional clubs to put on Championship shows each year. Obviously, the BTC show is a premier event in the breed calendar; in America such an event is called a national specialty.

The number of classes scheduled for Bull Terriers at Championship shows varies. A club show might offer eight or nine classes for dogs and, of course, the same number for bitches: for example classes might include Puppy (for dogs of six and not exceeding twelve months of age on the first day of the show); Junior (six and not exceeding eighteen months); Novice (for dogs that have not won a CC or three or more first prizes at Open or Championship shows, Puppy classes excepted); Post Graduate (for dogs that have not won a CC or more than five first prizes at Championship shows in postgraduate classes or above); Limit (for dogs that have not won three CCs under three different judges or seven or more first prizes at Championship shows in Limit and Open classes); Open (open to all dogs, Champions included); and Veteran (seven years or older on the first day of the show).

A general Championship show might offer only Puppy, Junior, Post Graduate, Limit and Open classes.

Assuming there are five or more dogs of sufficient merit in each class, the judge places them first to fifth, with a red card for first place, a blue for second and so on. (In America these colours are reversed, with blue going to the first placed dog and red to the second!) From the unbeaten exhibits, the judge selects the CC winners for each sex, presents them with the signed green cards signifying these awards and finally determines whether the best dog or bitch is Best of Breed (BOB). To become a Champion, a dog must win three CCs under three different judges, one when over the age of twelve months. Show results are published in the two dog fanciers' newspapers that are published each week, along with critiques from the judges. If the show-bug bites, you will want to subscribe to one or both of these publications to keep up with what is going on with Bull Terriers and the sport in general.

SHOWS IN AMERICA
Shows in America differ in several significant ways from those in the UK. The vast majority of AKC-sanctioned events offer Championship points, with relatively few matches (non-Championship) shows. To become a Champion, a dog has to accumulate 15 points, which must include two 'majors' of three, four or five points. The points awarded to the winning (winners) dog depend on the number of Bull Terriers he or she has beaten. Points are also gained for group or BIS wins and so, theoretically, a dog can become a Champion without ever having beaten a specimen of his or her own breed.

Another major difference is that Champions do not compete for these Championship points. Instead, they join the

Winners Dog and Winners Bitch in the Best of Breed or Variety class, from which BOB or BOV is selected before going forward to Group competition. A typical schedule of classes is: Puppy, Twelve-to-Eighteen Months, Novice, Bred-by-Exhibitor, American-bred, and Open, followed of course by the BOB or BOV class. The Bull Terrier Club of America (BTCA) and regional clubs also put on Specialty shows, which may be stand-alone events or held in conjunction with general Championship shows. Specialties can be preceded by a Sweepstakes, which is like a match only much more prestigious, and such events often schedule non-regular classes like Veteran, Stud Dog and Brood Bitch.

America is unique in classifying white and coloured Bull Terriers as separate varieties, so that there are Winners dog and Winners Bitch and BOV for each variety. At all-breed shows the white and coloured BOVs both compete in the Terrier group, while at independent specialties they come up against each other for BOB.

IN OTHER COUNTRIES

There are many variations on these show systems in other countries. The South African system is a variation on the British one, with open and Championship shows and Champions competing for the CCs; to become a Champion, a dog must gain five points, with a certificate counting for one point if there is competition from less than ten dogs, and two points for ten or more. The system in Australia is similar; Champions compete for challenge awards, for which the winners receive points towards their Championships. In European countries dogs are, in effect, judged twice, once to assess their quality (grading) and then competitively with the dogs being placed first to fourth in order of merit. The judge dictates a short critique on each and

every dog, a signed copy of which is given to the exhibitor. Top continental dogs often compete and win Championships in several countries. Also in Germany there are two titles – VDH and Klub (Club) Champion. VDH is the equivalent to the national kennel club; CCs can be won in both open and Champion classes – four (two of these at major shows) are needed to gain the title, with at least one year between first and last and under three different judges. The Club title is the more prestigious as it necessitates winning in the very best company at a Championship show put on by one of the two national Bull Terrier clubs.

International Champion is a title awarded by the Fédération Cynologique International (FCI) (as an aside, 'cynology' is the study of canines). Unlike the KC and the AKC, the FCI is not a registry; it is a for-profit show-giving organisation, whose headquarters are in Belgium. Formed primarily to encourage the standardization of shows in smaller countries, it has developed into a major international player in the sport in Europe and in both Central and South America. The FCI's equivalent of the CC is the Certificat d'Aptitude au Championnat International de Beauté (CACIB). To gain the title International Champion, a dog must win four CACIBs under at least three different judges in at least three different countries; the dog must be over 15 months of age, must win one CACIB in its country of residence and there must be one year and one day between the first and last CACIBs.

JUDGES AND JUDGING

Bull Terrier breeders and exhibitors are noted for being willing to travel long distances to seek out the opinions of judges who are fellow breeders. Vastly greater prestige accrues from prizes won under fellow breeders than those gained under group judges or so-called all-rounders, that is, judges approved for all terrier breeds. The Bull Terrier fraternity emphasizes type and positive virtues and are concerned that all-rounders tend to place too much importance on soundness and a lack of faults. The ideal, of course, is a balance between these two extremes – virtues plus soundness, rather than either virtues plus unsoundness or a faultless nonentity.

When you pay to enter your Bull Terrier at a show you are in effect seeking the judge's opinion of your dog. How well does your dog stand up against the Standard of perfection? All you can expect is the judge's honest assessment of the dog on that day. Whether the judge is impressed with your dog or not, it is incumbent on you to be polite and sportsmanlike. Sometimes your dog may be placed higher than you expected, at other times lower. You pays your money and you takes your chances, as the expression goes. I often remind myself of the story of the judge who told a novice owner "that's a very nice dog, but I'm afraid it's not a good Boxer." You may have the nicest dog around, but he or she may not be a super Bull Terrier according to the Standard. Remember, however, you get to take your dog, the same dog, home with you and that is more important than winning prizes.

OBEDIENCE EVENTS

Relatively few Bull Terriers take part in competitive obedience trials. With skilled training, these few perform well. In America several Bull Terriers gain their CD (Companion Dog) and one or two their CDX (Companion Dog Excellent) titles most years. While some take to it well, many do not; their exuberance and hard-headedness do not mesh with the rigorous training necessary for serious obedience

The versatile Bull Terrier tackles Agility obstacles.   Courtesy of Mary Remer.

Ch. Sunspar June Breeze UD, CGC, TDI practising Open Obedience.
Photo courtesy: Christine Burton.

Ch. Sunspar June Breeze, the first Utility Champion in the history of the breed, practising Utility Obedience.
Photo courtesy: Christine Burton.

work. Also, insensitive training methods can soon turn a happy-go-lucky Bull Terrier into a truly miserable creature. So my counsel is the same as that for showing dogs: if both you and your Bull Terrier enjoy attending obedience school and preparing for and competing in obedience events, then go for it; otherwise, find something else to do.

It is advisable to wait until your dog is fully mature before embarking on this venture into obedience. In addition, if you are involved in conformation, it is better – and certainly much less demanding – to wait until at or near the end of your dog's show career before turning your attention to obedience. I should add here that obedience is also an outlet for dogs that are not of show quality or have been spayed or neutered, as there are no requirements in these respects.

There are three levels at which dogs compete in AKC obedience trials. Novice classes are for beginners; in Novice A the handler must be the dog's owner and must not have previously handled or regularly trained a CD winner, while in Novice B the dog can be handled by the owner or any other person. Success at the next level, Open, also divided into A and B, results in a CDX. There is also a third and even more challenging level called Utility; only a handful of Bull Terriers have won a UD (Utility Dog) title. In Novice the dog has to heel, both on and off the leash at different speeds, come when called and stay still along with a group of other dogs. He also has to stand to be examined. The Open exercises are similar, but involve longer periods off the leash plus jumping and retrieving tasks.

To earn an obedience title a dog must gain three legs, each of which necessitates scoring at least 50 per cent on each of the exercises, and attain a total minimum score

of 170 out of a possible 200 points.

THE INCOMPLEAT SHOW GUIDE
HANDLING CLASSES
Many Bull Terriers are such extroverts that they take naturally to the show ring and it is their owners who are uptight and jittery when placed at the other end of the lead. And, of course, any nervousness is transmitted straight down the lead to the dog. This is where a good handling class is needed to accustom both dog and owner to what happens at shows. There are usually suitable classes put on locally expressly for this purpose; if not, you may have to make use of general training classes or whatever is available. At these classes, you and your dog will learn the elements of ring craft. Basically, your Bull Terrier must behave properly around other dogs, of every variety and disposition, and get used to typical ring procedures – standing correctly, walking around the ring, being examined by the judge and walking on a diagonal or in a triangle, all while showing himself off to best advantage. Remember treats and lots of praise, and have fun. For best results, you should practise what you learn during the classes for five or ten minutes four or five times a week. Also, take advantage of local fun matches to assess the progress you and your dog are making. Shows are held both indoors and outdoors – usually on grass – so you should prepare your dog for both.

A word regarding collars and leads. The traditional show lead for Bull Terriers in the UK is the white martingale (double loop) type. These are ideal for showing your dog on a loose lead. Another popular type is a simple white slip-lead, made from round braided material. Having used both of these types of leads over the years, I have now switched to a light choke chain with a clip-on lead made from thin cord; these can be

The loose leash technique at its best: Am. Can. Ch. Magor Matinee Idol, 1992 Silverwood Trophy winner.

employed for loose lead work and yet provide much greater control as and when needed. You should use whichever one you feel most comfortable with.

CONDITIONING AND GROOMING

The first essential for showing is that your Bull Terrier has been properly fed and conditioned, as a matter of course, resulting in the right weight for the dog, superior muscle tone and a healthy, gleaming coat. In other words, if you are doing well by your dog, there should not be much more that you have to do in the way of conditioning.

Unlike some of the coated breeds – for which preparations entail little short of a tour de force – Bull Terriers require minimal grooming for the show ring. In springtime, especially after a long cold winter, extra brushing will be needed to remove loose hair and perhaps to thin the heavy coat some dogs develop around their neck.

There are as many pre-show routines as there are exhibitors. As an example here is mine. I like to complete certain tasks several days before the show, namely nails, ears and tail. Nails should be checked and clipped or filed, if necessary. I do this early because I do not want my dog to associate nail clipping with shows. Ears should be checked and cleaned, if dirty. Next, I deal with the tail, for which a pair of barber's scissors is needed. I cut back the long hairs at the tip and then the straggling hairs along the side of and underneath the tail. My intention is to present a smooth, rounded appearance. (Trimming the tail requires practice, so you may wish to seek advice and also to practise long before your first show.) Two days prior to the show, I bath my dog in the bath tub, using warm water and regular dog shampoo and then, of course, dry him off with towels. (Incidentally, this is not the time to experiment with a new shampoo.) All of my dogs love to be bathed, but none like soapy water around their eyes or ears, so I wash the head afterwards with a washcloth. Some exhibitors trim the tail immediately after bathing the dog, because the hair is then softer. I prefer to do it earlier as the hair has a chance to grow out a little, so avoiding that just-trimmed look. The night before the show I cut off whiskers and I clean teeth. And that is it – I am ready for the morrow. On the morning of the show I rewash feet, if they are dirty, and slick down the coat with a towel.

View a line-up of white Bull Terriers and there will be nearly as many shades of white as there are dogs, ranging from that whiter-than-white popular on detergent commercials, through off-white, to coats with a definite yellowish tinge. Some variation is natural, but special shampoos are what produce those whiter-than-white shades. In days of yore, breeders used blueing or diluted bleach to cleanse and brighten coats. Today, pet stores carry a range of whitening shampoos that do this far more effectively; some use optical dyes, others enzymes. And, if you have coloureds, there are even canine shampoos that claim to brighten their coats.

Until now, I have studiously avoided mentioning the whole issue of chalk and other 'foreign' substances used to enhance the dog's appearance. When I began showing, dogs would enter the ring, shake themselves and become enveloped in a cloud of chalk. Later the KC clamped down on this practice and banned chalk and the like from the show site. AKC regulations state clearly that no dog shall receive an award if the natural colour, shade or markings have been altered or changed by the use of any substance and that any "cleaning substances must be removed before the dog enters the ring." In practice, such regulations do not preclude the use of white make-up or the traditional chalk, as long as it is removed before the dog is shown. Many exhibitors still use white make-up around the eyes, muzzle and underjaw and feet of a white Bull Terrier or on the white highlights of a coloured. They then remove the said white substance so that none comes off when the dog is handled by the judge. Inevitably, however, a thin residual white coating remains and this is a distinct improvement over using nothing at all.

I make no comment on the ethics of such practices; I am just saying that in the real world these things happen.

SHOWS AND ALL THAT STUFF
The best way for a newcomer to learn the ropes, so to speak, of shows and showing is, firstly, by attending shows as a spectator and, secondly, by enlisting the advice and help of an experienced exhibitor. This is a much more pragmatic approach than my trying to explain the details of which shows and classes to enter, then how to enter, what to do if your dog's registration or transfer of ownership does not come back in time and so on.

Some exhibitors set off for shows taking with them just about everything except the kitchen sink; others, and I count myself among them, like to travel light. The essentials are yourself and the dog, the entry forms and stuff for the dog – crate, show lead, treats, grooming materials, towels and, last but not least, water and a water bowl. You should plan to arrive at the show with time to spare – and remember, if you are late, the class will be judged without you. One final point, *never* leave your dog locked in the car in hot or even warm weather; a dog can overheat and die in less time that you could possibly imagine.

Showing your dog can be a delightful and absorbing hobby. Give it a try and find the niche that gives you and your dog the most enjoyment, whether it is serious competition on the Championship circuit, fraternizing with fellow Bull Terrier owners or contributing to shows and clubs in your home town.

8 CELEBRATION OF THE BREED

Lovers of the Bull Terrier are fortunate to have inherited a rich tapestry of tradition and lore – from heart-rending narratives to historic occasions, from anecdotes to fables, from the outrageous to the unbelievable. They are woven into the very fabric of our wonderful breed.

SIR WALTER SCOTT'S CAMP

It was of his beloved dog Camp that Sir Walter wrote "the wisest dog I ever owned was what is called a bulldog terrier." Born in 1800, Camp "was got by a black and tan English terrier called Doctor out of a thoroughbred brindled bull bitch." According to Scott, he was "of great strength, very handsome, extremely sagacious, faithful and affectionate towards the human species but somewhat ferocious towards his own". This last trait may be understated, as Camp "could only be kept from fighting," it was reported, "when his master's eye was upon him, so brought the two into many a scrape." Scott also commented on Camp's gift for gaiety, drollery and understanding of whatever was said to him. Camp accompanied his master on hunting trips; though "an amateur of coursing", Camp was "excellent at finding hares, and, since the breadth of his chest and the broadness of his paws made him a capital water-dog, would serve as a retriever" when Scott went shooting wild duck.

In old age, Camp sprained his back and could no longer accompany his master on trips, so he would lie waiting for the first hint of the way by which Scott would return. Camp was always the first to greet him. The devotion was mutual; when Camp fell ill, Scott nursed him back to health, as "the dog would take no food except the milk his master poured into his mouth by spoonfuls." A portrait of Scott and Camp, painted by James Saxon in 1805, is on display at the Scottish National Portrait Gallery.

Scott later built Abbotsford, the great house in the Scottish border country with which his writings and the Romantic revival are so closely associated. During the late 1920s the house was rented by the Johnstone family and it was in the library at Abbotsford that 'D' Montague Johnstone's first Bull Terrier, the brindle Sher Fustian, whelped a litter of puppies. Sher Fustian and one of the these pups, Romany Ringer, are behind all of the great Romany dogs

The Bull Terrier – a breed rich in folklore and tradition.   *Photo: van Kempen.*

and almost certainly can be found, albeit way back, in the pedigree of the Bull Terrier occupying your couch.

THE REMARKABLE PUSS

Pride of place as the matriarch of the breed must go to Puss – the first of the new pure white dogs exhibited by James Hinks. She was a remarkable specimen by any standard, as indicated by James Hinks, the son, who wrote "Old Puss was a wonder. No money would tempt my dad to part with her, and when she died he kept her skull as a memento of a wonderful bitch with a tremendous bite. When fighting she was a terror; she would hug her adversary like a bear, and bite him through."

Puss's arrival on the London show scene was recorded by Rawdon Lee in a 1894 publication: "James Hinks began to cross the patched, heavy-headed Bull Terrier, used for fighting, with the English white terrier,

and in due time he produced dogs handsome enough to make a name for themselves, and able to revolutionise the variety. Some of the old 'doggie men' said this new breed was soft and could not fight. 'Can't they?' said Hinks, when talking to a lot of his London friends at the Holborn Horse Repository dog show in May 1862, 'I think they can.' 'Well,' said one of the London school, 'let's make a match.' Hinks, nothing loth, did make a match and backed his bitch Puss – that day she had won first prize in her class – for £5 pounds and a case of champagne, against one of the short-faced patched dogs similar in weight.

"The fight came off that evening at Bill Tupper's well-known rendezvous in Long Acre. It took Puss half-an-hour to kill her opponent, and so little the worse for wear was she for her encounter that she appeared on the bench the next morning, a few marks on her cheeks and muzzle being the

76

only signs of the determined combat in which she had been the principal overnight. When accounts of this became bruited abroad, although it is not generally believed, the popularity of the long-faced dog was established."

Versions of Puss's 1862 victories in London differ in detail. Most authorities agree that the show probably took place at Ashburnham Hall, Cremorne, rather than Holborn. There was also disagreement as to whether Puss won her first prize ribbon before or after the fight. Grandson Carleton Hinks, writing more than 60 years later, suggested: "Probably one show that took place in London worthy of mention was the match between Hinks' bitch Puss, weighing 40lbs, and Mr Tupper's coloured bitch weighing 60lbs. An uneven match by all appearances but in the end Puss killed her opponent, returned to the dog show...caught the judge's eye and annexed the red." (Author's note: the weight difference is surprising, since dogs were usually matched at about the same weight.)

No doubt the story of Puss's victory has been embellished over the years. Indeed, there are those who would suggest it is apocryphal. Nevertheless, Puss and her exploits in London are woven tightly into the origins and folklore of the breed.

BIRMINGHAM – THE HOME OF THE BREED

The origins of the breed, as discussed earlier, are strongly rooted in Birmingham, the great industrial metropolis of the Victorian era. Indeed, with the likes of Carleton Hinks and Jimmy Thompson, the city remained a bastion of the Bull Terrier until the 1940s, when the mantle was assumed by the Thames valley, home to Ormandy and other great kennels.

What may not be realized is the proximity of the key breeders to the city centre during the 19th century. James Hinks lived at 53 Worcester Street, a stone's throw from the home of J.F. Godfree at 5 Bull Ring, and later opened a Canine Repository in Sherlock Street. Joe Willock was proprietor of The Barrel in Inge Street, J.F. Mayhew lived on Temple Row close to the cathedral, T. Satterthwaite on Hurst Street and the Lea brothers at 19 Cannon Street. Fred Hinks had several addresses, but registered most of his dogs from his home on Bath Row, while his younger brother James ran the Sportsman's Hostelry in Pershore Street. All of these addresses were located within easy walking distance of each other in the heart of the city. Of the principal players only Charles Boyce, several miles away in Balsall Heath, lived outside this central perimeter. No doubt the synergy created by so many breeders and dogs in proximity served to establish and consolidate the white cavaliers in those early days.

Unfortunately, in the guise of progress and modernization, the centre of Brum today bears scant resemblance to the city of yesteryear, or even, for that matter, of the haunts that were familiar to me as a schoolboy during the 1950s. Worcester Street suffered first from the expansions of New Street railway station and, more recently, essentially disappeared with the construction of the Smallbrook Ringway. Worse still was the impact of the Ringway on the old Bull Ring, where, by royal charter, markets had been held on Thursdays since the 12th century. A cobbled expanse falling away steeply toward St Martin's Church and the River Rea, the old Bull Ring was the heart and soul of the city to generations of Brummies.

Of course, much else has changed since Victorian times. The construction of Corporation Street and surroundings began shortly after James Hinks' death, replacing the unsavoury slums that were home to the notorious 'Birmingham rough'. In 1867 the rough were active in the religious riots that plagued the city; those were days when Brummies and their dogs had to be able to take care of themselves in the event of an altercation. When visiting modern Brum take a few moments to reflect on the vibrant centre of Hinks' day – especially if you are hopelessly lost in the one-way traffic system or on the egregious Ringway.

EARLY DESCRIPTIONS OF THE BREED

In the 1859 edition of *The Dog in Health and Disease,* Stonehenge provided the fancy with the first meaningful description of the Bull Terrier: "The points of the Bull Terrier vary greatly in accordance with degree of each in the specimen examined. There should not be either the projection of the under jaw, or the crooked fore legs, or the small and weak hind quarters; and until these are lost, or nearly so, the crossing should be continued on the terrier side. The perfect Bull Terrier may, therefore, be defined as the terrier with as much bull as can be combined with the absence of the above points, and showing the full head (not of course equal to that of the bull), the strong jaw, the well-defined chest, powerful shoulders, and thin fine tail of the Bulldog, accompanied by the light neck, active frame, strong loin, and fuller proportions of the hind quarter of the terrier...The height varies from 10 inches to 16, or even 20. Colour most frequently white, pure or patched with black, blue, red, fawn or brindle. Sometimes also black and tan, or self coloured red." In the next edition, "most admired white" replaced "most frequently white", intimating the near monopoly of pure white coats in the show ring.

The first description published in America, of which I am aware, appeared in *James' Terrier Dogs* (1873), which gave 'The Points and Properties of a Perfect Bull Terrier' as: "His head should be long, the muzzle sharp, the jaw level – not underhung, which is a disfigurement and also prevents a dog punishing his adversary. The under jaw should display great power and the neck should be long.

"The chest is wide, the shoulders sloping and powerful, the loins and back strong, the hindquarters and thighs muscular. The tail should be fine and sting-like but not bare, carried gaily but not 'hooped.'

"The fore legs should be straight with a slight angle at the pastern. The bone of the leg must be as large as possible and the muscle of the forearm, as well as the tendons of the pasterns and toes, proportionately strong. If the foot is not perfectly straight, it must turn in, not out. In shape it should be very round and cat-like, but very highly arched toes are apt to give way. Sole hard and thick. The hindquarters must be as strong as possible, wide as well as deep. Bone of pastern strong and large; hocks strong and straight.

"The coat throughout is fine and short, and it should lie smoothly as in a well dressed racehorse. Pure white, with a black eye and nose, is the most approved color, but white with colored ears or a patch on the eyes is highly appreciated. As in the Bull Dog the color should be 'whole' and, when spotted, correspond with the colors of the Bull Dog.

"His weight from twelve up to thirty-five pounds or more. His appearance resembles that of a terrier, except that he is wider across the skull and possesses more strength and stamina."

FIRE AND WATER

Thomas Knox's *Dog Stories and Dog Lore*,

published in New York in 1887, discussed what he described as a common peculiarity of the breed – its aversion to fire: "On a train leaving Chicago...a well-dressed man entered the smoker with a handsome Bull Terrier at his heels...A passenger at the other end of the car drew a cigar, put it in his mouth, lit a match and held it carelessly in his hand waiting for it to burn into a bright blaze...the dog saw the match, ran rapidly down the car, sprang at the match, and, catching it in his mouth, extinguished it in an instant. A roar of laughter greeted the exploit...The dog contentedly trotted back to his master's feet and sat down as if he had done a very meritorious act. Then the passengers began experimenting. Someone lit a parlor match and threw it in the air; the dog sprang and caught it before it fell. Matches lighted and thrown on the floor were extinguished in an instant by the dog with his mouth and fore paws...Someone took a piece of paper, crumpled it into a ball and lit it. When it was ablaze he threw it on the floor...The dog had been restrained with difficulty during the operation, and, being released, made a spring and came down on the paper with all four paws and nose in a bunch, extinguishing it easily...The owner said the dog was a Bull Terrier about two years old and added 'I use him as a watch-dog...and have not trained him...beyond his natural instincts. It struck me the trait was a good one; so I patted him on the head. He beats a patent fire-extinguisher all hollow.' "

Contemporary with this report are stories of the breed's affinity for water. Rawdon Lee recalled that a Mr Tom Pickett of Newcastle had a Bull Terrier named Wallace, a prize winner, which won a swimming match in the Tyne and "noted that his own Madman (one of many dogs of this name), was as good a swimmer as ever entered the water."

Such was the passion of one of Sir Harry Preston's Bull Terriers for water that when master and dog were crossing the river at Blackfriars atop an open omnibus, the dog jumped from bus to bridge and then into the Thames. In best storybook tradition, the dog survived to 'tell the tale'. The Bull Terrier's love of water, whether at the seashore, in a canal (or 'cut' as Brummies used to call them), or in the form of a bath (mud baths are fine too), has been maintained, even strengthened, through the years. The immediate reaction of Bess, my first Bull Terrier, to a beach in Wales was to run into the sea and take off swimming. Had I not swum after her, I am quite convinced she would have paddled her way across to Ireland. The same Bess wreaked havoc at a hitherto peaceful fishing competition taking place on the Duke of Bridgewater's canal in Cheshire – she dived into the murky water in pursuit of the bait as an astonished fisherman cast his line.

GARM – A HOSTAGE

That master of the short story, Rudyard Kipling, set this heart-rending tale of a soldier and his Bull Terrier in India during the days of the British Raj. First published in 1897, it is usually found printed together with *The Power of the Dog* from which come the familiar lines:

"Brother and sisters, I bid thee beware
Of giving your heart to a dog to tear."

Garm was "one of the finest Bull Terriers – of the old-fashioned breed, two parts bull and one part terrier...pure white, with a fawn-coloured saddle just behind the neck, and a fawn diamond at the root of his thin whippy tail." The story traces the separation of Garm and his penitent master through to their eventual reunion. Not unexpectedly Garm displays those singular qualities that owners have come to expect of the breed. My favourite scene has Garm marching the artilleryman, who had tried to steal him, back to the fort, to the amusement of one and all – several regiments had tried to steal Garm; naturally to no avail!

THE BAR SINISTER

Richard Harding Davis based this classic rags-to-riches short story on the real life of Kid, known more formally as Edgewood Cold Steel. Born in Canada, Kid's father was the registered Bull Terrier Lord Minto. His dam, however, was a 'black and tan', hence the dubious parentage, Kid being the only white pup in the litter. Kid was later purchased by Davis, for whom he won numerous first prizes. The first, beautifully illustrated, edition of *The Bar Sinister* was published in New York in 1903. Since then, the story has appeared in many editions, has been serialized and, in the 1950s, made into a movie.

The screenplay for the MGM film gave full range to the extraordinary talents of trainer William (Bill) Koehler, who handled the eight Bull Terriers and also supervised the 180 other canines used in the dog show sequences. The starring role of Kid, renamed Wildfire in the movie, was played by Cadence Glacier CDX (Companion Dog Excellent) with marvellous panache – hardly surprising since Bull Terriers are such natural hams. The film was released in 1955 as *The Bar Sinister*. However, the studio changed the title a couple of months later to *It's a Dog's Life* – apparently because someone thought the original sounded like a Western! 'Wildfire' deservedly won the PATSY award (Picture Animal Award Top Star of the Year), offered by the American Humane Association and voted on by film critics. Thanks to a bequest from Glacier's co-owner, the late Claudia Slack, this award now resides on the wall in my study.

In the 1960s Raymond Oppenheimer revived the name when registering the great Ormandy Souperlative Bar Sinister. James, as he was known to his friends, possessed an impeccable pedigree, with champion parents and grandparents. But he did bear a cross – only one of his testicles had descended, which precluded his being shown. Raymond, however, determined not to waste a dog so far in advance of his contemporaries and used him at stud with striking success. Later Raymond was able to argue successfully that faults such as monorchidism should be treated by the KC as a fault rather than a disqualification. Despite this change James himself was never shown, his place in history already assured.

JOCK OF THE BUSHVELD

This stirring adventure story of a coloured Bull Terrier in the Transvaal at the turn of the century was written by Sir Percy Fitzpatrick and first published in 1907. Jock enjoyed in abundance the many traits that made Camp and Puss so remarkable – intelligence, tenacity, unfailing loyalty and courage. Ted Lyon had become accustomed to coloured Bull Terriers such as Jock in India and it was to redress the lack of spirit and audacity that he began his crusade to reintroduce colour into the breed at about this time.

Richard Glyn studied the early efforts of Ted Lyon and his cohorts and published his conclusions in an article entitled 'The Seven Sources of Colour' which appeared in *Our Dogs* in 1933. He suggested "the chief winning strains of Coloured Bull Terriers" were descended from just seven coloured Staffordshires. Writing in 1950, Glyn revised his view of the "seven ancestors" to "six of which were Staffordshire, and the seventh (and one of the most successful) was a first cross between a brindle Bulldog

Jock of the Bushveldt.

and a Manchester Terrier. All of these seven were dead by 1925, and most of them long before that date." The rumour of a Bulldog-Manchester cross close up in the pedigrees of the early coloureds had been persistent, and now Glyn confirmed its veracity. Subsequent research has revealed the seventh dog to be none other than the brindle Jock of the Bushveldt (note the addition of a 't' to Bushveld), who was born in 1910 – the get of the brindle Bulldog Vulcan Prince and the tricolour Moss Rose. So a real-life Jock joins Fitzpatrick's hero in the annals of breed folklore.

TOY BULL TERRIERS
Lady Evelyn Ewart, a staunch patron of small members of the breed, writing around 1906 noted that "Toy Bull Terriers have fallen into popularity as pets, and it is chiefly in the East End of London or the mining districts of the Midlands of England that specimens are to be found...their lilliputian self-assertion is quite amusing. As pets they are most affectionate, excellent as watch-dogs, clever at tricks, and always cheerful and companionable. They have good noses and will hunt diligently; but

wet weather or thick undergrowth will deter them, and they are too small to do serious harm to the best stocked game preserve.

"One little dog which belonged to the writer would fly at cattle, and once got kicked by a cow for his pains. Equally he would fight any big dog, and the only chance of distracting him from his warlike purposes was for his mistress to run when a fight was impending. Fear of being lost made him follow his owner and abandon the enemy. After many narrow escapes he met his fate in the jaws of a large black retriever which he had attacked in his own kennel.

"The most valuable Toy Bull Terriers are small and very light in weight, and these small dogs usually have 'apple heads.' Pony Queen, the former property of Sir Raymond Tyrwhitt Wilson, weighed under 3 lbs, but the breed remains 'toy' up to 15 lbs. When you get a dog with a long wedge-shaped head, the latter, in competition with small 'apple-headed' dogs, always takes the prizes; and a slightly contradictory state of affairs arises from the fact that the small dog with an imperfectly shaped head will sell for more money than a dog with a perfectly shaped head which is larger.

"At present there is a diversity of opinion as to their points, but roughly they are a long flat head, wide between the eyes and tapering to the nose, which should be black. Ears erect and bat-like, straight legs and rather distinctive feet; some people say these are cat-like.

"Some Toy Bull Terriers have a curved back which looks as if the dog was cringing. This peculiarity has been attributed to the fact that they have been carried under the arm or even in the pockets of their owners for generations, and that finally nature has adapted the dog to its usual position. This is as it may be. Toy Bull Terriers ought to have an alert, gay appearance, coupled with refinement, which requires a nice whip tail. The best colour is pure white. A brindle spot is not amiss, and even a brindle dog is admissible, but black marks are wrong. The coat ought to be close and stiff to the touch. Toy Bull-terriers are not delicate as a rule. They require warmth, and never are better than when taking exercise in all weathers."

Jacko, the famous ratting bull-and-terrier of the 1860s, weighed about 13 lbs. He was said to have killed 60 rats in 160 seconds! Serious supporters of these small ones talked about the "true" 16 pounders. They decried the influence of the "toy" breeders, who by 1913 had succeeded in transferring the under-12 lb dogs to the Toy group; this weight limit was recommended by Lady Ewart. At 20, 16 or even 13 pounds, Bull Terriers retained many of the important breed characteristics and were still capable of dealing with vermin and giving a good account of themselves. The same was not true of the Toys. It was as if their devotees were living in Alice's Wonderland and, like many other upper-class institutions, the Toy breed failed to survive the realities of the Great War. Unfortunately by fragmenting support for small Bull Terriers, the Toy faction unwittingly brought about the demise of miniatures – the 12 to 20 lb dogs – which by the early 1920s were "struck off the Kennel Club's list as being defunct."

CHAMPION HAYMARKET FAULTLESS

Westminster Kennel Club held its first show in New York in May 1877, since when it has become a veritable institution. Nowadays it is staged each February at the 'Garden' – Madison Square Garden – just as

it was on that momentous day in 1918 when a Bull Terrier carried off the BIS trophy for the first and only time. The following contemporary report captures for Bull Terrier aficionados the excitement of that unique victory by the Canadian dog Haymarket Faultless. Although his pedigree traces back to top UK dogs like Ch. Charlwood Victor Wild, Faultless was distinctly North American in style – higher on the leg, narrower in chest, ears cropped and lacking the downfaced head that was all the rage in Britain. For better or worse, this cleaner, more terrier-like dog was destined to be superseded by the modern Bull Terrier that was then beginning to emerge in top British kennels.

"The greatest honor ever to come to the Bull Terrier was the winning of best in show at Westminster Kennel Club exhibition at Madison Square Garden, New York, February, 1918, when Humphrey Elliott came down from Ottawa, Canada, with Haymarket Faultless, a son of Champion Noross Patrician out of Champion Channel Queen. Faultless had been shown at the Mineola Show the previous summer and had created a sensation there. When he entered the ring at the Garden, Faultless was the cynosure of all eyes and easily topped the breed which numbered thirty-nine and was judged by Enno Meyer and then returned in the competition for best of show and best all breeds. The systematic group classification for Best of Breed competitors was not in vogue at the time.

"Two of America's greatest allrounders, Charles G. Hopton and the late Vinton P. Breese, by a process of elimination and joint collaboration, had narrowed down the contenders of a huge field to two, G. Elbridge Snow's celebrated Pekingese, Champion Phantom of Ashcroft, and Humphrey Elliott with the Bull Terrier

Haymarket Faultless. Although the Bull Terrier people had a deep conviction of the greatness of Faultless and an abiding faith in his merit, they never dreamed that he was destined to such heights. Mr Hopton held out for the Peke. Mr. Breese was adamant for the Bull Terrier. Therefore, all their hearts beat in unison with a single prayer on their lips when George S. Thomas was summoned as arbiter. Never was a best in show staged to quite so dramatic a tempo as when Mr Thomas, a truly great allround personality, nodded in the direction of Humphrey and Faultless. And then the crowd went wild. Never before was there a more popular Best in Show award.

"Now a word as to Haymarket Faultless, himself. All white from the tip of his big black nose to the end of his good straight tail, endowed with great depth of rib and girth, beautiful sloping shoulders and good reach of neck, with a true front and muscular rear quarters, his great forte was a matchless combination of type and balance. To be true he was not possessed of the now fashionable angulated foreface, mistakenly advanced by some fanciers as the downfaced type. Rather did he have a very strong foreface filled to his priceless small three cornered eyes; and, of supreme importance, he possessed a great sweep of punishing underjaw. The latter attainment is rarely found in the rabbit-like profile type so often met with today. About the only fault that critics of this great dog could consistently advance was his ring demeanor. Some called him the 'wooden dog.' The devoted pal of his owner, and essentially a gentleman both inside the ring and out, Faultless was a natural poser. It was due to this quality that he was sometimes wrongly accused of lack of fire. The following year, Faultless was again a near winner at Westminster. He was runner up to the Airedale, Briergate Bright Beauty."

SIR HARRY PRESTON'S SAMBO

Special, even extraordinary, relationships between dogs and their owners are legion. In the world of Bull Terriers, perhaps none were closer in spirit, indeed in all ways, than Sir Harry Preston and his Sambo. Active in the breed for more than half a century, Sir Harry's many other dogs paled against Sambo. He and Sambo were devoted companions for some 17 years. After losing Sambo, Sir Harry would ask friends to raise a glass to his memory, such was the mutual respect.

They were inseparable. When Sir Harry ventured away from his post as manager of the Royal Hotel in Brighton without his faithful companion, Sambo would wait at the front door – for several days if necessary. This was not, of course, necessary on occasions when Sambo anticipated his master's trips to London and would hide under the seat of the railway carriage. The hotel dining room was out of bounds to Sambo, but in best Bull Terrier tradition this edict rarely kept dog from master. Sambo would creep across the room, hiding underneath tables en route to his master's table at the far end of the room. Once there, he would announce his presence via a cold nose and settle down happily. On one almost disastrous evening, Sambo made his furtive journey to Sir Harry's table, but then, instead of pressing his nose against his master's knee, selected the knee of the lady who was a Sir Harry's guest. Indignant and glaring at her host, the lady rose from her seat. Fortunately, Sir Harry's intuition came to the rescue of his reputation; he looked under the table and pulled out the real culprit – Sambo.

In best tradition, master and dog grew alike and were noted for the remarkable similarity of their characters – friendly and lovable, courageous and loyal, gentle yet always ready for a scrap, fun-loving yet sometimes impatient. Friends even noted the likeness of their "beady little eyes".

COUNT VIVIAN HOLLENDER

From its beginnings the breed has attracted many remarkable individuals, sometimes eccentric, usually extrovert, invariably multi-talented and, of course, all sharing many of the characteristics of their beloved dogs. At the turn of the century there was the flamboyant Harry Monk, acknowledged as the best handler. "He came into the ring looking for all the world like a circus proprietor, complete with check suit, white spats, bowler hat, and buttonhole. Like a ringmaster mesmerising the animals, so he had the same effect on some of the judges, so well trained were his dogs." Harry's contemporary, genial Tom Gannaway, "was a well-known character at the shows, and surely loved by all, for his great sense of humour, wonderful powers of discretion and good nature."

Another extraordinary character and life-long devotee of the breed was Count Vivian Hollender. When he died in 1954, Raymond Oppenheimer wrote this tribute. "The Bull Terrier Club has lost a staunch friend in Count V.C. Hollender. Here indeed was the personification of a real dog lover and moreover one who was an outstanding judge of the breed. At times a certain hastiness of temperament could provoke in him a word or a judgement which later he would regret and criticise as harshly as his greatest detractors, but, at the end, whatever the circumstances, he possessed a wonderful ability for inspiring a genuine affection, probably because his character contained in such generous measure the virtue he so admired in the Bull Terrier – utter loyalty to his friends."

Another trait that the Count shared with his dogs was an innate ability to get into trouble. I am uncertain whether he enjoyed causing controversy or it was simply attracted to him, but he was involved in many controversial issues during his tenure as a judge. In 1919 he was the first to award a challenge certificate to a coloured Bull Terrier – Bing Boy. This was at a time when coloureds were viewed as little better than mongrels and were ostracized by the lovers of the then pure white breed. His decision caused an uproar. An unfailing supporter of the coloureds, the Count caused another sensation in January 1931 by awarding both CCs to coloureds at the National Terrier Show. The brindle Bull Terrier Lady Winifred was agreed by most to be thoroughly deserving of this, her third certificate; she thereby became the first coloured champion. What upset the establishment that day was his awarding the dog certificate to the red Hunting Blond. Tom Gannaway, who had previously handled Hunting Blond, was particularly critical of this decision, believing that the white dog that he was showing should have won. But Count Hollender was unrepentant, as indicated by his column in the Kennel Gazette:

"I seem fated to be placed in extraordinary quandaries, or give awards that are quoted as making 'history.' I have no doubt many (kind friends) say I like it, and put myself in that unenviable position.

"Just after the war a sensation was caused because I put up a brindle Bull Terrier over the white dogs. It was a blasphemy – ludicrous – outrageous. My decision was appealed against. The Committee of the Kennel Club were appealed to, but asked me one terse question: 'Was the dog in question (the famous Bing Boy) a Bull Terrier? Yes. Then why protest?'

"Well, this time I can do no better than quote Mr Tom Gannaway's criticism in *Our Dogs* in his report: 'It was a good entry assembled for that old-time lover of the breed, and the quality throughout showed a marked improvement. A most sensational incident occurred in the awarding of the Challenge Certificates, and never in the history of the breed is there a precedent where two coloured specimens won the coveted green cards.'

"Unfortunately, for many years there has been a growing erroneous idea that I prefer coloured dogs to whites. It is true that I tried to help to improve the coloured dog, but so I have the Staffordshire Pit Bull Terrier, but what it really amounts to is this, that I would try to help anything on four legs that comes under the classification of Bull Terrier, but because the colours have improved beyond all expectation, there has been jealousy in the ranks of the white owners.

"The sooner we realize that the Bull Terrier was never all white, originally, the better. I would like to state once and for all that I have bred and owned more white dogs than any others, and that my two greatest, truest, most intelligent and loyal pals were both all white."

Who can challenge Count Hollender's devotion to Bull Terriers – both coloured and white?

JIMMY THOMPSON AND RUBISLAW

Another Birmingham breeder came to prominence during the 1920s, namely Jimmy Thompson. Jimmy was a coal merchant and according to Tom Horner "had a rough exterior, but a heart of gold." I should add that, like many Brummies, his down-to-earth approach to life was accompanied by a dry, often incisive, wit that was probably completely lost on those who put on airs and graces.

Jimmy's first success came when he bred his Dauntless Duchess to Carleton Hinks'

Rubislaw.

Ch. White Wonder, which produced the Champion sisters Dauntless Beauty and Peerless of Brum. Later Duchess spawned a third Champion, Shure Thing, whom Jimmy co-owned with Carleton, and also Gladiator's Trigo, sire of the first Regent Trophy winner, Mrs Adlam's Ch. Brendon Becky. Later, Shure Thing was exported to America, but not before siring the key dog Ch. Beshelson Bayshuck. In turn, Bayshuck sired three outstanding dogs in his litter to Ch. Debonair of Brum – Champions Ringfire of Blighty (winner of the 1932 Regent trophy) and Aberdonian, both of whom were exported, and the uncrowned Rubislaw.

Jimmy wanted to buy Rubislaw. Unfortunately, he was not a wealthy man and did not have the ready cash. However, as a young man, he had been handy with his fists, winning a number of boxing medals. So he sold these medals and set off on his bicycle for Worcester, a journey of about 27 miles. Having consummated the deal, Jimmy set off to walk back to Birmingham – pushing the bicycle and leading Rubislaw. The history books tell the rest of the story. Rubislaw became the leading stud dog of his day, siring no less than seven champions, a pre-war record. He is also doubled up behind Raymond Oppenheimer's first great Champion – McGuffin. Rubislaw lived at Jimmy's coalyard, dust and all – not exactly the ideal environment for a white cavalier. Apparently, Rubislaw's grimy appearance had no effect on his fitness, his prowess as a stud dog, or his reputation as a canine gladiator. I suspect the contents of Jimmy's yard were absolutely safe with Rubislaw there to keep watch.

Though Jimmy carried on breeding under his Dauntless affix into the 1950s, he failed to move with the times. While others developed flashier, more elegant show dogs, Jimmy continued to produce the same tough – and by then comparatively coarse – Bull Terriers for which he had become so well-known in days of yore.

PATSY ANN

Marvellous tales of Bull Terriers are legion, but perhaps none is more extraordinary than that of Patsy Ann – the Greeter of Juneau. Born of pedigreed parents in Oregon in October 1929, she was shipped as a puppy to a family in Juneau, Alaska. Unfortunately, she did not settle down in that home or another in which she was tried. Defying all efforts to keep her at home, Patsy would slip her leash and take off to wherever there was a crowd of people; she loved people, the more the merrier. She was attracted in particular to the waterfront, where she took to meeting the steamships as they docked. Eventually she left home and took up residence near the docks. Never short of a meal or a place to stay, she frequented cafes and saloons and in winter toasted her toes in front of the pot-bellied stove at the Alaska Empire. Her favourite residence was the longshoremen's hall in Willoughby Avenue.

Why this strange behaviour, this refusal to stay at home? Patsy Ann was stone deaf

Patsy Ann   Photo courtesy of the Trevor Davis Collection, Alaska State Library.

and, for reasons best known to her, preferred the hustle and bustle of the waterfront. She invariably anticipated the arrival of ships long before their whistles could be heard, probably because she could sense the vibrations of their engines. Also, she had the uncanny knack of knowing where they would dock. Her dignified, friendly greeting of passengers endeared her to visitors and locals alike. In her younger days she would not allow any other dogs on the dock while the ship was in, but age brought a degree of tolerance in this regard. Patsy Ann turned into an institution; she became famous. Taxi drivers would point Patsy Ann out, stores sold postcards of her, while the newspapers provided regular updates of the Bull Terrier's exploits. In 1939, Carl Burrows published a booklet devoted to her.

Patsy Ann died peacefully in her sleep in March 1942. The next day her coffin was lowered into the waters of the Gastineau Channel over which she had watched so diligently for those many years. Fifty years on, thanks to the efforts of the Gastineau Humane Society and The Friends of Patsy Ann, the Alaskan Legislature passed the following citation in her honour:

"The Seventeenth Alaska State Legislature takes great enjoyment in recognizing the contribution of Patsy Ann, 'Official Boat Greeter of Juneau, Alaska.' She did not seek fame, only to bestow friendly greetings to all she encountered – a job she undertook with dignity, persistence, and single-minded dedication. Fame found her on its own.

"Born totally deaf, she nevertheless anticipated not only the arrival of all incoming steam ships, but also at which of Juneau's docks they would be tying up. Cynics surmised she was attracted by the occasional morsels of food tossed through the portholes by kindly travelers; but the truth was, she loved people. The bigger the crowd, the better. Baseball games were her favorites; her penchant for charging the field and absconding with the ball earned equal amounts of players' ire and spectators' delight.

"Patsy Ann was as much a fixture of beer parlors and hotel lobbies as any paying guest. She was pointed out by cab drivers and photographed by tourists. Her image adorned postcards sold by curio shops. She even appeared in a talent minstrel show for which she endured the humiliation of a bath.

"Her distinctive gait slowed over the years due to rheumatism brought on by unscheduled dives into the cold Gastineau Channel. Still, she always headed for the docks on the double whenever steam ship whistles shook the Juneau boardwalks. Human Alaskans will forever hold Patsy Ann's name dear – longer, certainly, than those of many so-called bipeds amongst them."

In addition, the Friends commissioned a sculpture of the Official Greeter from my wife Anna Burke Harris. A white, one-and-a-half times life-size bronze of Patsy Ann now adorns the docks at Juneau, so that she is now able to welcome visitors again in form as well as spirit.

MISS MONTAGUE JOHNSTONE'S WAGER

The pioneers of the coloured variety were Ted Lyon and Walter Tumner. The cause was then taken up by Mrs Violet Ellis, the breeder of Hunting Blond, and it was Mrs Ellis in her turn who was responsible for steering Miss 'D' Montague Johnstone toward the coloureds. In Miss Johnstone's words: "I saw her in the ring with two red and whites (one of them the important Dam, Red Binge) when I had just returned from a last term at school and remarked on them to Mr A.J. Harrison, then Secretary of the Bull Terrier Club, and most kind and helpful to a keen youngster. He told me to leave them alone and stick to Whites, so, being perverse, I bet him I would breed a Coloured Champion in ten years and went straight off to see Mr Lyon, from whom I bought my first Coloured that day, in the late fall of 1927. She was six months old, dark brindle, very light in bone, and quite flat-sided. Her head was much more like a Fox Terrier's than the modern Bull Terrier's, with rose ears, and she had a poor coat. To her credit, she had a lovely little black eye, a perfect mouth, and was the gamest thing on four legs. Her name was Sher Fustian, and, directly down from her, by using the best of the White blood without losing the colour, emerged Ch. Romany Rhinestone in April 1936, so I had won my bet."

The other of Miss Johnstone's youthful pastimes was motoring. Even in her later years she enjoyed speeding around the Berkshire lanes, as I found to my cost on one occasion. As usual, D was driving the battered Morris Minor Traveller, with her partner Meg Williams in the passenger seat and River Pirate – by then a veteran – bouncing around in the back. Unfortunately, I was at the wheel of my old 2.5-litre Riley, which, with its long wheelbase and slow-revving engine, was ill-equipped for those narrow, twisty back roads, replete with passing places. D was in fine form, hurtling around blind bends with the horn warning of her approach – other motorists were supposed to get out of the way (I'm not sure how!). I too enjoyed driving 'flat out'; but it was all I could do to keep the Morris in view. I was not in the least surprised when, at the end of her tour de force, D complained that she had had to slow down for me.

Perhaps the single most important mating of coloureds prior to World War Two, in D's words, "broke all the rules". She allowed Rhinestone to mate the lovely brindle Ch. Jane of Petworth behind a screen at the Kensington show in April 1938. The resultant litter produced two key coloured bitches – Stronghold Jeanette, the great granddam of Ch. Romany Reliance, and Stronghold Lollipop, who founded Mrs Violet Marchant's Blanmerle kennels (another Birmingham breeder). Both Jeanette and Lollipop are behind the great Ch. Beech House Snow Vision, and thus probably behind every Bull Terrier around today. As Raymond Oppenheimer commented some 40 years after the illegal event (matings are not permitted on show premises): "Under the circumstances I think the Kennel Club will invoke the statute of limitations and pardon the offence."

These brief anecdotes shed some light on the remarkable and colourful (no pun intended) life of Miss Johnstone. She and Meg dedicated their lives to their dogs and to the breed in general. Their kennels were arranged not for their own convenience, but for the benefit of the dogs. They set and maintained the highest standards, ones we can but attempt to emulate.

THE WHITE CAVALIER'S LAST STAND

Following the crowning of the first coloured champion in 1931, the variety began to make steady if unspectacular progress in England. Naturally, coloured Bull Terriers began to find their way abroad

Typical Romanys.

Photo: Fall.

and, inevitably, white dogs bred from these coloureds began to be shown. Initially, leading figures in the breed were confident that coloured blood would never be allowed to taint the purity of the White Cavaliers, as when Tom Gannaway enlightened new fanciers of the breed thus:

"The American breeder is in fear of the coloured dog being so interbred with the white that all and sundry will fall under one heading, and a pure white dog with an unadulterated line of white ancestry will become a thing of the past.

"But have no fear, Uncle Sam! We here in England are just as concerned as you are, and not only is our front line of real white ones as safe and intact as ever it was, but you can rest assured that it will remain so."

In a reversal of stereotypical roles, it was American breeders who fought for tradition, for the status quo, for maintaining the purity of their bloodlines. The British, on the other hand, though opposed in principle, continued to permit the use of their top white studs on coloured bitches and were satisfied with the safeguards of the white stud book – policies surely guaranteed to lead to the eventual acceptance and equality of the coloureds. But not so in America, where the establishment fought a magnificent rearguard action, trying every ploy to keep their white cavaliers as a distinct and separate breed, even revising the Standard to specifically exclude colour behind the collar. Given the firm stance of the AKC, however, the best the BTCA could manage was to delay for a number of years acceptance of the coloureds as one of two varieties of the Bull Terrier – the other, of course, being their beloved whites.

Leading the fight during the mid-1930s was BTCA president, The Reverend Francis J. Heaney. One of his parishioners – and a wonderful character in his own right – Jim Boland described Father Heaney as "a sainted man, a Catholic priest who bred, exhibited and imported top Bull Terriers. Forty years after his passing he is still revered in his parish here on Staten Island. His profession was forgiveness. He could absolve murderers, arsonists, burglars, muggers, thieves, rapists, but he could neither understand, tolerate nor forgive breeders, importers or exhibitors of coloreds." Father Heaney's 1936 BTCA presidential message established the stance of the club for a decade to come:

"I would ask members to have patience and to take a broad view, a liberal view, on the question of coloreds. While it is true that 99 per cent of the fancy prefer the whites and detest the coloreds as a degeneration of a noble breed, we must have patience. The Board of Directors of the AKC has passed a ruling which, to my thinking, is utterly illogical and stultifying, yet we must wait with all the patience we can till we can make the directors see clearly. When logic shall have displaced misunderstanding, I am sure the men of the board have the moral courage to right the wrong that has been done. Those that want the coloreds can have them, surely, but we want no interbreeding. Let us take a stand, show under white judges only – clubs giving shows do not have to schedule classes for coloreds – we can see that they do not.

"As a matter of fact, I look upon this question as a passing fad, conceived of pique, nourished by poor sportsmanship, encouraged by mean, low ambition for commercial profit, by men who really do not mean the breed any good."

Accompanying Father Heaney's message

in the club's 1936 annual were these verses by 'Ready':

> "For seventy years my coat has been white,
> Now some restless mortals say I am too light,
> And they're bringing from England a dog they call me,
> So's the dirt in his coat will be harder to see.
>
> That my color's important is certainly clear,
> Else why do they call me the White Cavalier?
> In fighting and friendships, I've gained quite a fame,
> Now Kennel Club rulings say, 'What's in a name?'
>
> My sons will be brindle, my girls will be red,
> Oh, why cannot someone make use of his head?
> The mutt's an imposter, yet it's questions like these
> That make us White Dogs feel covered in fleas!"

WAR-TIME DOGS – MAJOR MAJOR AND THE REAL WILLIE

Many Bull Terriers have accompanied their owners to war, proving themselves – not surprisingly – loyal and steadfast companions, esteemed by those who knew them. The much-travelled Major was one such dog. Born in Australia in 1937, Major was purchased by Suzanne Crockston as a gift for New Zealander Lieutenant Errol Williams with whom he returned to Christchurch. When Suzanne and Errol were married shortly after the outbreak of World War Two, Major was adorned – much to his disgust – by a white ribbon and awaited the couple on the steps of the chapel. A few weeks later, Suzanne waved farewell to Errol and Major as they departed to join the ANZAC troops in the North African campaign. Suzanne was destined never to see either of them again.

Major became the mascot of his New Zealand battalion and was clearly officer material – he had learned to distinguish the brown boots worn by officers like Errol from the black ones worn by the soldiers, presumably by the smell of the different polishes. Also walking in the Egyptian heat was not for Major; he much preferred to be driven around. Major's promotion to second lieutenant was delayed because of a brawl in which he took on five Egyptian curs. The local dogs knew they had been in a fight, but Major was bitten badly around the head and was left with one floppy ear.

In typical Bull Terrier fashion he loved frolicking in the Mediterranean with the men. Unfortunately, one day he finished second in a sprint race and thought the men were jeering at him; thereafter woe betide anyone who swam ahead of him – they would find Major's jaws attached to one of their ankles.

The desperate fighting in North Africa began to take its toll of the New Zealanders. At Tobruk, in November 1941, Errol was killed and Major wounded. The following summer at El Alamein Major was injured again, by shrapnel. Though he recovered from these injuries, the veteran dog was steadily losing the comrades with whom he had travelled those many miles from New Zealand. There were lighter moments, such as the rapturous affair with a Pekingese from a Royal Navy ship, with which he celebrated his promotion to captain. Later, he became Major Major, a rank he temporarily lost when he went AWOL – returning a week later bedraggled and in the company of a lady dog.

Efforts were made by his friends to return the ageing dog to New Zealand, despite the official restrictions. Ministerial approval was finally obtained, though he could not go home until the end of the war. Meanwhile, the New Zealanders sailed for Italy, inadvertently leaving Major behind. The day was saved, however, by a lieutenant who smuggled him aboard ship in his trunk and Major was reunited with his regiment. Unlike many dogs, Major had not been unduly concerned by the shelling and aircraft during the desert campaign. But the war was beginning to take its toll, and in Italy Major became 'shell happy' – rushing at still-smoking craters – causing him to be sent south to the New Zealand base. One more attempt was made to return Major to his regiment, but he came down with pneumonia and died in December 1944, despite the devoted care of his mates. He was buried as a soldier, wrapped in a blanket, in a grave near Rimini.

Major's story was recorded in 1986 in a book called *The Four-Legged Major* written by Graham Spencer – a fitting tribute to the indomitable spirit of this gallant dog and the brave men with whom he served.

General George S. Patton Jr. purchased his Bull Terrier from the widow of an RAF officer in March 1944. Willie, as the General named him, had accompanied the officer on six missions over Europe, but had missed the fatal seventh flight. The General's constant companion, Willie had free run of Patton's Headquarters until the day he jumped on General Bradley's lap – not the thing to do to your master's boss. Apparently, Patton made frequent reference to "the comfort of Willie's snoring" in letters home to his wife. The General also wrote "to him I am always right" – such was Willie's devotion.

After Patton's death in December 1945, Willie was flown home to the family estate in Massachusetts, where he lived to the ripe old age of 13. He never forgot his master and was reported to have run around in search of him when shown one of the General's helmet liners. In later years, the dog would sit out on the grass and enjoy barking at nothing in particular for an hour or so.

Of course, most of us associate Willie with the canine character portrayed in the movie *Patton*. This is a terrific movie, except in one regard – its outrageously inaccurate depiction of Willie. This was not the real Willie. Through mutual friends, Miss Claudia Slack "heard how Willie had adjusted to his new circumstances and had become a much-loved member of the household..

"Years later, when the film was released, I was told Mrs Patton was quite indignant about the way Willie was portrayed. Her comments were along the line that Willie would have tackled anything, up to and including a tank, in defense of his people and home.

"The word around Southern California, where I then lived, was that someone connected with the picture thought it would be 'cute' to show Willie as a coward. Mrs. Patton was consulted about her husband's life and character, but either she was not asked about Willie, or her testimony was ignored.

"This bit of Bull Terrier lore would not matter if Willie had been a fictional character, but he was real: a good, honest Bull Terrier who deserves better than to be remembered as a craven buffoon."

Lovers of the breed can rest assured that the real Willie was a typical Bull Terrier. Just one question remains to be answered and that is his background – with the prevailing wartime conditions, the General received no papers on Willie. The Patton

Museum has tried, without success, to discover when and where he was bred. All we know for certain is that Patton purchased Willie in Cheshire in March 1944. The museum would greatly appreciate receiving any and all information on Willie's background.

MRS GLADYS ADLAM

When George Adlam presented his fiancée Gladys Inglis with a Bull Terrier puppy, little did he realize that the breed would become a passion – and I do not employ the word lightly – for her remaining sixty-odd years. By 1909, she had become a member of the BTC and, in 1910, judged her first championship show, awarding the dog ticket to one of the great showmen, Ch. Bloomsbury Cheeky, handled of course by the one and only Harry Monk. She won her first CC in 1913 with a four-and-a-half-month-old puppy (!) and made up her first champion, Brendon Floss, in 1922. But it is with the great Ch. Rhoma, whom she bought on the advice of Tom Gannaway, that history will always associate Gladys Adlam. Rhoma produced three Champions, including Brendon Becky, the 1930 winner of the first Regent Trophy. By then, Mrs Adlam had become an internationally renowned figure in the breed, a position she retained throughout her very full and active life.

A few years later, Raymond Oppenheimer began affectionately to call her 'Grannie Adie' – a name by which she was known to generations of fanciers. Grannie Adie cared, passionately so, never losing her intensity and commitment. She cared about the Miniatures when few others did. She cared enough about the breed to break rank in 1950 and second a successful motion to delete the pledge that BTC members should not use colour as the basis of a white strain. There was also a humorous side to her nature. Eva Weatherill noted that Grannie Adie's greatest asset was her ability to make people laugh, especially after a disastrous day at a show. She was also ever-ready with words of advice and encouragement for newcomers, to generations of whom she was the grand old lady of the fancy.

Mrs Adlam took time out to write *Forty Years of Bull Terriers,* copies of which are much treasured today; it was published in 1952. She then carried on for another 17 years, never missing the really important things like reading the weekly dog papers. Indeed, she sent her son out to fetch them, when, thinking she was too ill to want them, he arrived at the hospital without them shortly before she died. Besides her book, Grannie Adie bequeathed us a wealth of comments and expressions: "They change so, dear" referring to puppies; "Bless his heart, give him a ginger biscuit" when looking at a pup; "After all, dear, you know it's all such fun!" after a new white (or coloured) hope has just been beaten. In a tribute to this remarkable woman, Eva wrote "I hope with all my heart I can go on thinking like her, a woman as game as the dogs she loved so well. Grannie will never really leave us, who knew and loved her."

'DOC' MONTGOMERY

Searching for a breed figure who was truly larger than life is an easy task. At six feet seven inches in height and reputedly weighing 525 pounds, there was only one Dr Edward S. Montgomery of Pennsylvania. The 'Doc' became actively involved with the breed during World War Two and subsequently imported a number of top English dogs – including outstanding coloureds like Abraxas Oldtrinity Spaniard, Romany Ritual and Dulac Heathlands Commander – as well as maintaining a large kennel of his own Monty-Ayr Bull Terriers. His dogs were invariably among the top winners until he gave up breeding in the early 1960s; among his best were Champions Heir-Apparent, Radar and Dancing Master of Monty-Ayr, all BIS all-breeds winners. He also compiled a comprehensive book on the breed, which was published in 1946. Again, nothing in short measure for the Doc – there are 414 pages of *The Bull Terrier.*

Doc Montgomery often wore a flamboyant red cape to shows, as if his own physical stature was not enough to make him stand out in a crowd. For the last specialty show he judged, he appeared in a resplendent yellow outfit, all part of the Doc's image. Stories about him are legion and, in most cases, it is difficult to separate fact from fiction. Here are a few of these tales, all guaranteed absolutely true by those who told them to me.

At one show the Doc disqualified a Fox Terrier for having its ears 'fixed'. Asked by an AKC representative how he knew the ears had been fixed, he explained that he personally had operated on them!

He trained and promoted a professional boxer; unfortunately, the boxer did not pay attention to his instructions and, in the ensuing argument, the Doc knocked the man out. At another show, the Doc terminated a dispute with an AKC representative by picking up and depositing the man in a large trash bin. Quod erat demonstrandum.

The Doc often employed handlers. At one show weekend, unhappy with a handler's performance, he hung the man out of a hotel window – by his ankles; I am told it was a third floor window.

His goals as a breeder appear to have been twofold: firstly to produce top-winning Bull Terriers and, secondly, to be able to write out pedigrees in which every dog carried the Monty-Ayr affix. I have several examples of the Doc's four-generation pedigrees, in which all 30 dogs carry his affix, believe it or not!

These brief notes serve to sketch a picture of this amazing man – indisputably the breed's largest character.

CHAMPION ABRAXAS AUDACITY
In February 1972, when Raymond Oppenheimer wrote his weekly column for *Dog News* – in case readers thought it was a slip of the pen – he repeated the news from the opening paragraph: Ch. Abraxas Audacity was BIS at Crufts! For the first and only time a Bull Terrier was the Crufts Supreme Champion.

Bred and owned by Miss Violet Drummond-Dick, Audacity (or Kim as he was known to his friends) was the product of supremely great parents, Ch. Romany River Pirate and the incomparable Ch. Abraxas Athenia. Violet was, and is, renowned for the wonderful temperaments of her Abraxas dogs and Audacity was no exception. He was a delightful character and, like his sire, a fabulous showman. He raced to his title during 1970 with eight BOBs, then the following year took another BOB at Crufts under Miss Johnstone and swept the trophies, winning both the Regent Trophy and Ormandy Jug. Raymond Oppenheimer wrote of him: "It is true that unlike many great dogs one can find each separate feature of his make-up in more outstanding form in some other dog, but I have rarely, if ever, seen a dog so devoid of faults and with such abundant virtues."

With this fanfare behind him, Audacity settled down to entertaining the finest bitches in the land at Violet's kennels in Surrey. Unfortunately, his performance at stud was rather disappointing with only one English Champion, Souperlative Bettina, to show for his efforts. However, he did make an enormous impact in the second

93

Ch. Abraxas Audacity, Cruft's Supreme Champion, 1972.   *Photo: Fall.*

top terrier judge Joe Cartledge and then BIS under the highly respected Arthur Westlake. In *Dog News*, Raymond commented:

"In only one respect do I think that Audacity was lucky and that is he arrived at the show in the early morning distinctly overweight but, due to the efficient heating at Olympia and to the very mild weather, the conditions in the National Hall Gallery, where the breed was judged, were more reminiscent of a Turkish bath than of a dog show so that, by the time he went into the big ring, he sweated off a good five pounds, looked a picture, showed like a bird and was beautifully handled by his owner, Miss Drummond-Dick.

"The drama and excitement throughout the whole affair was almost unendurable. Finally, he and a charming and beautiful Miss Whippet, were pulled out before the eyes of the massed thousands and this was very much to Kim's taste, so much so that I thought we might be going to see the start of a new breed, Bullets or Whipperries. I think I would have liked to own one!".

A year or so later when I visited Abraxas, I found Audacity happily sitting on a box, watching a litter of pups scampering around. Without apparently making any effort, Kim simply radiated personality and it was easy to see how this delightful dog had captivated the judges and the audience at Olympia. One little-known fact about Kim is that he almost went to Ralph and Mary Bowles in America. It was a close call, but ultimately his outstanding half-brother Ch. Abraxas Achilles went in his stead.

generation, by siring the dams of three of the most celebrated stud dogs of the seventies and early eighties – Ch. Badlesmere Bonaparte of Souperlative, Ch. Souperlative Jackadandy of Ormandy and Am. Can. Ch. Magor The Marquis. So your current couch potato may well carry one or more lines back to Audacity!

He was entered in only one more show and that was Crufts in 1972. There, he took BOB over a small but tremendously strong entry. In his critique, breed judge George Cousins, who had been associated with Bull Terriers for some 50 years, noted that: "It was a great thrill for me to witness my BOB, Ch. Abraxas Audacity, being awarded BIS. This is the greatest award any dog can receive."

Audacity went on to win the group under

SPUDS MACKENZIE

Little did I realize when I stayed with friends Dick and Peggy Selk near Chicago in June 1983 that the three-and-a-half-week-old litter in the next bedroom contained a puppy destined for national, indeed international, fame. Peggy asked which of the bitch pups I would keep if they were mine. Having given every conceivable reservation – I did not know the breeding; they were at a terrible age to decide anything, and so on – I plumped for one of the bitches. This was not the one with a brindle patch over her left eye, the one that was later registered as Honeytree's Evil Eye and went to Jacqueline and Stanley Oles. I did not select Ch. Honcytree Evil Eye, alias Evie, alias Spuds MacKenzie, though Dick and Peggy have been far too polite to remind me of this. Still that is history, so let us get on with the story.

The following spring an advertising agency, retained by Anheuser-Busch, contacted the local specialty club requesting a white Bull Terrier to pose for photographs for a Bud Light poster. When the agency staff noted they would need to paint a patch over one eye, the club was able to go one better and put them on to the Oles. At the appointed time, a taxi arrived to transport Jackie and Evie for a photo session. Evie was so laid-back she was a natural at posing in front of the camera, and she just loved being dressed in a T-shirt. The photographs were a hit at Anheuser-Busch and Evie's career as Spuds MacKenzie, their 'Party Animal' or, more formally, the 'Original Bud Light Party Animal', was off to a flying start.

Partygoers found a kindred spirit in Spuds, although I should note that they thought Spuds was a he not a she. Evie, I mean Spuds, appeared on posters and calendars and eventually auditioned for a television commercial. Again, Spuds was a big hit. The ads were tried out in California and other markets. Then Spuds made 'his' national debut during the 1987 Super Bowl broadcast. 'He' was not just the original, 'he' was the ultimate party animal, happy to be dressed up, sitting on a motor cycle, in the middle of a crowd, indeed anywhere there was festive event.

Everyone loved Spuds and, to the uninitiated, Bull Terriers became 'Spuds' dogs. This was a boon to the breed at a time when Pit Bulls were receiving really bad press and a large segment of the public could not tell a Pit Bull from a Bull Terrier. Spuds changed all that; the public now knew that Spuds and Bull Terriers were fun-loving party animals. Unfortunately, they did not realise that few Bull Terriers are quite as easy-going and tractable as Evie. It is not that Bull Terriers do not love fun, people and parties; simply that for every Evie there are probably 999 other Spuds dogs whose idea of a party is completely different from hers – words like rumbustious, riotous, rowdy, unruly, chaotic and disorderly come to mind. Hey, perhaps Bull Terriers have a lot to teach the public about real parties! But, regardless of all this, Evie – in the guise of Spuds MacKenzie – is now a legend.

9 HEALTH CARE

KEEPING YOUR DOG HEALTHY

An ounce of prevention is worth a pound of cure, we are told. So keeping your dog fit and happy – and both are vital to good health and longevity – should be the number one priority. Here are some others.

1. Correct feeding, regular exercise and spending quality time with your dog should all go without saying; they are the basics.
2. Keep your dog's vaccinations up to date.
3. Next come the maintenance issues such as clipping claws, cleaning teeth and grooming the coat. Quita Youatt, from whom I purchased my first Bull Terrier, told me that God makes Bull Terriers but owners make feet. Exercising on hard surfaces like pavements will reduce the frequency, but, nevertheless, your dog's nails need clipping or filing regularly.
4. Modern diets are not conducive to healthy teeth; indeed dental care is a fast-growing facet of veterinary work. So brush your dog's teeth with a canine toothpaste on a routine basis; this will also help to reduce bad breath. Older dogs tend to develop plaque. I use a dental scraper to remove this; you may wish to assign the task to your veterinarian.

5. By their very nature Bull Terriers garner their fair share of cuts and scratches. Cleaning and treating a cut pad or bloody scratch immediately will avoid infections and complications.
6. Some dogs develop impacted anal glands, which need to be emptied. Again, you can learn to do this yourself or take a trip to the vet.

Dogs cannot tell us when they feel ill, so, having done all we can to keep our dogs healthy, our next responsibility is to observe them and their behaviour for any symptoms of sickness or ailments. Unfortunately, the same Bull Terrier that shrieks at the mere sight of the nail clippers is capable of withstanding great pain with remarkable fortitude and minimal fuss. In addition to indications like coughing, vomiting, diarrhoea or obvious pain and distress, you should be checking your dog for more subtle changes in behaviour such as lethargy, sleeping much longer than usual or reduced tolerance to exercise.

Taking your dog's temperature with a common mercury thermometer is an easy and a valuable diagnostic aid. Ensure the mercury is shaken down, grease the bulb

Sequoiah the Bajan: Correct feeding and regular exercise are essential to your Bull Terrier's health and well-being.

with Vaseline, gently push the thermometer, bulb first, into your dog's rectum and leave it there for at least two minutes; I hold the dog's tail in one hand and the end of the thermometer in the other. Your dog's temperature should be between 101 and 102 degrees Fahrenheit (F), circa 38.5 degrees Centigrade (C), though it may go higher temporarily after strenuous exercise. If your dog's temperature settles at above 103 degrees F (39.4 C), contact your vet.

It is important to establish a good relationship with a local vet as soon as you bring your puppy home. Ensure the veterinarian likes Bull Terriers and that your dog enjoys visiting the clinic. My dogs are always happy to be driven to see our vet, never seem to mind receiving injections and

view being examined as great fun. Ask your veterinarian to carry out a routine check each time you take your dog in for vaccinations. This way when there is something seriously wrong, your dog is used to seeing the vet and does not suffer additional stress when rushed off to the clinic. Finally, remember, if your dog becomes ill, or if you are worried about your dog's condition, contact your vet without delay.

EMERGENCIES
Sooner or later, and usually at the most inconvenient time, your Bull Terrier will require immediate treatment. Boy Scouts are taught to be prepared. This should be your motto for emergencies. Keep at hand

the location and telephone number of your nearest 24-hour emergency clinic. If a crisis does occur, immediately call your own vet or, outside office hours, the emergency clinic number and seek advice. If your dog is in shock, keep him or her warm with a blanket and, if necessary, a hot-water bottle. In the event of physical injury, improvise a stretcher by laying a towel or rug next to your dog, then pull him or her on to it by the scruff of the neck.

Many household products are poisonous to dogs, as are a number of common indoor and garden plants. If you suspect your dog has been poisoned, seek veterinary advice immediately. In America, the National Canine Poison Control Center at 1-900-680-0000 is available around the clock.

Disbelieve those who tell you Bull Terriers are afraid of snakes; mine certainly are not. If your dog could come into contact with a venomous snake, be prepared to follow the same regimen recommended for people: expel as much poison from the wound as you can, reduce the spread of the remaining poison by keeping your dog still, and get to a vet as soon as possible.

INFECTIOUS DISEASES

The availability of effective vaccines has made us far less concerned about viral diseases like canine distemper and infectious canine hepatitis than perhaps we should be. But make no mistake about it, these are killers, particularly of puppies. Immunization schedules vary according to risk factors and the age of the puppy at vaccination. Typically, multivalent vaccines are administered at two-to-three-week intervals from six weeks until 16 weeks, followed by annual re-vaccination. The exact sequence will depend on the local prevalence of these diseases. A common

scheme is injections at six, nine, 12 and 16 weeks of age with combination vaccines. Consult your vet for the sequence appropriate to your puppy and do not fail to complete this important protective care.

DISTEMPER

Prior to the development of effective vaccines distemper was the number one killer of dogs. It is highly contagious and primarily, though not exclusively, affects puppies up to the age of twelve months. For this reason, early and regular shots are essential. An unvaccinated puppy who comes down with distemper may recover, but is likely to suffer permanent neurological damage. Initial symptoms such as watery eyes, loss of appetite and lethargy are often mild. As the disease progresses, the dog usually develops a dry cough accompanied by vomiting, diarrhoea and fever. Secondary infections are common and the condition may take months to run its course. Broad spectrum antibiotics are usually prescribed. There is, however, no specific cure.

INFECTIOUS CANINE HEPATITIS

This is a viral disease of the liver to which puppies are highly susceptible. It is spread through mouth-to-mouth contact and via urine and faeces, in both of which traces of the virus are found long after a dog has recovered. Symptoms are similar to those of distemper. Hepatitis is often fatal, so vaccination is again essential.

LEPTOSPIROSIS

This is a bacterial disease of the liver and kidneys, spread primarily by rats. Leptospirosis can be transmitted to humans, so those caring for an affected dog must take precautions against infection. There are two forms of the disease, canicola and ictero-haemorrhagic; the latter is far more serious. Common symptoms include dullness, loss of weight, stiffness of the hindquarters and redness of eyes and gums. The principal symptom of the ictero-haemorrhagic type is jaundice, with progessive yellowing of the eyes, gums and eventually the skin. Although antibiotics can clear up this disease, preventative inoculation is a wise precaution.

PARVO AND CORONA VIRUSES

These highly contagious viruses belong to a group of diseases that all produce similar signs of explosive haemorrhagic (bloody) diarrhoea, usually accompanied by vomiting. They are usually transmitted dog-to-dog, but parvovirus is believed to have been transported from America to the UK during the 1970s on the clothes or shoes of visiting judges. The viruses are remarkably resistant to most disinfectants, and so are difficult to eradicate from the house, kennel and garden. Very young puppies are particularly susceptible and, to make matters worse, the initial immunity to parvovirus they usually receive from their mother's milk has to dissipate before protection from vaccinations kicks in. For this reason, it is important for puppies to have a series of shots up till the end of their sixteenth week. (I keep mine quarantined till after this injection.) Infected puppies become severely ill and, without treatment, a high percentage die from dehydration and protein loss through intestinal damage. Treatment consists of intravenous fluids and supportive care.

PARAINFLUENZA

Better known as kennel cough, this viral infection causes a hacking cough, which has a more debilitating impact on puppies than on adults. Vaccine can be administered via nasal spray and is recommended if your dog will be around a lot of other dogs, for example at a show, or prior to being boarded at a kennel; indeed, some kennel owners sensibly require vaccination against parainfluenza.

RABIES

This is the most serious of canine diseases. It is caused by a virus that attacks the central nervous system and is invariably fatal. The virus, which is transmitted when an infected animal bites another, attacks all warm-blooded animals – including humans. In areas where rabies is endemic, vaccinations are usually prescribed by law. Generally, the first shot is administered at about six months of age, with re-vaccination every twelve or thirty-six months. The UK, like Australia, is currently rabies-free and therefore dogs do not have to be vaccinated. It takes from two weeks to as long as several months for the symptoms to appear. They take two forms, depending on which part of the nervous system is attacked: the dumb one, in which the infected dog is relatively passive, and the furious form, which produces the vicious, aggressive behaviour we associate with rabid animals. Whichever form the disease takes, the victim dies within three to seven days after the symptoms appear.

PARASITES

There is a entire spectrum of parasites that attack canines – external ones (ectoparasites) like fleas and ticks that live on the body or skin, and internal ones (endoparasites) comprising various worms that live inside the host dog. Ectoparasites cause itching, to which dogs respond by scratching or even biting themselves; when infestations are severe or allergic responses are generated, such scratching can result in serious damage to the skin. Fortunately, these parasites can be managed much more effectively today with the aid of the new medications that are replacing the traditional powder and dip treatments. Keeping your dog free of endoparasites necessitates a routine worming programme. Your vet will be able to advise you as to which parasites your dog will be exposed to in your locality and recommend appropriate medications.

ECTOPARASITES

EAR MITES: Sometimes called ear mange, these mites live in the canal leading to the eardrum and cause intense irritation. They can be treated with proprietary medications. Since moving to America my dogs have not had ear mites, but have occasionally suffered from infections caused by yeast. Such infections can be cleared up with an appropriate antibiotic ointment.

FLEAS: In areas where they proliferate, fleas can make your dog's life a misery. Those most commonly found are dog fleas; however, others such as cat fleas will breed on dogs if no felines are to be found. Fleas cause irritation simply by their movement on the dog's skin and also, of course, through their bites, to which some dogs become allergic. Fortunately, there has been a steady stream of new and improved treatments in recent years. Regular dustings of the dog and its quarters used to be necessary; flea collars then helped to keep the fleas at bay; now your vet can supply programme drugs that are given on a monthly basis. Some of these programme treatments, though effective at killing fleas, do not prevent them from first biting the dog and potentially causing allergic reactions. However, a once-a-month topical treatment that kills and repels both fleas and ticks has recently come on to the market, and is already proving itself a winner in flea-plagued areas of America.

LICE: These parasites are perhaps more often a problem in large kennels. If your dog does become infested, the lice can be killed with a specially formulated shampoo and then removed with the fine-toothed comb that usually accompanies such shampoos.

MANGE: Two types of mange are found in dogs – demodectic and sarcoptic. Demodectic (follicular) mange is the less serious ailment of the two, typically manifesting itself as bare patches on the head and causing only minor irritation. It is, however, extremely difficult to eradicate. Some families of Bull Terriers are prone to mild attacks of this mange as puppies, often developing a bare thumb-print on the forehead. The cases I have seen were not serious and cleared up of their own accord as the puppies grew into adolescence.

The mites that cause sarcoptic mange burrow deeply into the skin and lay their eggs there. Once the infestation develops, scabs form – hence the common term 'scabie' – with loss of hair and thickening and wrinkling of the skin. Itching becomes severe. If scabies is left untreated complications set in and death may follow within a few months. It is no longer the killer it once was; nevertheless the sooner an affected dog is taken to the veterinary clinic and treatment begun, the better. Sarcoptic mange mites are small and can be difficult to find even in a badly infested dog. Determined scraping of the skin with a sharp blade is needed to remove them for identification under a microscope. Persistent and prolonged treatment is essential for the elimination of mange mites, so follow the instructions of your veterinarian to the letter. It is reported that humans can contract sarcoptic mange, though I have never heard of such a case.

TICKS: Dogs can be host to a variety of ticks. In the UK, dogs sometimes pick up sheep ticks from grazing land, while in

America dogs have to contend with several forms of dog-specific ticks (the common brown tick being found in most areas) as well as deer ticks. Both male and female ticks attach themselves to the dog's skin, become engorged with blood and then mate. The females then detach themselves, lay their eggs on the ground and the cycle repeats itself. In America there are some very serious tick-borne diseases that can be contracted by humans as well as dogs; these include Lyme disease and Rocky Mountain spotted fever. It is essential to immediately remove any ticks found on your dog; they are often attracted to the ears. Do not pull a tick directly from your dog's skin as the head will remain buried in the skin. Application of surgical spirits (isopropyl alcohol) will cause the tick to release its grip, so that it can be safely removed and disposed of. As reviewed in the discussion on fleas, new tick and flea repellants are a highly effective preventative measure.

ENDOPARASITES

HEARTWORMS: These are transmitted during their larval stage by mosquitoes and are endemic to tropical and subtropical areas. They occur only rarely in the UK and Europe, but in America, where they were once thought to be confined to the southern states, they are steadily expanding their range. The larvae (called microfilaria) enter the dog's bloodstream and develop into worms that lodge in the heart where they interfere with the pumping of blood. Symptoms include coughing and general lethargy. The presence of microfilaria can be detected by examination of a blood sample. Treatment for heartworm infestation is a risky procedure, involving as it does killing the worms while avoiding clogging the heart and blood vessels with their residues. Clearly, prevention is the way forward. This used to necessitate a daily tablet throughout

the mosquito season. However, the advent of a drug based on Ivermectin has reduced this frequency to just once a month.

HOOKWORMS: These are small (typically less than one inch, or 2.5 cms, long), thread-like worms that live in the small intestine, where they suck blood. Affected animals become anaemic, with puppies and ill-nourished dogs being more susceptible. Huge numbers of eggs are passed in the faeces, contaminating the ground with larvae and resulting in re-infestation of treated dogs. For this reason, medication should be repeated at intervals and contaminated soil should be sterilized and kept well drained.

ROUNDWORMS: Roundworms are by far the most common endoparasite. Up to eight inches (20 cms) in length, their presence in the dog can be detected by microscopic examination of the faeces. Dogs ingest eggs from the ground; the eggs travel to the intestine where the larvae develop. Symptoms include unthriftiness, digestive problems and, in puppies, pot bellies. Early treatment is important, as one form of roundworm (Toxacara canis) can enter the lungs, causing susceptibility to pneumonia. Removal of infected faeces and a high standard of hygiene are essential. A word of warning: humans, especially children, can ingest and become infected with roundworms.

TAPEWORMS: Another intestinal parasite, of which the type most frequently found in dogs grows to more than one foot (30 cms) in length and requires an intermediate host, usually a flea or louse. Effective treatment of an infected dog requires the complete worms to be eliminated, as any heads remaining embedded in the intestinal wall simply grow new bodies.

WHIPWORMS: As the name suggests, they are shaped like tiny whips, usually about two inches (5 cms) long. Eggs swallowed by a dog hatch in the small intestine and migrate to the caecum (equivalent to the appendix in humans). Most worming medications can kill whipworms, but to do so they must reach them hidden away in the caecum. Mild infestations do not appear to have serious consequences. However, re-infestation due to contaminated ground can be a problem, necessitating removal of faeces and at times of the topsoil. In this regard, the ultraviolet rays of direct sunlight are the dog's best friend, sterilizing the ground and killing off whipworms, roundworms and their kin.

OTHER AILMENTS

ATOPY (SKIN ALLERGIES)
Bull Terriers, like a number of other terrier breeds, suffer from their fair share of skin problems. These allergic reactions result from a variety of sources, including flea and mosquito bites, plants, diet, coat dressings and shampoos, household cleaners and garden products. The effects range from minor, with just local and temporary irritation, to generalised inflammation of the skin and loss of hair with consequential intense itching and the potential for secondary infections. Removal of the cause, if it can be found, is obviously the best approach. As discussed earlier, much-improved programmes are available for warding off fleas and mosquitoes. Identifying the offending plant is difficult at best but, if it can be done, the dog can be desensitised to that particular allergen. Switching foods clears up a surprising number of persistent skin problems. Proprietary dog foods are often the cause; unfortunately, in time, the dog may become just as allergic to a new variety. In this event, a more natural diet is called for.

Skins problems tend to run in families and so perhaps should be included under the heading of genetic diseases. Also colour seems to be factor, though I have no scientific evidence of this. In general, white Bull Terriers appear to be the more sensitive to skin problems than coloureds. Among the coloureds, brindles and black brindles have the least problems. However, this may not be true in specific cases.

GASTRO-INTESTINAL BLOCKAGE
Most Bull Terrier puppies and quite a few adults will chew and swallow just about anything. Their digestive systems are remarkably tolerant of foreign objects that pass through them, but occasionally blockages do occur. For example, plastic toys are a favourite and, potentially, a deadly favourite. When a blockage happens, the dog often shows minimal symptoms for the first few days. As soon as signs such as general lethargy and vomiting appear, the dog must be taken in for surgical removal of the offending object *without delay*.

INTERDIGITAL CYSTS
Some Bull Terriers are susceptible to cysts that develop between the toes. These hard lumps become infected and cause the dog great discomfort, often resulting in incessant licking. Antibiotic tablets seem to produce minimal and, at best, only temporary relief. Cortisone-based drugs alleviate the condition, but the cysts reappear as soon as the treatment is stopped. (I have ample evidence that such cortisone treatments can result in personality changes and, in particular, increase the dog-aggressive tendencies of previously easy-going Bull Terriers, so I will not use them on my dogs.) Cysts usually appear seasonally, possibly due to grass or weed allergies. In this sense, they appear to be related to general skin allergies and, like them, may be inherited. Certainly, they tend to run in families. The optimal way of

dealing with cysts is to find out what is causing the allergic reaction and then put the dog through a course of desensitising injections. In serious cases, cryogenic techniques can be used to freeze and remove the cysts. For minor occurrences, keeping the cysts clean and dry and applying antibiotic creams is about the best that can be done.

GENETIC DISEASES

Bull Terriers, like all other dogs, pure-bred and mongrels alike, and indeed humans, are prone to diseases that are inherited. Their parents may or may not suffer from a particular disease, but if they are both carriers, then their progeny may develop it. Only a very small percentage of the total Bull Terrier population inherits these diseases, though this is scant consolation for afflicted dogs or their owners. Space precludes discussion of the underlying principles of genetic inheritance and for such information I refer readers to one of the excellent texts devoted to this topic, such as Malcolm Willis' *Genetics of the Dog* (Howell Book House, USA). In most cases, however, we do not know with any degree of certainty the exact mode of inheritance and so, for practical purposes, the most important factor is an awareness of those genetic conditions from which our dogs may suffer.

The following diseases are usually genetic in origin, though some can also result from trauma or in the case of kidney ailments from poisoning.

DEAFNESS
From the earliest days of the breed, deafness has occurred in Bull Terriers, as it does in many white animals. Dogs can be deaf in both ears (bilateral) or just one ear (unilateral). Bilaterals are, of course, what we term stone-deaf, whereas unilaterals can hear, but lack the ability to determine the direction from which the sound originates. For many years, deafness was thought to be confined to the white variety but, in recent years, occasional instances of unilateral deafness in coloureds have been confirmed.

Researchers in America have pioneered the use of BAER (Brainstem Auditory Evoked Response) testing to determine deafness in dogs. Each ear is tested separately. The screening can be carried out on puppies as young as five weeks of age. Responsible breeders in America are now testing all of their puppies before sale. Australian breeders are showing an interest in BAER testing and it is anticipated that it will become more generally available.

LUXATING PATELLAS
Slipping patellas result from malformation of the groove in which the kneecap (patella) is located. If the groove is too shallow, the patella can slip off to the side, causing lameness. Authorities have described the Bull Terrier as a Bulldog on terrier legs; as such, active youngsters put their joints under tremendous strain and so are likely to expose any potential patella weakness. Vets can grade the seriousness of the malformation. In mild cases, restricted exercise and, according to some breeders, high doses of Vitamin C help to ameliorate the condition. However, such use of Vitamin C is perhaps more effective as a preventative measure. In more severe cases, arthritis soon sets in and surgery may become necessary.

KIDNEY DISEASES
Two genetic kidney conditions have long been known to occur in Bull Terriers: renal dysplasia, which causes incomplete development of the kidneys during the first few weeks of life and leads to early renal

failure, and hereditary nephritis, which results in progressive failure of kidney function. Both conditions are invariably fatal. The age of onset of hereditary nephritis is highly variable (from as early as two or three years up to six or seven years), as is the rate of progression of the disease. Symptomatic of this condition is excessive consumption of water, though this may not be noticeable until the disease is quite advanced. A better indicator is an elevated level of protein in the urine, which can be determined by measuring the ratio of protein to creatinine in a urine sample. Asking your vet to include this straightforward test in your dog's regular check-up is a sensible precaution. If kidney failure is diagnosed, your dog should be placed on a special low-protein diet; this and TLC (tender loving care) are the best prescriptions. Ill treatment or trauma can hasten the onset and progress of the hereditary nephritis.

Recently, a third hereditary condition, polycystic kidney disease (PCKD), has come to light. This condition is not accompanied by high protein levels and definitive diagnosis requires ultrasound screening of the kidneys. Dogs with this disease may show no obvious symptoms while young and live comparatively long lives. PCKD is often accompanied by valvular heart problems. The disease is believed to be caused by an autosomal dominant gene. If this is so, it should be possible to eliminate, or at least minimize, its occurrence by breeding only from stock which has tested clear of PCKD.

BEHAVIOURAL PROBLEMS
Compulsive behaviours – like constant licking, fixation on an object such as a ball, spinning and tail-chasing – have been shown to be heritable in Bull Terriers. All such behaviours worsen if the dog becomes over-excited, is confined in a crate or left alone in a kennel for prolonged periods. Adjusting the dog's environment and seeking expert advice are recommended. In mild forms, these behaviours may represent little more than boredom and lack of exercise. However, a dog showing excessive compulsive behaviour may have to be put down. Recent researches indicate that these problems may be related to seizure disorders and some have been treated successfully as such.

ACRODERMATITIS
This is an immune problem associated with an inability to metabolize zinc correctly. Puppies with the disorder lose interest in nursing and often die when just a few days old. With hand-feeding, such puppies can be kept alive, though they remain small. Later they develop splay feet and cow hocks and then skin lesions that become infected. Zinkies, as they are called, tend to have nasty temperaments and unnatural coat textures and colours. Left to their own devices, these puppies die young, which, I believe, is the kindest ending for them.

PYLORIC STENOSIS
Bull Terriers with this disease have difficulty passing food through the pyloric valve, from the stomach into the intestine. As puppies, when first given solid food, they can become rigid as the food reaches the valve. Later symptoms include a frothy vomit and literally throwing up food. Such symptoms become worse when the dog is under stress. The good news is that pyloric stenosis does not occur frequently in the breed and when it does, the symptoms can be alleviated with drugs that are used to control epilepsy.

10 BREEDING PRINCIPLES

SCIENCE AND INTUITION

There is a core of basic principles that applies to breeding all dogs as well as other domestic animals. Successful breeders have added to and refined these principles in their efforts to produce winning Bull Terriers. Nothing would please me more than to be able to lay out a set of scientific rules detailing how to do this. Unfortunately, though an understanding of the scientific underpinnings is increasingly important and, arguably, in this day and age, essential to success, breeding is as much – probably more – art than science. There are no substitutes for a keen intuition and having a good eye for a dog. Many of the great Bull Terrier breeders of yesteryear were extraordinarily superstitious and being

told some of them practised black magic would not surprise me in the least. Luck certainly has its part to play in the scheme of things.

BASIC GENETICS

There are several excellent texts available for those who wish to study the subject in depth and so my purpose here is simply to give a practical overview of the principles of genetic inheritance.

The basic building blocks of inheritance are chromosomes, of which there are 78 in dogs, compared to 46 in man. Each chromosome contains literally hundreds of genes, which are responsible for passing on inherited characteristics from parents to offspring. These structures have been

Top stud dog: Ch. Souperlative Jackadandy of Ormandy.

likened to beads on a string, with the chromosome represented by the string and the genes by beads. Both chromosomes and genes occur in pairs, with each parent contributing 39 chromosomes and their associated genes to each puppy and thereby bequeathing a unique set of genetic characteristics to each and every one of them.

The genes responsible for a certain characteristic, for example whether the coat is brindle or red, always occupy the same location on a certain chromosome and, as noted above, occur in pairs, one inherited from each parent. At any particular location, two or more different genes can occur; these are known as alleles. Within each series of alleles there is a pecking order, with genes being dominant or recessive to each other. (This simply means that the effect of a dominant gene, if present, will be seen, whereas – in the presence of its dominant allele – the effect of a recessive gene will not manifest itself, yet it can be passed on to the next generation.)

For example, a series of alleles determines whether a Bull Terrier is white or coloured. In this case the gene for colour is dominant to that for white, so that, if either of the pair of genes at that location is the one for colour, then the dog will be coloured. Because the white gene is recessive and cannot express itself in the presence of the colour gene, only when both genes are white ones will the coat be white. Therefore white Bull Terriers carry only the genes for white coats and, mated together, produce 100 per cent white puppies, never coloureds. With other traits, however, pairs of genes may be incompletely dominant or recessive to each other and the results are less straightforward.

Unfortunately, most inherited traits result not from the actions of a single pair of genes, but rather from the interactions of many different pairs of genes. The effect of such polygenic inheritance tends towards a continuous variation in the characteristic rather than the clear demarcation resulting from the colour/white gene pair. For example, height is polygenic in nature and so Bull Terriers vary in height continuously – within their typical range. Some genes have the ability to override or mask the effects of genes at other locations; this is called epistasis to distinguish it from dominance, which refers to the overriding impact of one gene on another at the *same* location. An example of epistasis occurs in black brindle Bull Terriers, where a separately inherited gene for black masks the brindle; this effect, of course, is incomplete as brindling can be seen around the edges of the black coat.

Although most polygenic traits vary smoothly through their range of expression, some are subject to a discontinuity in their expression. These threshold characteristics are thought to require a build-up of certain polygenes before they appear – the transition from three toes to four toes in guinea pigs is a classic threshold situation. Canine problems like patella luxation may well be threshold in nature in that we can mate two apparently normal dogs and without warning get puppies prone to slipping patellas. Other groups of polygenes appear to modify the expression of a primary gene. Such is the case with red/fawn coats; these are the same base colour, but with significant variations in the intensity and brightness of the pigment caused by the so-called rufus polygenes.

The hereditary information in the gene is composed primarily of the chemical deoxyribonucleic acid, better known to us as DNA. Researchers are now beginning to unravel the complexities of canine genetics. Already a saliva sample can be analysed to provide the DNA fingerprint of an individual dog, thereby uniquely identifying it. These fingerprints can also be used to confirm the parentage of a suspect litter. Based on advances in human research, a major project is underway in America to piece together the chemical structures of the dog's genetic makeup (genotype). Called the Canine Genome Project, the aim is to produce a map of all of the chromosomes in dogs, which can be used to map the genes causing disease and the genes controlling morphology and behaviour. Through the use of marker genes, associated with a particular heritable disease, we will be able to test our breeding stock for the presence of the gene(s) causing that disease. Several of these DNA tests – the first being for copper toxicosis in Bedlington Terriers – are now available, so we are not talking science fiction. Over the next twenty years or so, a battery of such tests will equip breeders with the ability to look into the genotype of their dogs in addition to their external characteristics (phenotype).

BREEDING FOR COLOUR

The mode of inheritance of coat colour in Bull Terriers has been well-established for more than 50 years. Here is a basic set of rules from my book *Full Circle* (1990).

1. All Bull Terriers carry colour; they are coloured dogs not albinos.
2. White Bull Terriers have a masking factor, which inhibits the expression of colour – except for marks that occur on the head or occasionally on other parts of the body.
3. Coloured Bull Terriers come in a variety of colours: brindle, black brindle, red, red smut, fawn, fawn smut and finally black and tan (which with the usual white markings is called tricolour).
4. Every white Bull Terrier carries one of this same spectrum of colours. In terms of

Top stud dog: Ch. Ghabar The Admiral.

inheritance, the colours carried by whites operate in exactly the same way as in coloured dogs. The colours, however, may not be apparent because of the masking factor.
5. Brindle is the dominant colour. For a dog to be brindle, or in the case of a white to carry brindle, at least one parent must be brindle or carry brindle. Combinations of other colours – reds, fawns (clear or smut) and black/tans, or whites carrying these colours – cannot produce brindles or whites carrying brindle.
6. White mated to white always produces 100 per cent white litters. White to white cannot produce coloured puppies.
7. For a dog to be coloured, at least one parent must be coloured. Although results of coloured-to-coloured and coloured-to-white matings are predictable statistically, in practice they vary widely from litter to litter in terms both of colours and markings.
8. Most coloured Bull Terriers sport a white blaze, a white collar and chest, white socks and a white tip to the tail. These are the most popular markings for show purposes.
9. A few Bull Terriers are nearly solid in colour. Such dogs exhibit minimal white – usually only a small amount of white on the chest and perhaps the feet, with little or

107

none on the muzzle. They result from the mating of two coloured dogs and are referred to as solid for colour. When mated, they produce 100 per cent coloured offspring. Even when bred to white mates, they never produce white puppies.

I should add here that the basic coat colour is any shade from rich red through to pale fawn. The brindle pattern, when present, is superimposed over this base colour, in which event the variation in tone of the base colour causes the brindle to range from rich mahogany to pale silver brindle. The black pattern may be superimposed on top of the brindle, resulting in a black brindle coat. Black superimposed directly on the base red or fawn produces black and tan, which with white is called tricolour. The smut pattern occurs in both reds and fawns and is characterized by dark-tipped hairs on the muzzle and along the spine and tail; in the absence of smutting, the coat colours are sometimes referred to as clear red or clear fawn.

TERMINOLOGY

Two terms frequently employed in articles on the genetics of breeding are homozygous and heterozygous. In general use, they refer simply to the degree to which a dog's genes are pure for their characteristics. Mongrels, for instance, have a largely disparate set of genes and so are heterozygous, whereas well-established strains of pure-bred dogs have much greater genetic purity (with many locations on the chromosomes carrying the same gene from their respective sets of alleles) and so are genetically homozygous. Our efforts as breeders focus on increasing the genetic purity or homozygosity of our stock and thus the predictability of their phenotypes.

We should also clarify some of the terms

Top stud dog: Ch. Kilacabar Rolling Thunder.

breeders use – and often misuse — in discussion. Strictly speaking **inbreeding** is the mating together of animals more closely related than the average within the breed. When doggy people talk about inbreeding, however, they usually mean very close matings like father-daughter, mother-son or brother-sister. We call the less close forms of inbreeding that most of us practise **line breeding**; typically we breed together relatives of a dog, or less frequently of a bitch, we greatly admire. **Outcrossing** (or outbreeding) is another term we tend to use rather loosely. By definition it is the mating of unrelated animals, one or both of which are inbred. Rarely are Bull Terriers unrelated once we get back a few generations, so in practice so-called outcrosses tend to be partial at best. Over time, some (celebrated) breeders are able to develop their own **strain**, which implies that their dogs breed so true to a distinctive type that we can recognize them in an instant; this was often said of the many wonderful brindle Bull Terriers from the Romany kennels. A favourite cliché among breeders is **prepotent**. This is not a scientific term, but is commonly applied to dogs that consistently stamp progeny with their virtues and so can be assumed to be homozygous for the said virtues.

BREEDING SYSTEMS

There are two complementary aspects of breeding animals, namely how we select the animals we want to use and the system we employ to mate them together. The ensuing discussion illustrates the separation between these two steps. But before we set off to breed our own dogs – hopefully to develop a distinctive line and perhaps even a recognized strain – we must first decide on our goal, our ideal Bull Terrier. In other words, before we start our journey we need to determine where we are going – our destination. It is not enough to say that we want to breed better dogs or the best Bull Terriers around. Every major breeder has slightly different priorities. The breed is a head breed, so what are we willing to sacrifice for a terrific head? To some breeders, expression is crucial; to others it is significant, but not number one priority. How important is overall balance? Do we want an absolutely middle-of-the-road type, or do we slightly prefer the more heavyweight or terrier side of the road? White or coloured, or does it not matter? How critical is movement? Where does temperament fit into all of this? These considerations cannot all be number one in priority. Consistently successful breeders have a clear vision of what they want to achieve, and they have their priorities firmly in place.

Once we have set our goal, we can move on to selection. Usually we have a bitch and we want to select the optimal male for her. The simplest approach is to decide, on the basis of phenotype, the male that in our judgement appears to have the most merit. This, of course, tells us little about his genotype – whether he is homozygous for those virtues (or characters) we find so attractive. Characters controlled by a single gene, such as the brindle coat, are readily apparent. However, most of the characters for which we aim are polygenic in nature and may even be controlled on a threshold basis. Although we cannot be sure of the sire's genotype, the closeness of his pedigree and a knowledge of the type and virtues of his parents and grandparents does provide an indicator of this. If we were breeding farm animals, we would carry out some progeny testing before committing ourselves to this male. With dogs, the best we can do is to wait till he has a reasonable number of puppies on the ground the better to determine whether he is prepotent for his key virtues. Perhaps he produces superb downfaces, but accompanied by quite a few incorrect bites? Is this acceptable to us? He may consistently pass on his outstanding bone, but with a tendency to slight shortness of leg, and so it goes.

The quickest and surest way to lock in one character is to select solely on the basis of that particular character. For example, if

Top stud dog: Ch. Kilacabar Cabin Buoy at Bullyvark.

we select and breed for great heads for several generations, we will make tremendous advances in heads, although (probably) to the detriment of the whole dog. However, once we have the heads we want, we can move on to the next character, focus on that and try – without losing the heads – to lock it in, then move on to the third character. Unfortunately, this tandem method of selection demands a huge breeding programme and so it is rarely employed. In practice, most of us take a more balanced approach, selecting on the basis of a number of different characters. We may grade the prospective males of suitable pedigree for these key virtues and then eliminate those that do not reach a certain standard in each. One danger with this approach is that an excellent dog may be ousted because it fails in one requirement, despite being superior in all of the others. To avoid such elimination, the textbooks recommend a points score method, grading each character on, say, a one-to-ten scale and then totalling the score. Whether we do it consciously or not, we each have our own method of evaluating and grading dogs for our breeding programmes. A better appreciation of the scientific basis for these methodologies cannot but strengthen our objectivity in applying them.

Next we come to systems of mating and, in my view, using each latest, greatest superstar is not a system at all. Such use of superstars may well result in some highly successful show dogs, but with the randomness of the genes involved it will not – unless by accident – produce consistent type and certainly not a homozygous line of Bull Terriers. The same is true of mating like to like; that is, dogs of similar type. It is a safe and sensible approach for beginners and will tend to reproduce that type, but the progeny will

not have the prepotency to impose their type on unlike mates.

A long-term breeding programme necessitates a planned approach to how the dogs we have selected are mated together. In their early stages, all breeds were developed by judicious inbreeding, which is the quickest and most effective way of fixing the desired type and also the genotype to reproduce it on a consistent basis. The danger with inbreeding is the increased possibility of bringing to light faults or diseases, which are nearly always polygenic in nature. With line breeding, there is a steady and progressive increase in homozygosity. It takes longer to lock in those genes, but has the advantage of permitting more time to breed out unwanted genes and avoid these recessive problems. Having decided on a dog to which they wish to line breed, breeders may initially take advantage of half-brother to half-sister matings, thereby doubling up on the said dog. Most breeders tend to maintain the line by selecting animals with this dog prominent in their pedigrees, though less closely than in the above half-sib mating. For someone starting out with a relatively poor bitch, in terms of show points, the best approach is often to 'grade up' by line breeding to a superior male. The success of line breeding is by no means guaranteed. A great dog can appear multiple times in the pedigree of a perfectly awful show animal. The breeder's skill in selecting the right dogs is the key to success.

Some breeders recommend outcrossing after a couple of generations of line breeding. However, geneticists argue that there is no point in outcrossing as part of a typical line breeding programme unless the need arises. Random outcrossing will increase heterozygosity of our line, potentially undoing much of what we have worked hard to achieve. That is not to imply that superior show dogs may not result from an outcross; often they do, but because of the multiplicity of the genes we have introduced, the gain may be short rather than long-term. The purpose of an outcross should be to remedy a problem that has arisen or is beginning to show itself, or perhaps to take advantage of the exceptional virtues of a particular dog. Experience and skill are at a premium when outcrossing. The bottom line is not to outcross unless we have a good reason to do so, and then to select very carefully.

A final word concerns Bruce Lowe, a 19th century Australian. Based on his studies of thoroughbred horses, Lowe proposed that the tail male and tail female tail (the top and bottom lines of a pedigree) are the most important ones and also that certain sires produced outstanding daughters rather than sons. There is absolutely no scientific basis for these proposals; the top and bottom lines contribute the same number of genes and have the same influence as the middle lines. Nevertheless Lowe's theories gained considerable favour among dog breeders and, to this day, are perpetuated by the significance attached to stud dog trophies and developing a line of champion males, which is not difficult for a powerful kennel attracting many bitches.

KEY BREEDING PRINCIPLES

The late Raymond Oppenheimer is viewed by many as one of the greatest of dog breeders and certainly his Ormandy Bull Terriers dominated the show scene for many a year. In 1957 Raymond laid out his approach to breeding as *Twenty Basic Breeding Principles.* Since then they have been reproduced countless times in publications around the world. Within the Bull Terrier fancy they have become little

Top stud dog: Eng. Am. Ch. Abraxas Achilles.
Photo: Bowles.

short of holy writ. Underpinning Raymond's doctrine was a focus on virtues rather than faults. Overt faults did not concern him, provided the animal possessed overwhelming virtues. Such was his view when he offered Ormandy Souperlative Bar Sinister, a dog far in advance of his contemporaries yet with one undescended testicle, at stud.

Ultimately, decisions on breeding come down to personal preferences and priorities. Raymond bred whites; Anna and I breed coloureds. We place temperament at the top of our list of requirements; not everyone does, and this is where lip service comes in handy. Some pay more attention to movement than others. Outside the breed, many of us are thought of as head freaks. And so it goes. Nevertheless, most of us subscribe to the principles that have enabled Raymond and other great breeders to consistently produce so many outstanding Bull Terriers. Here is my own interpretation of these basic precepts.

'THE TEN COMMANDMENTS'

1. **Always breed for the very best.** The maxim is – if it's worth doing, it's worth doing well. Do your homework. Seek advice from successful breeders; do not take advice from those who have no track record of success (though they are often the ones most anxious to give it). Use the best dog you can find, regardless of who owns it and whether it is conveniently located; never use mediocrities.

2. **Breed for a superb head.** Bull Terriers are a head breed and, yes, today's heads are exaggerated. So, if you do not aim for that unique egg-shaped head, you may get nice dogs, but you will not get good Bull Terriers.

3. **Breed for balance.** The head may be exaggerated, but otherwise the Bull Terrier is a well-balanced dog, without overstatement. To obtain correct type, you must aim for overall balance. You want substance plus quality, a terrific head plus soundness.

4. **Always aim for the best possible temperament.** The vast majority of Bull Terriers live as family pets, so their typical fun-loving character (mental health) is, like physical health, essential. Some pay lip service to this goal, but are willing to take undue risks in the search for their next trophy winner. There are always risks associated with breeding; however, do not risk temperament.

5. **Be realistic about faults and virtues.** To make progress, you must be honest with yourself about your bitch's faults and virtues and also about those of potential studs. As Raymond proclaimed, the perfect Bull Terrier does not exist, never has, never will. Choosing a mate for your bitch is

Top stud dog: Am. Can. Ch. Magor the Marquis.

always a matter of priorities, preferences and, ultimately, compromise.

6. **Focus on virtues.** In Raymond's words "Do not be frightened of breeding from animals that have obvious faults as long as they have compensating virtues." A lack of virtues is by far the greatest fault of all. Successful breeders seek dogs with positive virtues – virtues that for breeding purposes far outweigh the faults that such dogs inevitably possess. They scorn blameless nonentities.

7. **Breed together complementary types.** Simplistically, this is a matter of not breeding together those possessing the same faults and lacking the same virtues. But discerning type and recognizing complementary types is far more subtle than just identifying faults and virtues. As Raymond noted, it is a breeder's gift; it is the hallmark of every consistently successful breeder. Do not be fooled by the occasional exception, for example, two bad movers producing a puppy that moves well. Such exceptions only serve to prove the rule.

8. **Line breed.** Line breeding – of complementary types – has proven time and again to be the high-percentage path to success. Top breeders line breed on a consistent basis, making judicious use of the

Top stud dog: Am. Can. Ch. Jocko's Julius of Magor.

occasional outcross. However, as Raymond wrote, an indiscriminate outcross can produce an aggregation of every imaginable fault. If the latest, greatest trophy winner or import is an outcross, think twice before using him and, if in doubt, let other breeders with the same line test the outcross for you – as they surely will.

9. **Do not forget colour.** Experience has demonstrated the value of breeding colour, in particular brindle, back into white lines every few generations. So periodically use either a coloured stud, or a white one with colour close up in his pedigree.

10. **Trust your own intuition.** Initially, it makes sense to be guided by your mentor(s). But later, if you are to be recognized as a breeder of true merit, you must rely on your own judgement, acumen and instincts. You must learn by your own mistakes; it is the only way.

TEMPERAMENT

I have yet to come across a breeder who does not claim that temperament is at the top of his or her list of priorities. How could anyone say otherwise? Yet some breeders turn a blind eye to bad temperaments when it suits them. Perhaps I take an extreme position. To me, a Bull Terrier must be healthy in both body and mind; it is sine qua non. Even if we cannot all agree on this, I would argue that we do not have a choice. The experts tell us that heritable behavioural problems are more readily passed on – perhaps by as high a proportion as 50 per cent – than all of those physical traits so necessary to the successful show dog. In today's litigious society, how can any of us afford to place a potentially unreliable puppy in a pet home, or any home for that matter?

ETHICS

Discussion of unreliable temperaments leads directly into the whole question of the ethics of breeding dogs. The pleasure of breeding our own Bull Terriers brings with it responsibility for the welfare of the breed, to the dogs themselves and to their prospective owners. Are the puppies we breed healthy and will they mature into healthy adults both physically and mentally? Bull Terriers, like mongrels, other pure-bred dogs, and humans, carry genetic faults and have the potential to pass them on to their progeny. Inevitably, some of these problems will manifest themselves

Early in this century deafness was a major cause for concern, not surprisingly so, given the continued use of deaf stud dogs and presumably of deaf bitches, in breeding programmes. In 1909 the BTC took a firm stand on this issue, requiring members to sign a Declaration of Honour. This is the wording of the declaration as it appeared in the Club's 1931 Annual.

"All Members of the Bull Terrier Club do undertake not to exhibit for competition deaf Bull Terriers and, furthermore, that they will support the Club in every way practical to stop the exhibiting of deaf dogs, whether owned by a Member or anyone else. Members also declare that they will not offer for sale, or be in any way concerned in the sale or offering for sale, of deaf Bull Terriers...nor will any member knowingly use a deaf dog as a sire, or breed from a deaf bitch. Note: The Club considers any dog deaf that cannot hear perfectly."

This declaration has long since been dropped from the BTC rules, though it is equally valid and important today.

In recent years, the national clubs in both the UK and America have established more general ethical standards for their members to follow; the BTCA has a Standard of Ethics and both clubs have Codes of Conduct. They provide sensible guidelines for breeders and owners, emphasizing responsibilities and honourable behaviour. Neither are mandatory, and so they are dependent on example and peer pressure rather than legal enforcement. They cover a wide range of topics including: behaviour at shows; advice on breeding and on the buying and selling of puppies and adult dogs; not mating a bitch till she is mature; the goal of breeding being to improve the breed; not breeding from inferior dogs nor from those suffering from an inherited abnormality; stud dog owners not accepting bitches of unsuitable temperament; maintaining good records. It is a matter of honour and integrity.

BREEDING PRACTICE

FIRST THINGS FIRST

A surprising number of us did not buy our first Bull Terrier with intent to exhibit, and certainly with no thought of breeding. This was true of Anna and myself. Then somehow we start showing, get bitten by

Top stud dog: Am. Can. Ch. Monkery's Buckskin.

the bug and before we know it we decide to breed the bitch we initially acquired purely as a pet. However, it is one thing having some fun showing and getting to know our fellow Bull Terrier aficionados, but it is quite another making the commitment to breeding a litter with all that this entails – time, money, inconvenience, the problems of placing puppies in suitable homes and being prepared to take them back, for starters. It means taking a couple of weeks out of our lives to ensure the bitch whelps successfully and the litter thrives. And you should not bank on making money; with two or three litters over the lifetime of a bitch few of us do. Also, there are financial risks – paying a stud fee does not guarantee puppies and occasionally there may be large veterinary bills. But perhaps I am painting too bleak a picture, as there are few more rewarding experiences than raising a happy, healthy litter.

The above makes no mention of those of us who start out with a male. Unfortunately, few males possess the requisite virtues to justify their use at stud – based on breeding only the best. The vast majority of bitches are served by a limited number of top males. Handling a stud dog demands experience and so, if we are lucky enough to own a really outstanding one, it is best to seek assistance from the breeder or our mentor. However, it is not unusual to receive a call from the owner of a pet male – never shown and of nondescript pedigree – wanting to buy a really good bitch to mate to him. No ethical breeder is going to sell a bitch in that situation, though there are always puppy farmers prepared to sell 'guaranteed champions' to anyone willing to part with sufficient money.

DOING YOUR HOMEWORK

When preparing to mate your first bitch, much of the enjoyment comes from deciding on a suitable stud dog, the optimal one for her. You must first decide on your goal, on your ideal. Having done that, you need to assess honestly and realistically the virtues and faults of your bitch. From then on, it is a matter of doing your homework – going to shows, talking to knowledgeable breeders, visiting top kennels, reading everything you can get your hands on and studying pedigrees. In other words, you need to apply the theory discussed in the preceding chapter.

One of the practical issues that arises is how to go about fixing faults. Here it is important to breed to the correct middle-of-the-road dog. If the bitch has a gay tail, she

Top stud dog: Am. Can. Ch. Bulwark's Iceni Just William.

should be bred to a dog with a correctly-set tail, not to one with a tail set on too low. Similarly, if she is rather straight in stifle, she needs a dog with a correctly angled stifle, not one with an exaggerated bend. The goal here is to obtain the correct conformation, progressively getting closer to, and homozygous for, the ideal. Putting two extremes together is likely to result in every possible variation in the progeny and certainly will not lock in the desired trait. With heads, of course, we must forget all of this middle-of-the-road stuff. Here, we need length and strength of muzzle, a superb unbroken profile, a lower jaw that is deep

Top stud dog: Am. Ch. Banbury Benson of Bedrock.

and wide, plus a stunning expression. So we need to exaggerate in order to win with heads; indeed, some would argue we should go for broke.

SUCCESSFUL BREEDERS
During our quest for the ideal stud dog, we can do no better than study the approaches of our great Bull Terrier breeders and remember that anyone worth listening to will have a proven track record.

Raymond Oppenheimer served notice of his veritable genius when still a relative newcomer to the breed. He co-owned Ch. Cedran White Queen, one of many outstanding bitches by the crack sire Rubislaw. However, none of these Rubislaw daughters were coming up with the goods, despite being bred to the top-winning dogs of the day. Raymond deduced that he

needed to double up on Rubislaw and so, against the advice of the experts, sent White Queen to Rubislaw's best available son, even though the experts considered him "a common little dog". The result was Ch. Ormandy's Mr McGuffin, winner of the 1939 Regent Trophy and one of the pillars of the breed.

Here are the pedigrees of two celebrated stud dogs from the 1960s: the first is Raymond Oppenheimer and Eva Weatherill's Ormandy Souperlative Bar Sinister, one of the most famous dogs in the breed's long history; the second is 'D' Montague Johnstone and Meg Williams' wonderful brindle champion Romany River Pirate. Both are examples of focused line breeding.

Ormandy Souperlative
Bar Sinister

Sire: Ch. Souperlative Brinhead

Ch. Phidgity Phlasher of Lenster

Ch. Beech House Snow Visio

Ch. Phidgity Snow Dream
(by Snowflash)

Ch. Souperlative Summer Queen

Ch. Beech House Snow Visio

Souperlative Spring Song
(Snowflash's sister)

Dam: Ch. Souperlative Sunshine

Ch. Romany Romantic Vision

Ch. Romany Robin Goodfell

Ch. Phidgity Snow Dream

Ch. Souperlative Summer Queen

Ch. Beech House Snow Visio

Souperlative Spring Song

Ch. Souperlative Brinhead

Ch. Souperlative Sunshine (by Romantic Vision)

Ch. Souperlative Sea Captain

Sire: Romany Roving Sailor

Ch. Romany Romantic Vision (by Robin Goodfellow)

Romany Ruderpest (by Robin Goodfellow)

Romany Romantic Nomad

Ch. Romany River Pirate

Ch. Phidgity Phlasher of Lenster

Ch. Souperlative Summer Queen

Ch. Souperlative Brinhead

Dam: Ch. Romany River Witch

Ch. Romany Robin Goodfellow

Torrid Tempest

Budshead Bramble

The most successful breeder of the mid 1930s, Harry Potter (Gardenia), was a proponent of the classic half-brother to half-sister mating, followed by a judicious outcross and then back to half-brother to half-sister. As mentioned earlier, most leading show Bull Terriers were and continue to be pretty closely related and so Harry's outcrosses were only partial ones.

THE BITCH
However enthusiastic we may be to breed our bitch, there are a number of prerequisites – issues that must be resolved. The key questions here are: Is she of the type and quality to warrant mating? Is she healthy and free from apparent genetic problems? Is she from a line of good

mothers? Answering the first of these is simply a matter of being honest and objective and, if needs be, seeking expert advice. The second necessitates working closely with your vet. The bitch needs to be fit, at the correct weight, up to date on all of her vaccinations and in general good health. In addition, it is important to check on potential hereditary problems, in particular kidney, heart and thyroid function and patella joints. She should also be checked for normal bilateral hearing. The third question is important because bitches appear to learn from their own experiences as puppies in the whelping box. If their dam is a good mother so, usually, are they, and most Bull Terrier bitches fall into this category. Alas, a few are bad mothers and

Top stud dog: Am. Ch. Banbury Bellringer.

Top stud dog: Aust. Ch. Westbul Rolling Stone.

their daughters may be the same, which could necessitate hand-rearing the litter. If the answers to any of these questions are negative, then I would recommend not breeding the bitch.

But let us look on the bright side and assume that she passes with flying colours. The next question is on which day(s) of her season she should be bred. I maintain a record of every season for all of my bitches, and have found that each bitch is remarkably consistent in terms of the duration and characteristics of her seasons. Most Bull Terrier bitches first come into heat at eight to ten months of age and at about eight-month intervals thereafter, though a few come in every six months and others less frequently. The length of a season is typically 18 to 21 days. The first indications are swelling of the vulva, accompanied by a bloody discharge. If the bitch shows this bloody colour early in the morning I count that as the first day of her season; if later in the day, I count the next day as her first. This phase of the season is called pro-oestrus and usually lasts for up to ten days. The bitch's discharge then begins to turn straw-coloured and less mucus-like, which indicates true oestrus has begun. During the first four days of oestrus, the

bitch releases her ova (eggs). The ova take 2-3 days to mature to the stage at which they are ready for fertilization by the male's sperm, and then they remain viable for 48-72 hours. Another good indicator is the bitch's vulva, which typically becomes softer and increases in size when she is at her most receptive.

In practice, many Bull Terrier bitches are most receptive to the dog somewhere between the thirteenth and sixteenth days of their season. The challenge is to determine the optimal day or days for our maiden bitch. All of my own bitches over the years have fallen within this 13-16 day range. One would only stand for the dog on the thirteenth day, while another – though she whelped to the fifteenth day – would try to mate herself to any available male until the twenty-third day of her season.

When we started breeding in England, it was usual to drive the bitch to the stud dog and return the same day, with just one mating. Two matings 48 hours apart are preferable though by no means essential, provided both dog and bitch enjoy normal fertility. So, based on observations of previous seasons, if our bitch appears most receptive on her fifteenth day, we should plan to mate her on that day, or, if there are to be two matings, on her fourteenth and sixteenth days.

This approach to deducing when to mate a bitch has worked well for me. The acid test, however, is whether the bitch is receptive to and will stand for the dog, and so your best-laid plans may go astray. This is why some kennels prefer to keep the bitch for a few days and to rely upon the expertise of an experienced stud dog in deciding when she is ready. On the other hand, experts in reproduction place little faith in these external indicators – probably because they often have to deal with problem bitches rather than normal ones. The bitch's oestrus cycle is a complex affair controlled by the interaction of multiple hormones, most importantly of progesterone and luteinizing hormone (LH). A surge in the amount of LH triggers ovulation. Research has shown that the bitch is most fertile five and six days after this surge. Therefore, tracking the LH level provides a more accurate indication of readiness. Should a bitch fail to display normal external signs, then a vet can monitor the progress of her season via the tests that are now available and determine when she should be mated.

THE STUD DOG

Having agonized over choosing a stud dog, you have, hopefully, now settled on a suitable male Bull Terrier well before your bitch is due to come into heat. If the choice is the dog around the corner, a decision that often seems singularly attractive to novice owners, I suggest re-reading the previous chapter and starting all over again. I would make the same recommendation if the selected dog is the cheapest around; ultimately it pays to breed to the best available dog, regardless of whether we like the owner or not, whether the dog lives

Top stud dog: Nl Ch. Polytelis Silver Convention.

Top stud dog: Am. Ch. Iffinest Local Hero.
Photo: Burns.

conveniently close or not and, within reason, regardless of the cost of the stud fee. Next, I need to mention a couple of practical considerations. With a maiden bitch it is imperative to take her to a proven stud dog, handled by an expert; this is not the time for maiden dogs or lack of experience. Some stud dogs are extraordinarily prolific, seeming to get every bitch sent to them in whelp while, at the other end of the scale, some miss quite often. Such prolific dogs are a big advantage when it comes to getting that first litter of puppies on the ground.

Top stud dog: D Ch. Union Jack von der Alten Veste.   *Top stud dog: D Ch. Merlin von der Alten Veste.*

Once your decision is final, you should contact the dog's owners to determine whether they will accept a maiden bitch and to discuss arrangements; doing this well ahead of time avoids last-minute surprises and disappointment. Increasingly, stud dog owners are demanding the battery of health checks discussed above, and rightly so in my view. Such requirements, of course, oblige the owners of the stud dog to provide evidence that he has tested clear of these same health problems. When the bitch comes on heat she should visit the vet to be checked for any vaginal stricture plus any other necessary tests; in America most kennels require a brucellosis test (a simple blood test) and some want a guarded swab culture and sensitivity, which checks for the presence of abnormal quantities of

*Top stud dog:
N/S Ch. Quest
Giancana.*

infectious organisms such as beta-haemolytic streptococci.

You should also discuss travel arrangements. Will there be one or two matings? Is the dog close enough to jump in the car and drive there when the time arrives? In the USA and other geographically large countries it is often necessary to fly the bitch to the dog. Some kennels prefer to have a bitch a few days early and keep her till they are sure she is going off. The stud dog owners may ask for a puppy in lieu of the stud fee. It is much simpler to pay the fee, but this is a personal decision. The fee is payment for the stud service and implies no guarantee of puppies, so it better to clarify in advance whether or not a free return service will be provided if the bitch does miss.

Artificial Insemination (AI) is becoming an increasingly practical alternative to natural matings, especially if the bitch would have to travel a long distance. Two options are available – fresh-chilled semen or frozen semen. Chilling decreases the lifespan of the semen from the four or more days that it survives in the uterine tract, when naturally inseminated, to about two days, with one of those usually taken up by shipping. This necessitates much more accurate prediction of when the bitch is ready, so that ovulation testing is essential, as are two inseminations. Freezing and

Top stud dog: SA Ch. Bonaparte of the French Border at Kingstonia.

subsequent thawing further reduces the motility and lifespan of the sperm, and so places even greater emphasis on getting the timing right. For this reason, it is usual to make one surgical insemination of the semen directly into the uterus, followed by a vaginal insemination. As expertise is developed with AI techniques, the success rates are steadily increasing. In the long term, AI will overcome the barriers imposed by distance and outdated quarantine restrictions, and open up our choice of stud dogs to the best available on a worldwide basis.

THE MATING

As soon as the bitch comes into season – I usually wait 24 hours to ensure she is really on heat – you should make final arrangements. Contact the stud dog owners and agree times and dates. Then book her in for the veterinary check-up. The bitch's urine will attract males from far and wide, so she needs to be virtually imprisoned to avoid a misalliance. Initially, the bitch will fight off any attention from males, but later she may be just as keen on reaching that mongrel the other side of the fence as he is on reaching her. Stud dogs are creatures of habit and, when your bitch arrives, the owners will enter into the routine that has proven successful for their dog. They are in charge and they may or may not ask for your assistance. Sometimes it is better for owners to be out of sight so that the bitch's natural instincts take over. Despite being 'ready' the sweetest pet bitch may refuse to let the male mount her and attempt to take a chunk out of him, in which event she will have to be muzzled; some kennels do this as a matter of course.

A typical routine may entail allowing the two animals to get to know each other while separated by a chain-link fence; they can urinate, sniff and flirt to their hearts'

content. Next, secured on collars (not too tight-fitting) and leashes, they are brought together. Then, assuming the bitch is receptive, she will be held by the collar and the male allowed to mount her. After a few exploratory attempts, the male will usually thrust and enter the bitch, at which point a maiden bitch may well yelp and attempt to extricate herself. An experienced male will hold on to her and soon they will be 'tied'. During the tie most males will turn, initially standing alongside the bitch, and then rear-end to rear-end. The tie is unique to canines and results from a swelling in the dog's penis which is held as the bitch constricts her vaginal muscles. The tie may last for just a few minutes or for as long as 20 or 30 minutes. It is not necessary for the animals to tie, but it is a natural and desirable function. If a tie is not obtained or the dog slips out after only a short tie, it is advisable to elevate the bitch's rear-end at an angle of about 30 degrees to the horizontal and keep her in this position for about 15 minutes. When the mating is completed, the bitch should be crated and kept quiet; she should not be allowed to urinate for at least an hour.

After those careful preparations and making every effort to breed her at the optimal time, with any luck you should be able to look forward to the arrival of puppies in about 63 days.

11 BREEDING A LITTER

A PERSPECTIVE

No doubt some Bull Terriers are quite capable of whelping and raising puppies unaided. This, however, is a high-risk approach, with the likelihood of losing puppies and the possibility of the bitch getting into difficulties. We raise our dogs in an entirely unnatural way, and so we should not expect them to manage the event without our assistance. This is the key: we should be available to help them and the newborn puppies as and when needed. Some bitches expect us to do most of the work, while others just like us to be there to give the equivalent of moral support. Maiden bitches may well be shocked into inaction when their very first whelp arrives and wait for us to do something with it.

Anna and I usually whelp our bitches in a bedroom, and stay with them or within earshot for the first week or so. We still prepare for litters in the same way that we did 25 years ago, with our battered copy of *The Third Bull Terrier Book* containing Eva Weatherill's acclaimed article on whelping and rearing to hand, together with material and advice we have gathered from 'D' Montague Johnstone, Quita Youatt, Winkie

Mackay-Smith and others. The vet is the bitch's best friend in case of a problem, so we always keep ours abreast of happenings and ensure we can obtain emergency help around the clock should the need arise.

The following notes detail how Anna and I whelp our bitches. Every breeder has variations on the general 'how to do it' theme. We suggest reading through our notes several times and highlighting the important points, so that they can be located in a hurry, then doing the same with other articles written by other breeders. There are also some excellent general books available for first-time and experienced breeders alike – there is always more for us to learn.

PREGNANCY

After mating our bitch, we relax and enjoy her company. She needs to continue her regular 'high-quality' diet, plus the usual supplements – we add vitamin C tablets for the first few weeks. Her daily exercise is just as important as her routine diet. Indeed routine is the most important factor throughout her pregnancy. This summary of events may help those breeding their first litter.

WEEK ONE: After mating, she is still in season and so we must guard against an accidental mating, either to our own male or a fence jumper.

WEEKS TWO, THREE AND FOUR: She may become lethargic and sleep heavily. She may also have morning sickness and be fussy about food. She may be confused by the major hormonal changes she is experiencing and demand even more attention than usual; we indulge her whims. Again, we are careful to maintain her routine to the greatest degree possible, with the usual meal-times and exercise. We try – not always successfully – to put a stop to any roughhousing with people or other dogs and also to avoid car journeys and any such potentially stressful situations.

WEEKS FIVE AND SIX: She may feel the puppies beginning to move and find this quite perplexing. Towards the end of this period, there may be a clear or slightly cloudy mucous discharge from her vulva. This is normal and the sign of a good healthy litter. However, any odour, trace of blood or yellowness of pus may indicate an infection, so we check her temperature and get in touch with our vet immediately. Some breeders recommend checking for pregnancy via X-ray or ultrasound. We do not. She is either in whelp or she is not. More importantly, sick dogs go to vets and we do not want to risk her picking up an infection in the waiting room.

WEEKS SEVEN AND EIGHT: By now, she should begin to look bulgy around her mid-section with her teats enlarged and possibly milky. At this stage, sometimes earlier, most of our bitches become fussy about eating. We feed them smaller quantities more frequently and, if they refuse food, we even resort to hand-feeding (yes, I know we are not supposed to do this). We give an extra multi-vitamin pill in the evening, but we do not give other

'Gump' pictured seven weeks into her pregnancy.
Photo courtesy: The Henderson family.

supplements and especially *not* any calcium additives. As discussed later, Bull Terriers are prone to pseudo-eclampsia, a tendency that is exacerbated by feeding calcium additives during pregnancy. We simply maintain our normal diet, which contains ample natural calcium. Also, we do not change her diet as we want to avoid diarrhoea or stomach upsets.

WEEK EIGHT: By the start of this week, we have her whelping box set up in a suitable draught-free room; this becomes *her room*, free from other dogs, visitors and disturbances. We encourage her to spend time in the box, if necessary sitting there with her. We keep a watchful eye on her, though she will not produce puppies until close to the normal 63 days from the date of conception. However, we are fully prepared well ahead of time, as puppies born up to five days prior to this, though premature and delicate, can be viable. Two or three days either side of the expected date is fine. It is important to keep her exercised even if it is only a stroll up and down the street – remember she needs to be up to walking back. We let her eat when she likes and, because of the pressure on her bladder, ensure she can get outside whenever she wants to.

We avoid giving any shots or other medication during pregnancy (all of this should have been taken care of beforehand), with the exception of the monthly heartworm tablets that are essential in parts of America. Neither do we clip claws, with all the hysteria that can accompany this. For runny bowels or upset stomach we give her a child's dose of a mild human medication. Our goal throughout is to keep the pregnant bitch stress-free, happy and, hopefully, free from the usual array of dog ailments and injuries.

Finally, a word of warning: a bitch is quite capable of convincing herself and her novice owners that she is in whelp even though she is not, going through most if not all of the stages outlined above. Some bitches are prone to such false pregnancies, even without being mated. On several occasions, we have been called in by desperate novices convinced their bitch should have whelped by then, only to find that she was was not pregnant and did not appear so to an experienced eye.

GETTING READY
We try to get everything ready for the whelping at least ten days ahead of time; nothing is left till the last minute if we can avoid it. This is the checklist we use for these preparations.
1. We telephone to remind our vet of the impending litter, discuss issues, and ask any questions we have. These days, we give our own subcutaneous injections of soluble calcium in case of pseudo-eclampsia, but previously we ensured that our vet understood the breed's propensity to this problem. We also make sure the vet will make a house call in an emergency. If, for some reason, we absolutely have to take our bitch to see the vet, we insist on *carrying* her straight from the car to the treatment room.

2. We set up the whelping room, along with the whelping box, and move her into it 7-10 days before the due date. Ideally the room should have easy access to the garden, so that the bitch can go in and out without running the gauntlet of other dogs and strangers. Currently, we use a spare bedroom.
3. Whelping boxes vary in design and construction. Our current one is adapted from a wooden packing box (32 ins or 81 cms in each dimension), minus the top and with one side panel cut away to 5 inches (14 cms) in height. It is raised about two inches (5 cms) off the ground on wooden studs and the whole painted with a white emulsion. There is also a board that we can use to partially cover the top of the box and a detachable pig or guard rail that fits inside the box. The rail is about three inches (7.6 cms) wide and raised about three inches from the floor of the box; the rail prevents the pups being crushed against the sides of the box when the bitch lies down. We move the bitch's usual bed next to the whelping box and cajole her into taking up residence in the box.
4. Temperature control: The whelping room should be kept free of strong draughts that might chill the puppies. Eva Weatherill recommends an ambient temperature of about 60 degrees F (16 C). Rather than measuring the temperature, we simply ensure the whelping area is comfortably warm. We employ two means of heating the box itself – an infra-red lamp hung above and an electrical heating pad placed underneath the box – turning them on and off as needed. Although adjustable in height above the box, the lamp tends to overheat the bitch; so we place the cover over the top of the box and use it for background rather than direct heating. We rely primarily on the heating pad, with which we keep an area towards the front of the box warm. If

the pups get cold they migrate to this warm area; if they are too hot they move away from it. Hypothermia is a serious concern with new born pups; at the right temperature they will snooze contentedly, if too cold they will huddle together and whimper. They can also get too hot and become dehydrated, but this should not be a problem. A warning about air-conditioning: in hot, humid climates the cool breeze from the air conditioning that feels comfortable to us may chill the pups. We also keep a clean cardboard box with a hot-water bottle, which we wrap in a towel, for holding one or more pups in case of an emergency.

5. There is a collection of miscellaneous items that we lay out on a low table next to the box: a tray holding a rectal thermometer (plus a spare); scissors; a haemostat and thread (for tying umbilical cords); cotton wool; petroleum jelly; isopropyl alcohol; an iodine-based topical antiseptic; and an eyedropper, plus a small quantity of brandy (this is to assist in getting a seemingly moribund puppy to start breathing). We also have at hand some towels (preferably old ones as they may get stained), a roll of paper towels and a box of tissues. Finally, we bring in the kitchen scales so that we can track the puppies' weights. We weigh shortly after birth and then every couple of days – a gain of about one ounce (30 gm) a day means a pup is doing fine.

6. Newspapers and old blankets are valuable commodities. Clean newspapers can be used as a disposable lining for the floor of the whelping box. We also have an ample supply of dog blankets, cut to fit the box, and a plastic garbage bag for disposal purposes.

7. Sleep is always at a premium while whelping a bitch. We have pillows and a blanket handy so that we can catnap right next to the box. Once things have settled down, we can migrate to the bed and still keep an eye or ear on the pups.

8. Fortunately we have never had to hand-feed our puppies, though occasionally we have supplemented their mother's milk. Regardless of this, we still lay in the supplies necessary for hand-feeding the litter. There are a number of proprietary foods available for newborn pups, though we have never actually used any of these formulas. For supplementary feeding we have found goat's milk, diluted half and half with water and heated to wrist warmth, works well. If the pups are receiving no milk from their mother, it is essential to give them some natural yogurt (containing live bacterial culture) in order to provide their bowels with necessary bacteria. We also keep goat's milk around for the bitch. For tiny pups, we feed with an eyedropper, for stronger ones we use an ordinary baby's bottle, having enlarged the hole in the teat.

9. A nearby telephone is essential. Above it we tape a list of important numbers – vet, calm and reliable friends who can help in an emergency, experienced breeders, and so on.

10. Last but not least, we keep all of our whelping information and reference material handy, together with a notepad and pencils – to record *everything* that happens, both times and events. We also write down our initial impressions of each puppy.

WHELPING

As D-day approaches, the bitch will give a number of signs of her impending labour. About five to seven days beforehand, her puppies will 'drop' – that is, her muscles will relax and she will appear less tight. Also the vulva will become swollen and flabby. Closer to the time, she will become increasingly restless, start to dig up the blankets and newspaper in the whelping box (which we let her do), pant incessantly and generally to appear worried. With some bitches, this goes on for just a few hours, with others for days and, with a minority, not at all. Some bitches go off their food just before whelping; however, most of ours have not done so. A more reliable indicator, in our experience, is a steady drop in her rectal temperature. This may hover around 100 degrees F (37.8 C) for a day or so, then eventually it will drop to *and remain at* about 98-99 degrees F (36.7-37.2 C). Our bitches have invariably gone into labour within 12 hours of reaching this lower temperature range. If the bitch did not start whelping within 12 hours we would consult our vet; in any case, a courtesy call to the clinic is in order to update the vet that whelping is imminent.

Some of our bitches have whelped a day or so earlier than we expected; none have been more than a day late. No doubt we have been lucky! However, bitches can conceive as long as three days after their final mating, so we add this three days as well as the normal 63 days to estimate her latest due date. If nothing has happened by this estimated date – and she was definitely in whelp – we would again consult our veterinarian.

But let us assume that her temperature is down and she is showing every sign of going into labour. At this point we put a soft collar on her, so that we can control her if she gets too rough with the pups. She is probably shredding the contents of the whelping box to make herself a nest; this is a good sign. She may be panting and, in between times, shivering. The pressure on her bladder may cause her to have to take frequent trips outside to urinate. We go out with her and watch carefully, having twice had bitches drop a puppy while on such expeditions. Also, she may have decided to make her own arrangements and have

begun digging a nice hole under the house. At this stage we smear petroleum jelly under her tail and on her back legs, which helps to prevent bloody fluids sticking to her coat. We offer her a light meal – warm goat's milk mixed with an egg and a few drops of glucose. This is standard fare throughout the whelping. Some bitches will not accept anything; others are grateful for a snack, especially after delivering several pups. Of course there is a bowl of water near the whelping box throughout.

Eventually the shivering intensifies and the bitch will go into labour, alternately panting and then pushing. These contractions occur at shorter intervals; soon the water bag appears and usually bursts open as it is expelled. The first puppy is usually born within a few minutes of the water, though the bitch may go on straining for 20-30 minutes before delivering her firstborn. However, if she continues to strain for more than an hour without result it is time to telephone the vet.

The bitch may drop the first pup quite suddenly, but more often it appears first as a bulge just above the vulva. This gives us time to get ready to receive it in a towel as it drops. The whelp is usually presented head first within a bag (sac) of fluid and attached by the umbilical cord to its placenta (afterbirth). The bitch, especially a maiden, may be in shock at this point and so we need to take charge. Holding the pup on the towel, we quickly break the sac and remove it from the pup's head. Holding the pup with the head pointing slightly downwards, we use the towel to strip any fluids from its muzzle, by which time it is usually screaming its head off. We then offer the pup to the bitch who should lick off the remainder of the sac and begin eating the placenta, biting the cord close to the pup's belly. She will want to continue to lick it, which is a good stimulant. Should the bitch get too rough with the pup at this point and we cannot calm her down, we clamp and cut the cord ourselves. Incidentally, it is a myth that undershot bitches cannot sever the cords; they do it with their molars, as do the majority of our bitches.

With the pup safely delivered, nursing is the next priority. We roll the bitch on to her side and start the pup nursing immediately. Some are easy to get going, others need a little perseverance. We find squeezing a little milk from a nipple and then placing the pup's mouth over that nipple helps. Strictly, this is colostrum rather than milk; the bitch's milk does not come down for a couple of days. It is *vital* that the pups receive the colostrum; it contains maternal antibodies that provide protection against infectious diseases through their first few weeks. It also acts as a mild laxative, prompting the puppies' initial bowel movements. The pups' nursing will stimulate the bitch's mammary glands. Next, dispose of the soiled top layer of newspapers and replace the blanket.

A couple of general comments are in order here. This first pup is the bitch's most important possession ever, so we do not take it out of her sight; we praise her and we ourselves try to keep as calm as possible – an excitable human is the last thing a bitch needs right then. Incidentally, spectators and visitors dropping by just to see the pups are 'verboten'. Other authors discuss the pros and cons of the bitch's eating the placentas – every one of our bitches has eaten every placenta she produced. This is completely natural behaviour and provides the bitch with concentrated protein and iron.

Typically, puppies are then born at intervals of between 20 minutes and one hour. Each time she produces a whelp, we go through the same routine. Some bitches

leave most of the work to us, others want to do everything themselves, which is fine by us. Most articles on whelping Bull Terriers recommend removing the existing pups each time the bitch gets ready to deliver another, keeping them in a cardboard box over a warm hot-water bottle wrapped in a towel or blanket, then returning them to the bitch after the next one is born. We have found that this upsets the bitch, so we just move the pups to the front of the box over the area warmed by the heating pad. With each new pup we immediately get it hooked up and nursing, then get all of the others nursing too; this tends to have a calming effect on the bitch. Often, after whelping three or four pups, the bitch will decide to take a nap. We let her do this and take advantage of the break to tidy up the box and ensure our notes are up to date. For each pup, we have the time when major contractions began, the time it was born, a description (male, female, weight, colour and markings) and quick first impressions, which we find valuable indicators of potential with our line. We also keep count of the placentas to ensure that she has expelled them all; a retained placenta can lead to infection and threaten the bitch's life. After safely delivering the last pup, she will probably accept a liquid meal – goat's milk and eggs or chicken broth and rice. Then she will almost certainly settle down for a very long nap. Curiously, the pups often sleep at the same time. But before everyone settles down for this snooze, we clean out the whelping box, replace the blankets and fit the pig rail, tucking the corners of the blankets under the feet of the pig rail to help keep them in place.

Nine times out of ten, bitches whelp into the night and so we become exhausted. However, this is where the round-the-clock routine begins, so having two of us working 'shifts' is a boon. The pups need to nurse every two hours around the clock and with a large litter it can be difficult at first to get them all hooked up at the same time, especially if the bitch is not co-operative. We say soothing words and, if necessary, hold her by the collar to keep her on her side. Soon she will relax and let her milk down, at which point the pups appear almost rigid with concentration. At the same time, they need topping and tailing – in other words getting their bladders and bowels working. Initially, the pups cannot do this themselves and so the bitch should lick them till they urinate and defecate. Usually bitches have favourites that they tend to clean over and over again, to the detriment of the others; so we make sure she has topped and tailed all of them after each nursing, holding each of them in turn for her to do her stuff. Their initial bowel movement is particularly important, expelling as it does that smelly black material called meconium. A constipated pup will cry constantly, upsetting the bitch and disturbing everyone. We need to keep the pups at a comfortable temperature, adjusting the heating pad and, if in use, the lamp, as necessary.

The bitch will not want to leave her precious babies, except for a quick rush to the great outdoors and a high-speed return. We take advantage of these trips to clean the box and change the blankets. The bitch needs food high in fat, protein and carbohydrates while she is lactating. We feed her cottage cheese, goat's milk, scrambled eggs, rice, chicken, and biscuits plus pretty well anything she really likes, provided it is not likely to cause diarrhoea. Initially she gets a little food often, then, as she settles down, we give her three meals a day. She will not want to leave the pups, so we hold the food bowl in the box for her, but we do not leave it there as she might

become aggressive with the pups – happily none of our bitches have been so.

Bull Terriers bitches from some lines have reputations as bad mothers. We have been fortunate; all of our bitches have been super mums, though I have to admit that the smaller ones are typically more efficient at managing the litter and need less assistance from us. Our bigger bitches, particularly those over about 60 lbs (27 kg), have been prone to lying on pups and, without attention, such bitches may accidentally injure them. Regardless of size, however, we sleep next to the whelping box for at least a week, longer if need be, and we are always within earshot during this time.

WHELPING COMPLICATIONS

In the previous section we discussed a whelping that went pretty much according to plan. Unfortunately, this is not always the case. Sometimes a bitch is unable to deliver one or more of her pups without assistance because the whelp is badly presented or particularly large. Symptomatic of such situations is when, after prolonged contractions, the bitch appears to be making no progress. The whelp may be felt above the vulva when she contracts but then returns to the uterus as soon as she relaxes.

BREECH PRESENTATIONS: Many breech presentations, that is with the pup's hindquarters first, are born without difficulty; but occasionally the pup will become stuck, which is dangerous, as the umbilical cord may be flattened or severed, cutting off the supply of oxygen. In such situations, we try to help with the delivery. After washing hands thoroughly in germicidal soap, we *gently* take hold of the pup's rear legs between finger and thumb and, as the bitch pushes, pull steadily downwards. Some breeders recommend holding the legs between a wad of cotton wool. The key words here are firm, gentle and steadily – more haste means less speed and can harm the pup. Once the hips come out and can be held, the rest of the body is then fairly easy. We adopt a similar approach to large pups that become stuck or to those presented at a difficult angle (usually with the head to one side). Sometimes the sac breaks prematurely, causing the pup to dry out and thus become lodged; in this circumstance, smearing obstetric jelly or fluid around the vaginal passage is helpful. Although, through long experience, breeders learn how to help the bitch with such difficult deliveries, they are truly the province of the vet and should not be attempted by novices. Eva Weatherill – a veritable genius with whelping and puppies – was adamant that if the bitch had been straining for an hour or more without result, we should call the vet and not attempt to do anything ourselves.

REVIVING PUPPIES: After having the mucus removed from around the nose and mouth, most newborn pups will almost immediately start breathing normally, as well as exercising their vocal chords by crying. Others, particularly those that have undergone arduous, prolonged births, may have initial breathing difficulties or may show no signs of breathing at all. Winkie Mackay-Smith recommends holding such a pup in a towel, carefully supporting its head, and swinging it downward in an arc from shoulder height to between our legs, thereby expelling much of the fluid from its lungs. We also rub the pup gently but vigorously between folds of the towel. Such actions usually do the trick. If not, then we try a drop of brandy on the pup's tongue. If all else fails, we try mouth-to-mouth resuscitation, being careful not to blow too hard and over-inflate the lungs. Having revived a pup, the first priority is to get it nursing. Such pups are often very weak, so

we pay special attention to them till they are stronger.

Upsetting as it may be, we all occasionally lose a pup. Pups that are born blue and apparently dead can sometimes be revived, but unless this can be done quickly the lack of oxygen will result in brain damage. Experience has taught us to let such pups go; this is much better than raising them and then facing the heartbreak of having to put them down later. Sometimes the bitch rejects a pup and we have found that she is invariably correct. She must recognize instinctively that it is 'not quite right' and we have learnt to accept her judgement. Also, we check the pups for cleft palates (incomplete closure of the roof of the mouth); such pups cannot suckle and must be put down.

UTERINE INERTIA: A bitch who exhausts herself with one or more difficult presentations may simply stop having contractions, even though there are obviously more pups to come. She has gone into uterine inertia. This is more likely to occur if the bitch is overweight and unfit, but it is usually brought on by whelping difficulties. Inertia may also be a family trait and this emphasises the importance of having a bitch from a good whelping line. Inertia is a matter for the vet, who may elect first to give the bitch an intramuscular injection of the calcium solution used for treating eclampsia. If this fails to stimulate more contractions, the vet will probably give an injection of pituitary extract.

CAESARIAN SECTION; Due to a variety of problems, including inertia, the veterinarian may advise that a caesarian section is necessary; in other words, the unborn pups will be removed by surgery. The timing of such a decision is crucial to the health of the bitch as well as to the survival of the pups. Though, none of our bitches have had to undergo a section, we still keep our vet updated on the bitch's progress, just in case surgical intervention becomes necessary. We have been fortunate in having a very good whelping line and also in having good-sized litters, the smallest being five pups and the largest nine.

POST-WHELPING COMPLICATIONS
Close monitoring of the bitch's health after the litter has been born is essential. If she has retained a placenta or a dead pup, septicaemia may occur. This is why we keep count of the placentas and, if one is missing, we ask our vet to give her a shot of pituitary extract to help clean out the uterus. If she has had some difficult births, necessitating manual intervention, it may be advisable for her to be given an antibiotic injection too. We take her temperature regularly during the first few days. Usually her temperature will go up to 102-103 degrees F (38.9-39.4 C). But if gets above 103 degrees F (39.4 C) and stays there, she may have an infection and we call in the vet without delay.

PSEUDO-ECLAMPSIA: It is not unusual for Bull Terrier bitches to exhibit, just after the pups are born, symptoms similar to those of eclampsia (milk fever). At their worst, the symptoms include hysteria, constant panting, increasing anxiety, digging up the blankets and rushing around with a puppy in her mouth; nothing seems to calm her down. This is not true eclampsia, which occurs due to calcium depletion about two weeks after whelping. The syndrome appears to be peculiar to Bull Terriers and, within the breed, is referred to as pseudo-eclampsia. A subcutaneous shot of soluble calcium will give complete and almost immediate relief; one or more additional injections may be needed if the symptoms recur. One experience of an eclamptic bitch will be enough to convince anyone of the necessity of these injections. Unfortunately, some vets will not accept the breeder's recommendation for treatment because it is not true eclampsia, which would not occur till a couple of weeks later. So it is important to sort all of this out with the vet beforehand. It is possible that some bitches found to be jittery around their pups and thus viewed as poor mothers are actually experiencing mild pseudo-eclampsia.

MASTITIS: With a vigorous litter of pups, a bitch is in little danger of getting mastitis (inflammation and hardening of her milk glands). However, a daily check is in order to ensure that this does not happen. If the pups appear to be neglecting a particular teat, we put a vigorous pup to work on it.

HAND-FEEDING: Hand-raising a litter is an exhausting challenge. Initially the pups must be fed every two hours around the clock and then topped and tailed. It seems that as soon as one session is finished, it is time to prepare for the next. Proprietary puppy formulas come with clear instructions on quantities and preparation. At first, weak pups may need to be fed with an eyedropper, but, with patience and persistence, they will take to suckling a baby-bottle like their stronger siblings. We use cotton wool, lightly moistened with warm water, to top and tail each pup in turn, simulating the action of the mother's licking to get them to defecate and urinate.

Even when the bitch is doing a pretty good job with pups, supplementary feeding may be appropriate. We use our goat's milk preparation rather than a puppy formula. We also supplement the stronger pups, leaving more of their mother's milk for the weaker ones.

THE FIRST THREE WEEKS
Getting the bitch and her pups successfully through the first few weeks is a matter of

For the first couple of weeks the mother will provide for all the puppies' needs.

good animal husbandry. Our schedule looks like this:-

1. Days one to three, all of the pups need to nurse and be topped and tailed every two hours. We feed the bitch as often as she wants – lots of fluids. We take her temperature and check her teats daily. We use a wash cloth, baby soap and warm water to keep her rear end clean, something she cannot do herself. She will not want to leave the pups and so must be persuaded to take brief trips outside. We do not leave her and the pups for more than a few minutes at a time. We try to maintain a calm, reassuring atmosphere, often just sitting there enjoying watching her and the pups. Soon we all settle into a routine.

2. If dewclaws are to be removed this should be done at about three days.

3. For the next ten days, we are always there to assist the new mother and the pups as needed; some bitches take over managing the pups, others enjoy letting us do some of the work. We insist on getting all of the pups hooked up and nursing every three to four hours. Healthy pups will be gaining about an ounce a day. A pup that gains weight then loses it and starts to fall behind is in trouble; we ensure that it gets plenty of its mother's milk and stays warm; if it continues to fall behind we seek veterinary advice – the pup may have a congenital defect. The pups should have their claws clipped after eight to ten days and about weekly thereafter. The bitch's meals are progressively cut back in

Make sure all the puppies are getting their fair share of milk.

Photo courtesy: Ibbitson.

frequency. We keep an eye on her temperature and teats. If possible, we try to induce her to spend some time out of the whelping box, if only to sit on the bed, from where she can watch her precious babies.

3. At about two weeks, perhaps sooner, puppies will begin to open their eyes. Having done so, they begin to wobble around, exploring their box and showing their first signs of independence – probably to their mother's consternation. All this activity means that she is more likely to accidentally lie on them, and so we are particularly vigilant just after their eyes open. This is a wonderful time just to sit and watch the pups.

4. By three weeks, the proud mother will probably begin to show signs of boredom and will begin to spend time away from the pups. This leads us to the next stage – beginning to wean the litter.

WEANING AND REARING THE PUPPIES

AT THREE WEEKS

By three weeks the pups are becoming increasingly active and interested in exploring the world about them. Meanwhile, their mother is usually spending some time away from them. We take advantage of the bitch's absences to start feeding the puppies. We used to begin with milk feeds, but we now find it quicker and easier to start them off with meat. Eva Weatherill recommended scraped beef; we use finely minced beef – the leanest available, as the typical ground beef sold in supermarkets contains far too much fat. With mother away and the pups hungrily awaiting her return, we try to feed each of them about a teaspoonful of wrist-warm minced beef. This first attempt may not go too well, so patience and perseverance are at a premium. Initially we feed each puppy by hand, effectively letting it suckle at the meat – small amounts only, as larger quantities will get stuck to the roof of its mouth. Often, the big pups who are thriving on their mother's milk do not take to the meat, whereas those further down the pecking order take to it immediately. Following these early endeavours, the bitch will be happy to clean up all of that wasted meat and soon persistence pays off.

Next we introduce the pups to a warm milk feed, consisting of goat's milk thickened with a little high-protein (human) baby cereal. Again, we feed them individually. Often we have to gently push the pup's nose into the milk bowl to get it to lap. As with scraps of meat, the bitch will be delighted to clean the pups' muzzles and finish off the leftover milk.

Feeding the pups prior to nursing means they demand less milk from their mother and so she begins to produce less. The process of weaning the litter is under way. At some meals, individual pups may eat very little; this does not concern us too much, as our goal is to prepare them for the following week, when we begin to wean them in earnest.

It is never too early to start house-training the pups. Each time they wake up, and after every meal or nursing, we let them run around on newspapers (or outside in good weather) until they have completed their ablutions. This keeps their box cleaner and drier. Typically, they begin to climb out of the box during this period and so we place a pen around the box, with a play area and, in one corner, the inevitable patch of newspapers. If necessary, we remove the front rail from the box.

This is a wonderful time to sit back and enjoy watching the pups as they toddle around and play with each other. We observe their different personalities and give

132

A litter of eleven puppies all lined up and eating! This litter provided Kay Marshall with five Champions, including a Silverwood winner.

them as much individual attention as we can. We also respect their need for lots of sleep.

WORMING THE PUPS
Recommendations on when to worm pups vary. Some breeders treat them for roundworms when they are three weeks old; we prefer to wait till four weeks of age. We mix the worming medication with their individual meat meals. Then we repeat the same dosage ten days later.

AT FOUR WEEKS
By the time the litter is four weeks old, we have them on a regimen of four meals a day – milk feeds for breakfast and dinner, meat for lunch and supper. We encourage the bitch to stay away from them for longer periods and ensure that they do not nurse till after their meals. For breakfast each pup gets *about* a quarter of a cup of goat's milk mixed with a raw egg yolk (no white) and a tablespoonful of baby cereal. We feed the litter together, using a large bowl raised off the ground to their shoulder height. They get the same again at dinner time. At lunch time each pup receives about an ounce of meat, mixed with multi-vitamin powder. This we feed separately to ensure that each pup gets its share. We feed the same amounts again at supper time. We prefer to

end the day with a meat meal as part of their house-training – they are better able to last through the night without urinating.

During the week we start to supplement the meat feeds with moistened puppy meal, increasing the amount until it is equal to the beef in volume. We tend not to measure quantities of feed exactly, relying on our experience to provide the pups with the appropriate amounts. After a meal they should be nicely full but not plump or bulging, which of course they will tend to be, given a choice. We are careful to ensure the meals are all wrist-warm.

Our bitches generally begin to spend much more time away from the pups at this stage. We make sure mother is away from them for at least an hour before each meal. As soon as they have finished eating we let her in to nurse them. And, of course, we keep a constant check on her for any signs of mastitis.

FIFTH AND SIXTH WEEKS
Our goal by the fifth week is to have the pups pretty close to being weaned. We also want them reasonably well house-trained, which means thoroughly familiar with the routine of going outside every time they wake up and after every meal (or in bad weather trained to newspaper). Our bitches usually have relatively little milk by now

The puppies learn valuable lessons through play.

Photo above courtesy: Dettmar.

Photo right courtesy: Simpson.

and so can enjoy the pups without the strain of having to feed them, other than allowing a quick milk snack two or three times a day. Often the bitch will take the whole litter outside to explore or she will sit up high, out of their reach, and watch them play. Our philosophy is to lighten the strain on the bitch before the pups drag her down too much. After five weeks of caring for the pups, a bitch has usually lost her coat and is in need of the best of care and feeding to get her back in shape. Some breeders prefer to leave the pups on the bitch till she weans them herself; we do not.

We move the pups to more spacious quarters, leaving a radio talk-show on for them during the day as part of the socialization process. The more attention the pups receive, both collectively and individually, the better. We continue to spend as much time with them as we possibly can – probably more. They are so much fun and this is when we start preparing them for their families, training

It is not long before individual personalities become apparent.   Photo courtesy: Burton.

them not to nip with those needle-sharp little teeth and getting them used to lying upside down on our laps – by far the easiest way to hold a Bull Terrier. At the same time, we are assessing their characters and personalities, mentally fitting them to the homes that we have waiting for some of them. We do not want a big boisterous puppy going to a quiet older couple, any more than a retiring one to a large family with active, noisy kids. We want to fit the puppy to the home. Most of our adult dogs, males and females, enjoy playing with the pups, and they seem to know their parts in teaching pups the house rules and generally providing a civilizing influence. The diet and regimen remains the same, with quantities steadily increased, since the puppies grow like weeds.

SEVENTH AND EIGHTH WEEKS

The pups should have their first vaccinations during this period – at exactly six weeks of age if our vet is concerned about the prevalence of viral diseases locally, later if not. Obviously we want a pup vaccinated a few days prior to a family coming to pick it up.

At seven weeks, we give each pup about two ounces of beef, plus an equal volume of moistened meal at each meat meal. By eight weeks we have increased the quantity of beef to 2 ounces and the meal

proportionately. At each milk meal, we feed about half a cup of goat's milk, mixed with a raw egg yolk and two heaped tablespoons of baby cereal. The pups also get multi-vitamins appropriate to their weight.

We expect to have them essentially house-trained by this stage. It is much easier to do this earlier rather than trying to change bad habits later. This is why we make the effort to train and socialize them as early as possible.

Only at eight weeks will novice breeders recognise the time and effort needed to whelp and raise the litter, if the job is done well. By eight weeks the pups are full of energy and increasingly demanding, so much so that their mother and other adult dogs are anxious to be left in peace. The pups are ready for their new homes. If we are keeping a pup ourselves, the decision always seems to be made very soon after the pups are born. We have never regretted such early decisions, though textbook advice is to wait as long as possible before making the final decision. Many breeders 'run on' pups for several months in order to decide which one to keep. Unfortunately, finding a good home for a four or five-month-old puppy who has lived till then in a kennel is not an easy task. Most families want a house dog and, for obvious reasons, seek a much younger pup.

12 THE BULL TERRIER IN BRITAIN

BACKGROUND

For many years the breed in the UK, and indeed around the world, was dominated by a handful of major British kennels. Inevitably, these great breeders, after a life devoted to Bull Terriers, have passed on or have retired. Their legacy is the breed as we know it today, all of our current dogs tracing back many times over to Champions bearing such illustrious affixes as Ormandy, Souperlative, Romany, Abraxas and Phidgity.

The Ormandy/Souperlative kennels of Raymond Oppenheimer and Eva Weatherill were the greatest of these. Renowned throughout the canine world, Raymond's genius, together with Eva's consummate skills as a breeder and especially at raising and conditioning the dogs, produced an incomparable clan of top-winning and top-producing Bull Terriers. Champions like Ormandy's Snowflash, Souperlative Summer Queen, Souperlative Rominten Rheingold, Souperlative Jackadandy of Ormandy and many more – not least the fabulous Ormandy Souperlative Bar Sinister, so called because he was a monorchid – have engraved their names in the canine history books. Raymond and

Eva's counterparts in the coloureds variety were 'D' Montague Johnstone and Meg Williams of Romany, whose acumen, devotion and perseverance brought us generations of wonderful dogs like Rhinestone, Reliance, Robin Goodfellow and River Pirate. No-one who saw the ebullient Ch. Abraxas Audacity sweep all before him to become the first and only Bull Terrier to win BIS at Crufts will ever forget Violet Drummond-Dick and her world-renowned ambassadors of the breed. In their heyday, Hazlefield, the Lenster/Phidgity/Harpers kennels of Mrs Mankin and Misses Graham, Weall and Vick, were a force to be reckoned with, as was Phyllis Holmes (Monkery).

Not all of the success accrued to the large kennels. Both Joy Schuster (Contango) and Margaret Sweeten (Agates) consistently produced dogs of the very highest quality from relatively small breeding programmes. More recently, we have lost the services of Jack and Betty Mildenhall's kennel of grand Hollyfir stud dogs and the enormous influence, during the 1980s, of the Ghabar dogs of Audrey and the late Bill Edmonds.

So there has been a passing of the old guard and, with them, the large kennels on which breed progress had relied for so long. Fortunately, a cadre of new talented breeders has emerged to take their place. It is this cadre, together with some longer-established breeders, who will take Bull Terriers into the next millennium.

REGENT TROPHY & ORMANDY JUGS
Within the Bull Terrier fancy, the breeder-judge reigns supreme. His or her views are held in much higher esteem than those of even the top all-rounders. The highest accolade is not winning a group or BIS, but victory at the Regent Trophy competition. This trophy was presented to the BTC in 1930 by Dr Geoffrey Vevers, to be awarded to the best Bull Terrier – dog or bitch – first shown during the previous year. Initially, the BTC committee simply made the award, but for many years now the trophy has been judged in conjunction with the Club's February open show. In 1946, Raymond Oppenheimer added the Ormandy Jugs to the trophy competition, one jug per sex to be awarded to the best exhibit shown at a Championship during the previous year, whether for the first time or not. The primary purpose of both awards is to stimulate the breeding of better Bull Terriers, and neither Geoffrey or Raymond could have foreseen in their wildest imaginings their success in this regard. The trophy show, as it is called, is the highlight of the year and attracts visitors from around the world. The concept of a special trophy for the best dog and/or bitch of the year has been duplicated in many other countries with similar positive impacts on the overall quality of their Bull Terriers.

Recent winners of the Regent Trophy
1990: Lemon's Ch. Ghabar Bliss of Hamanos (Roller Coaster Jed of Ghabar ex Ch. Ghabar Silver Sea).

1991: Lancaster's Ch. Srissa Centurian (Ch. Mapalee Inoxydorable ex Mapalee Lady Delphinium).
1992: Henderson's Ch. Cheeky Tail of Topkine (Failsworth Triple Trouble at Topkine ex Amatol Tick Tack).
1993: Thornley's Ch. Kilacabar Kasablanca of Warbonnet (Ch. Warbonnet Buckskin ex Joan La Pucelle).
1994: Lambert's Ch. Caliber Cabin Class (Ch. Kilacabar Cabin Buoy at Bullyvark ex Caliber Crumpet).
1995: Lambert's Ch. Swagons Roll of Caliber (Ch. Swagman's Roll of Eirdred ex Adventurer of Caliber).
1996: Clowes' Ch. Laura Belle at Ishaba (Ch. Kilacabar Stand and Deliver ex Ishaba Hopscotch).

BRITISH KENNELS
ARICON
Since breeding the great Eng. Am. Ch. Aricon Chief Eye Shy, the 1981 Ormandy Jug winner, Eric Stanley has established Aricon, in Durham, as Britain's leading kennel. A string of celebrated Bull Terriers includes Look Me in the Eye who garnered six CCs by the age of 12 months during 1996. Eric's dogs have proven themselves not only distinguished but also distinctive. In Eric's own words, he has moulded "a line to balance middle-of-the-road type with a head, conformation, first-class movement and beautiful temperament". He does not want a head without movement or vice versa.

Eric began back in 1968 with Tracvals Barney Boy, who became the UK's first mismarked Champion. After spending several years in Canada, Eric returned and set about developing his own line. His successes stem from two kennels – Brobar, which he admired for style, showmanship and super heads, and Monkery for construction and outstanding movement.

Ch. Aricon Eye Spy, 1986 Ormandy Jug winner.

He bought Mamteeka Amelinda, a daughter of the great Ch. Brobar Elite, and mated her to Monkery's Corduroy of Javelan. From this came the key red bitch Aricon Spanish Eyes, who, to Ch. Brobar Backchat, produced Eye Shy. Next, from Eye Shy to another Amelinda daughter, came Ch. Eyeshiner of Aricon, who, to Ch. Kenstaff Shirley, sired the famous Eng. Am. Ch. Catrana EyeOpener of Aricon.

Many Aricon Champions have followed – too many to cover in detail. Aricon Captain Birds Eye (a grandson of Eyeshiner and EyeOpener) and Spanish Eyes produced the shapely and superbly made Ch. Eye Spy, winner of the 1986 Ormandy Jug and the Charlie Girl Trophy for movement, and runner-up in the Regent Trophy. In turn, Eye Spy sired the lovely bitch Ch. Eyes of a Star and the top German winner Camquest Theo Sylvander Aricon. Incidentally, despite having bred some very good bitches, Eric is

much better known for his dogs; he considers his best bitch to be the Eye Spy daughter Aricon As I See It. Eric mated his Eye Shadow of Aricon (a grand-daughter of Eyeshiner and EyeOpener) to Ch. Bullivar Real McCoy (an Eye Shy grandson) and, from this litter, got another Champion dog – One and Only. To the coloured Boco Patsy, One and Only sired the top-winning brindle Eng. Am. Ch. Boco Be Good of Aricon, who carried off the 1989 Regent Trophy, the Ormandy Jug and, in typical Aricon style, also the movement prize. Down from Boco Be Good, Eric has made up a line of Champions, namely Eye Bet (ex an Eye Spy daughter), sire of Roldaines Eye at Aricon, sire of Bryontezz Eyeci Spici of Aricon (ex a One in the Eye daughter), sire of his latest Champion Look Me in the Eye (1996 Ormandy Jug winner).

Space precludes discussion of the impact of Eric's dogs overseas. Suffice it to say that the Aricon bloodline can be found around the world and, of course, a number of the best ones have found their way to America. Eric is a breeder's breeder; there can be no higher praise.

BROBAR

The late Arthur and Joyce Miller made up their first Champion, Brobar Warpaint, back in 1958. Some eighteen more Brobar Champions were to follow, among them some key stud dogs and many wonderful bitches. Though Joyce and Arthur were very much a team in other respects, it was

Ch. Brobar Hotline, Arthur Miller's favourite bitch.

Arthur who handled and presented the dogs, in which respect he was simply the best. His rapport with the dogs was a joy to behold and an example to all of us. Experts and novices alike were always welcome at their Manchester home to see their dogs and discuss the breed. They were at their peak in the 1970s, producing Champion bitches like the stunning Elite (Ch. Maerdy Maestro ex Brobar Horatio) and Joyce's favourite, Clever Clogs (double Bonaparte). In 1978, Champions Jill (Jackadandy out of a sister of Clever Clogs) and Wild Rose (Jacobinia ex Ch. Keyhole Kate of Brobar) dominated the Trophies, though Arthur still preferred the third Brobar bitch competing that day – Hotline (Brobar Grisley ex Horatio) – and, in terms of follow-on, he was right. Not surprisingly, other breeders took advantage of their superb bitch line. Eric Stanley's foundation bitch was a daughter of Elite, while Bill and Audrey Edmonds restarted their highly successful breeding programme with Silver Satin (a Clever Clogs daughter). The last two Brobar Champions, Joker (a grandson of Troubleshooter and Clever Clogs) and Hot Tip (a grand-daughter of Silver Satin), were crowned in 1987.

Fortunately, the line did not end with the passing of Joyce and Arthur, as their eldest son Jimmy Henderson has taken over the Brobar affix. Jimmy had always helped with the dogs and he maintained his involvement after marrying Angela. In 1979, Jimmy and Angela started their own breeding programme with Brobar Babaji (another Clever Clogs daughter and littermate to Champions Backchat and White Satin) under the Topkine affix. From Babaji they bred the CC-winning bitches Tap Shoes and Tilly Trotter. Four generations on from Tap Shoes, came the 1992 Regent Trophy and Jug winner Ch. Cheeky Tail at Topkine (Failsworth's Triple Trouble of Topkine).

Jimmy and Angela are now line breeding to Cheeky Tail, with a litter on the ground by Turshead Saracen of Kilacabar (a Cheeky Tail grandson) out of a daughter of Brobar Back Stabber (Cheeky Tail). So we can look forward to more Brobar winners in the years to come.

BULLYVIEW
In 1982, John and Mandy Young, who live in Essex, became the proud owners of their first Bull Terrier, a white daughter of Ch. Hardra's Prince Hal. They bred her to Recoco Ringleader and, of course, as a result of this first litter, got the bug. Later, they purchased Silver George of Bullyview, a Crusader daughter, and bred her to The Admiral, thus doubling up on Crusader; this produced their first Champion, Bullyview Gentle Breeze, winner of 11 CCs and runner-up in the 1990 Bitch Jug. They then bred their coloured bitch, Elsa's Pride, to The Admiral, who obliged by siring their second Champion, the lovely red Bullyview Flash Dance, winner of the 1991 Sandawana trophy. Next came the black brindle Ch. Crossguns Checkmate of Bullyview, runner-up in the Regent trophy and winner of the Sandawana trophy in 1993. By Ch. Megavar Moderator (Local

Ch. Crossguns Checkmate of Bullyview, 1993 Sandawana Trophy winner.

139

Hero) out of a Boco Be Good daughter, Checkmate was John and Mandy's choice out of a litter of eight pups they helped to whelp. Since becoming involved with the breed, John and Mandy have seen many improvements, among them better heads and, most importantly, better temperaments.

CALIBER

Having been raised with Bull Terriers, Bill Lambert and his wife Carolyn bought their first one in 1978 and were soon bitten by the showing bug. The next year they purchased Jobrulu Zizania (Ch. Jobrulu Moss Campion ex Ch. Jobrulu Xhibitionist), who became their foundation bitch. Mated to Ch. Aricon Chief Eye Shy, Zizania produced Caliber Pepper Anderson, who in turn, to Jackadandy, produced Caliber Jackuzzi. In her second litter, to Ch. Ghabar Crusader, Pepper Anderson came up with the sisters Cruella and Crumpet; Cruella was a consistent winner at Championship shows, while Crumpet's success came in the whelping box as the dam of no less than three Champions.

Bill and Carolyn limit themselves to five dogs, all living happily together at their Surrey home. They sell puppies as pets first and show dogs second, often to friends so that they can maintain an active interest in them. True Bull Terrier temperaments are of prime importance in their breeding programme and they also place correct movement high on their list – goals with which I can readily identify. I should add that with the demise of the big kennels it is on devotees like Bill and Carolyn that the health and progress of the breed now depend.

Jackuzzi, in whom they had retained an interest, whelped a litter to The Admiral containing Ch. Admiration of Caliber, who won BOB at Crufts and was invited to compete in the trophies. In 1989 they mated Crumpet to the Admiral and were rewarded with their first home-bred Champion – Caliber Adorable. Two years later Crumpet, to Ch. Kilacabar Cabin Buoy at Bullyvark (one of the best in Bill's opinion), produced two more Champions, Cabin Class and Cabin Wench. Cabin Class, owned by Eve and Peter Lambert, swept the 1994 trophies and also won the Charlie Girl Cup for best mover – a surprise, since his sire was noted for indifferent movement. The following year Bill and

LEFT: Caliber Cruella.

BELOW: Ch. Caliber Adorable, the Lamberts' first home-bred Champion.

Ch. Auguside Yuletide Ghoste on Curraneye, 1988 Regent Trophy winner, owned by Joyce and Harry Marley.

Carolyn won the Regent Trophy and Charlie Girl Cup with Ch. Swagon's Roll of Caliber. He and his sister Ch. Swagony Aunt of Caliber, who was runner-up in the trophy, are by Ch. Swagman of Eirdred out of Adventurer (a littermate of Admiration) and thus doubled up on The Admiral. Since then Bill and Carolyn have campaigned the brothers Marker Boy and Sea Buoy of Caliber (Cabin Buoy ex Adventurer) with success, and now have their first coloured, Bagstock Hot Black Caliber, out of a daughter of Adorable.

CURRANEYE

John and Edie Micklethwaite purchased their first Bull Terrier, a fawn smut bitch, back in 1953. Although they kept her purely as a pet, they did join the Yorkshire Bull Terrier Club, attended shows and got to know the members. In 1960 they bought a daughter of Wilsmere Gold Dust, whom they christened Curraneye (Cur an I) Que Sera Sera – 'what will be will be' – which has remained their motto over the years. They had a lot of fun showing her. Curraneye Pattoo, a grand-daughter of Que Sera Sera, mated to Regent Trophy winner Ch. Ardee Resolute Defender, produced a single puppy, Solitaire, who, in 1968, became their first of many Champions. From Solitaire's litter to Langville Pilot Officer, John and Edie kept Ch. Curraneye Independence (the sire of our foundation bitch), who later went to South Africa.

Their wonderfully strong bitch line also comes down directly from Solitaire. A grand-daughter, Curraneye Elegance, mated to Independence, produced Lively Lady who, in turn, to Sunstar, rewarded Edie and John with the 1975 Regent Trophy winner, Ch. Curraneye Schoolgirl, and a Champion brother, Salute. After siring Ch. Lordsfield Defender, Salute went to Holland. Elida, a litter sister of Elegance, was also put to

Independence and from this mating came Int. Ch. Venture Hardlad of Curraneye, who went to the Imperator kennels in Germany. From Schoolgirl's litter to Jackadandy, John and Edie kept Curraneye Sweet Reflection and Ch. Jackieboy Master. A daughter of Sweet Reflection, Curraneye Gorgeouse Gussie, went to Harry and Joyce Marley and had two litters for them. From her first, to Ch. Meregis Jack Knife, she produced Ch. Auguside Giggling Ghoste of Curraneye. Giggling Ghoste to Ch. Burandi Black produced Yuletide Ghoste on Curraneye. Yuletide Ghoste won the 1988 Regent Trophy and Ormandy Jug. From Gorgeouse Gussie's second litter, to Explorer, came Ch. Auguside Sparkling Ghost of Curraneye, dam of Curraneye Pffindus. From Jameses Pert Fancy, a daughter of Jackieboy Master, John and Edie got Curraneye New Love, dam to Eyeshiner of Ch. Curraneye Wonderba at Debitus, the winner of the 1985 Ormandy Jug. Another Pert Fancy daughter, mated to Bullyboy, produced Ch. Curraneye Ajemma and John and Louisa Fletcher's much-loved brindle Am. Ch. Curraneye Allbritt. Pert Fancy, to Arcanum Jack in a Box (a Jackieboy Master son), produced the solid brindle bitch Curraneye Van Blaize. Mated to a son of New Love, Van Blaize produced Brian and Andy Hill's lovely brindle Ch. Curraneye Imperial Arcanum and top New Zealand stud dog Curraneye Ijak. Currently, Edie is campaigning Dextra Dove, a daughter of Rolling Thunder and Curraneye Xpialidotiouse, who goes back to Pffindus and New Love on her dam's side.

John and Edie talk about the fun and games they have had with their 'pets' over the 36 years. They are true stalwarts of the breed, always active and supportive in club affairs. Curraneye Bull Terriers have made their contributions to the breed around the world, while at home John and Edie have managed to maintain an exceptional bitch line. Movement is a strong point of the Curraneye dogs, with three – Jackieboy Master, Wonderba and Giggling Ghoste – all having received the Charlie Girl award as best movers at the trophy shows.

FOYRI

Brian Foy, born and bred in the Black Country, bought his first Bull Terrier – a Miniature bitch – in 1965. From her, he bred a Champion. Next he purchased, from Maureen Bell, the standard bitch Ionem Silver Mist of Geham, a lovely daughter of Ch. Bank Top Julius. Silver Mist soon proved herself in the whelping box. In her first litter, to Ch. Ionem Corvette, she produced Foyri Gin Ye Daur, sire of Ch. Foyri Ocema, and then, to Ch. Hollyfir

Dog-in-a-Doublet, the outstanding Ch. Foyri Electrify, a top winner in Britain and America. Both Electrify and his son, Ch. Foyri Verify, are members of that select band of Bull Terriers who have won the terrier group at an all-breed Championship show – Electrify at South Wales KC and Verify at WELKS (the West of England Ladies' Kennel Society).

To a litter sister of Ch. Souperlative Jackadandy of Ormandy, Verify sired the magnificent Eng. Am. Ch. Rambling Rose of Foyri. Doubling up on Verify produced Ch. Clifton Tommy of Foyri, who went to South Africa. To a coloured bitch coming down from Am. Ch. Brummagem the Brigand, Verify sired the brindles Am. Ch. Foyri Powder Puff and her brother Ganzee. From Ganzee, Brian bred a successful line of coloured studs, including Foyri Pemberton Boy, Eye of the Tiger Foyri, and Duke Jerome Foyri.

Brian has bred or owned eight UK Champions plus numerous CC winners. Today he makes available a strong stud force through dogs placed in co-ownership around the Midlands. Brian breeds for sound, good-moving dogs and is perhaps unique among Bull Terrier folk in letting the heads take care of themselves. He has a good eye for a dog and is a popular judge at home and abroad. Not least among Brian's attributes is his incisive wit and impish sense of humour. He has a fund of wonderful dog stories, and travelling with Brian to a show is always great fun.

KEARBY

A New Zealander by birth, Quita Youatt settled in the UK after World War II, and purchased her first Bull Terrier, a red bitch,

Eng. Am. Ch. Rambling Rose of Foyri – they don't come any better than this magnificent heavyweight bitch.

Photo: Roslin-Williams.

Ch. Kearby Jonah at Aricon, 1996
Sandawana Trophy winner.

via Harrods in 1947. Some fifty years on, Quita has lost none of her enthusiasm for and dedication to the breed. Her primary interest has always been the coloureds and she is the only breeder – since perhaps the days of Ted Lyon – who has never bred two whites together, always selecting at least one coloured parent for each litter. Not surprisingly, Quita's first Champion, Kearby's Kiwitahi in 1956, was a coloured, as have been many of her subsequent Champions. The best-known Kearby Champion was Temptress, who swept all before her in 1976, winning seven CCs, becoming the Daily Express Pup of the Year and the first coloured bitch to take BIS at an all-breed Championship show, and also taking the runner-up spot in the Regent trophy. In recent years Quita has bred Miniatures with great success, but she has kept her hand with standards, the brindle Kearby's Jonah at Aricon completing his title in 1996. He is a son of Eyeci Spici out of Kearby's Money Penny. Unable to handle large, boisterous dogs these days, Quita placed him with Eric Stanley.

Quita has never kept more than about eight dogs at home. However, she could always be relied on to support open and limited shows in the Midlands and North with multiple entries, even though this meant setting off in her trusty Land Rover in the wee hours of the morn to collect extra dogs from their co-owners. I recall a decision to delay the start of one limited show in the early 1970s because Quita and Maureen Bell (Geham) had not yet arrived and they had half the entry between them. Over the years, the Kearby dogs gained a reputation for soundness and really good temperaments, which Quita has always made a priority. Like most successful breeders, Quita practises line breeding, preferring to have a potent dog that produces good stock on both sides of the

pedigree within two or three generations. Temptress, the result of a half-brother to half-sister mating (doubling up on Maestro), was as close in as Quita breeds. Her current role as president of the BTC is a tribute to Quita's fifty years as a devotee of the breed.

KILACABAR
Chris and Carole Kilpatrick of Blackburn became involved with the breed in 1980, initially as pet owners. They began showing in 1987 with Joan La Pucelle, by Grealltop Matador (Bully Boy) out of Grealltop Sayani (Druridge Augustus). But it was as a brood bitch that Joan proved exceptional. For her first litter she was mated to Flagship, a complete outcross, but in Chris and Carole's words "both were very typy and had excellent temperaments." From this litter came Champions Kilacabar Rolling Thunder and Cabin Buoy, the leading stud dogs of 1994/95. In her next litter, to Eng. Am. Ch. Warbonnet Buckskin, Joan produced 1993 Regent Trophy winner Ch. Kilacabar Kasablanca of Warbonnet. Then, to Kilacabar a Kind of Magic at Bullyview (a Joan grand-daughter), Rolling Thunder sired Ch. Kilacabar Stand and Deliver – winner of the 1995 Jug and sire of the 1996 Regent Trophy winner.

They describe Kilacabar as "a small

143

Ch. Kilacabar Stand and Deliver, 1995 Ormandy Jug winner.

family-run kennel". Puppies are introduced to their five children from day one, and are soon socialized and ready to face anything their adult lives may bring. Kasablanca comes closest to the type for which Chris and Carole aim. Temperament is also very important to them. The kennels most influential to their breeding programme were those of Arthur and Joyce Miller and Bob and Audrey Edmond.

SEQOUIAH
John and Gaye Branch of Middlesex have owned, bred and shown Bull Terriers for nearly 40 years. Indeed Gaye, as the daughter of Bert and Grace Crowland, has been around them all her life and was first introduced to Raymond Oppenheimer when she was just three weeks old. John and Gaye made up their first Champion, Souperlative Dancing Star (Sunstar), in 1975. Her grandson, Sequouiah County Game (Commander), was equally successful in the show ring and at stud. To a daughter of Dancing Star, County Game sired Ch. Sequouiah Delight of Merlindan and Sequouiah Stumpy, so called because his dam bit off his tail in his first day of life which meant he could not be shown. However, Stumpy sired a number of Champions.

In their breeding programme, John and Gaye have often used half-brother to half-sister matings and gone outside their own line only twice in the past 25 years. They are not advocates of rushing to the latest big winner and they put temperament first, second and third in priority; since the Dangerous Dogs Act of 1991 it is even more important. In their view, while good heads are now commonplace, movement and hindquarters need attention; pigmentation on the nose is also becoming a problem. Two of their current dogs – The Bajan (a grandson of Stumpy) and his grand-daughter Something Speedy – are coloureds. John and Gaye still enjoy their dogs and cannot imagine life without them!

TERJOS
Terry and Jo Hylands bought their first Bull Terrier, a brindle bitch, in 1968 and later owned a Bar Sinister grand-daughter. However, the show successes of their kennel in Northern Ireland date from the acquisition, from Bill and Audrey Edmonds in 1988, of Ghabar Clearwater of Terjos, who is one of five Champion bitches Terry and Jo have made up in the past six years, a remarkable achievement by any standard.

Ch. Sequouiah County Game.

Ch. Ghabar Clearwater of Terjo's.

Clearwater, a littermate of Flagship, has three lines back to Brobar Silver Satin and thus it is no surprise that she has proven herself in the whelping box. Mated to Warbonnet Buckskin (Flagship), she produced Ch. Terjo's Masquerade, German Ch. Terjo's Crystal Water and Deep Water, the best in the litter except for an incorrect bite. Masquerade has been described as having the best head in the breed today, with Crystal Water not far behind. In an earlier litter to Buckskin, Clearwater produced the CC-winning dog, Highlander. The kennel also carried off the 1995 Ormandy Jug for bitches with the lovely Ch. Hillcairn Jasmine of Terjos (Rolling Thunder).

The Terjos line is based on Ghabar breeding, a fact of which Terry and Jo are very proud. They do not want to breed comfortable dogs with not much wrong with them, their aim being to produce outstanding virtue. Also, they want to reverse the trend towards heavyweights (what Terry calls the 'thuggy' type), preferring to return to the tall, cleaner lines of the 1950s and 60s, albeit with the wonderful modern head.

TYEBAR

Andy Stubbs of Manchester purchased his first Bull Terrier, a black brindle bitch of Curraneye breeding, in 1978. Mated to Jackieboy Master, she produced a good brindle dog, Bo Jack. It was while showing Bo Jack that Andy met and became friends with Arthur and Joyce Miller. It is on their Brobar dogs that his Tyebar line is primarily based, plus a dose of Eyeshiner for expression and Foyri dogs for their superb coloured jackets. His brindle male, Tyebar Trouble Brewing, comes down on his sire's side from Cobra Sharpshooter (double Brobar Troubleshooter), while his dam is a daughter of Ch. Brobar Joker of Emred (another Troubleshooter grandson). Trouble Brewing is proving an excellent producer; in 1994, mated to a bitch of Aricon breeding, he sired the Jacksons' Ch. Quiet Storm of Tyebar and two lovely bitches, Rebecca of Oldham at Tyebar and Silver Dreams of Tyebar. All of them are whites carrying brindle. Andy is currently campaigning Credetta Storm Brewing of Tyebar, a brindle son of Trouble Brewing. In his coloureds, Andy breeds for the correct expression, which results from wicked eyes and correct ear placement and carriage, and even markings without splashes. He wants fit, shapely dogs and disapproves of the current confusion of excess weight with proper substance.

Silver Dreams of Tyebar

13 THE BULL TERRIER IN NORTH AMERICA

INTRODUCTION

North America has long been a stronghold of the breed. Indeed, the Bull Terrier was listed in old texts as the national dog of Canada, though of course this is no longer the case. Both America and Canada are well-served by their national and regional clubs. The BTCA celebrated its centennial in 1997, while the Canadian national club operates in British Columbia as well as in Ontario. Another Canadian club, the Bull Terrier Fanciers Association, stages the annual Bronze Trophy show. There are about 25 regional clubs in America, some like the Bull Terrier Club of Philadelphia, long-established, others relatively new.

The AKC registers in excess of one thousand Bull Terriers annually; in 1995 the number was 1096, in 1996 it was 1034. Given the availability of so many all-breed Championship shows (1245 and 1220 respectively in 1994/95), a much higher proportion of registered dogs become Champions than in the UK. For example, 80 Bull Terriers gained their titles in 1994, and 78 the following year, the majority by showing under all-round judges.

SILVERWOOD TROPHY

The introduction by the BTCA of the Silverwood Trophy in 1970 marked a turning point for the breed in North America. Modelled on the Regent Trophy, it was the brainchild of Bill and Hope Colket, after whose Silverwood affix the competition was named. Tragically, both Bill and Hope died in accidents before they could bring their idea to fruition, but, with the encouragement of Raymond Oppenheimer, the BTCA initiated this annual trophy show.

It is open to Bull Terriers bred in North America, which, for this purpose, includes Mexico as well as Canada. The rules governing the trophy have varied in detail through the years, but essentially dogs qualify at specialty or supported shows or by becoming an AKC Champion. The competition is divided by colour and sex into four classes. There are three judges, selected from the ranks of breeders. In the morning round, the judges determine which dogs shall go forward to the finals, a process known as the 'cut'. In the afternoon or final round, the best and reserve in each class are selected and these then compete for the trophies. The Silverwood Trophy is awarded to the best North American-bred Bull Terrier, the Lovell to the runner-up; there are also trophies for the best of opposite variety and the best of opposite sex (BOS), and one for the breeder(s) of the Silverwood winner.

The BTCA describes the purpose of the competition thus: "to bring together at one time in one place America's outstanding Bull Terriers so that their virtues may be assessed and appropriately recognized. In this situation, breeders will have the opportunity to inspect America's top Bull Terriers and talk to breeders from other sections of the country. They will be able to relate their own progress to the breed as a whole and make decisions concerning future matings that should move the breed forward at an accelerated pace. It is hoped that through this activity better understanding and closer cooperation will develop throughout the entire Bull Terrier fancy."

This could well serve as a model description for the many Bull Terrier trophy shows that now take place around the world. The Silverwood competition has been remarkably successful in achieving its goals. Without question, it has succeeded in focusing breeders and dramatically raising the quality of American-bred Bull Terriers, who can now match the best in the world on a consistent basis.

The Silverwood weekends are now arguably the premier social gathering for Bull Terrier aficionados around the world, attracting increasing numbers of overseas visitors. They are organized by regional clubs using the facilities of large hotels, which provide not only accommodation for people and dogs, but also space for staging the trophy show, the associated national specialty, the banquet and other events. For many people, Silverwood is an annual pilgrimage.

SILVERWOOD TROPHY WINNERS
1990: Berez and Goldberg's Am. Ch.

Am. Ch. Action the Phantom, 1993 Silverwood Trophy winner, co-owned by the breeder, Franne Berez, with Frank and Maggie Alhino.

Action Big Shot (Am. Ch. Zodiac Private Eye ex Am. Ch. Action's Leading Lady).
1991: Murphy's Am. Ch. Jarrogue Geez Louise (Action's Newsflash of Booksale ex Am. Ch. Zodiac Jarrogue Prima Donna).
1992: Smith's Am. Ch. Magor Matinee Idol (Am. Can. Ch. Emred Top Gun of Brobar ex Am. Ch. Wykes Magor Miss Marple).
1993: Berez and Alhino's Am. Ch. Action the Phantom (Jarrogue's O Gee ex Am. Ch. Action Carbon Copy).
1994: Kovash and Berez' Am. Ch. Action Rajin' Cajun (Am. Ch. Carousel Black Tie Windfall ex Action Standing Room Only).
1995: Murphy's Am. Ch. Jarrogue's Jim Dandy (Action Newsflash of Booksale ex Am. Ch. Jarrogue's Ms Jennifer Jones).
1996; Lyon and Smith's Magor Moonshine (Am. Ch. Mere Matador ex Am. Ch. Magor Maggie Mae).

RECOGNITION OF MERIT
In order to recognise Bull Terriers of exceptional virtue and breeding potential more effectively than by breed wins and group placements, the BTCA established the Recognition of Merit (ROM) award and here much credit must go to Ralph Bowles. To receive the ROM award, a dog

must accumulate the requisite points, currently 10, at specialty and supported shows under breeder-judges. The awards were introduced in 1980, though Ralph did tabulate recipients back to 1970. Initially, the number of Bull Terriers receiving ROMs each year corresponded roughly to the number of Champions in the UK and conveyed equivalent status. Now there are more qualifying shows and more ROM winners. Nevertheless ROM-pointed shows continue to foster high-quality competition and the awards have done much to strengthen the base for breed progress. Meanwhile, Australia has instituted its own ROM system with similar success and the Auckland Club in New Zealand is experimenting with one.

IMPORTS

American breeders have enjoyed the advantages of a constant stream of imports from the UK, including a number of the most influential sires. These include the great Eng. Am. Ch. Abraxas Achilles (imported by Ralph and Mary Bowles), Am. Ch. Souperlative Special of Ormandy (Winkie Mackay-Smith), Am. Can. Ch. Monkery Buckskin (Bob and Lynne Myall), the sire of a record 76 AKC Champions, Eng. Am. Ch. Catrana EyeOpener of Aricon (Pete De Flesco), and Am. Can. Ch. Emred Top Gun of Brobar (Dale and Christine Schuur). Bob Thomas has employed his eye for exceptional dogs to good effect, bringing over to his Trebor kennels such outstanding British dogs as Eng. Am. Champions Aricon Chief Eye Shy, Bulivar Real McCoy and Boco Be Good of Aricon; his most recent import was trophy winner Ch. Kilacabar Stand and Deliver (now owned by Bill and Becky

Poole). Michael and Roberta Kaslow have based their Picklefork kennels on a number of fine Brobar dogs, while Bill and Becky Poole (Rocky Top) offered at stud the Jobrulu Champions Yukon Frank and Gilderoy and, more recently, imported Am. Ch. Hillcairn Duke of Terjos.

With such outstanding imports readily available, it comes as no surprise that the majority of leading American Bull Terriers have British dogs close up in their pedigrees.

AMERICAN KENNELS

ACTION

Franne Berez acquired her first Bull Terrier in 1979, after which she spent several years researching the breed before going to George Schreiber and Peter and Carol Larkin in England for the foundation bitches of her Pennsylvania kennels. From George she bought Am. Ch. Zodiac Star Attraction (Benson ex Lady Madonna), who at 18 months was a multi specialty and group winner and mother of ten pups. Bred to Am. Ch. Jocko's Jack Frost (Silver Chancelor ex Jaquenetta), Star Attraction produced Am. Ch. Action Leading Lady and, to Am. Ch. Cinema the Omen of Westbrook (another Silver Chancelor son), the brindle Action Ticket to the Roxie. Mated to Am. Ch. Zodiac Private Eye – thus doubling up on Lady Madonna – Leading Lady provided Franne with Am. Ch. Action Big Shot, who was best white

Am. Ch. Action Leading Lady.

dog at Silverwood in 1988 as a youngster and the overall winner two years later, with his daughter Carbon Copy runner-up. Franne sold Roxie to Stanley and Cheryl Clemmenson, who became close friends and now share her affix with the Action (West) kennels. Roxie has proven a remarkable brood bitch, with six Champions to date.

Franne purchased Am. Ch. Booksale Action and Drama, who was doubled up on Ch. Charlsdon Commander, from the Larkins in 1983. After a successful show career, Action and Drama set about producing no less than ten specialty, group-winning and BIS offspring. From her first litter, to EyeOpener, came Am. Ch. Action Mabelene of Montford. Then, to Private Eye, she whelped the fabulous Am. Ch. Action Hot Item, to whom I had the pleasure of awarding the 1989 Silverwood Trophy. To Big Shot she produced Carbon Copy and, to Int. Ch. Explorer of Prince Advokat, the important sire Action Newsflash at Booksale. From Hot Item's first litter came Champions Birnhamwood Class Action Suit and Action Packed and, in a later litter to Bullyview Rytham Dancer, the lovely coloured bitch Ch. Action Hot Tomato, of whom I am sure we will hear more.

Recent Action winners include the 1993 Silverwood winner The Phantom (the Newsflash son Jarrogue's O'Gee ex Carbon Copy) and runner-up Eureka (a daughter of Ticket to the Roxie), and the 1994 winner Ragin' Cajun (out of a Star Attraction grand-daughter) and runner-up Glamor Pix (by a Roxie son ex a Mabelene daughter). Glamor Pix was also Silverwood runner-up in 1995 with Good 'N' Plenty (The Phantom ex a Leading Lady grand-daughter) best coloured. Franne is currently campaigning Captain Chaos, a very promising coloured out of Action Kit Kat, a

daughter of O'Gee.

Franne believes these extraordinary achievements would have been impossible without her close alliance with Cheryl Clemmenson, with whom she shares the same vision of packing the most power, bone and substance into the typiest compact package. They are concerned about temperament and want their specialty winners to be able to compete successfully under all-rounders by ensuring good bites, soundness and movement.

BANBURY/BEDROCK

Winkie Mackay-Smith began her Banbury kennel in 1967 with the acquisition of Banbury Brick, whom she showed to his Championship. Winkie next imported the bitch puppy Kashdowd Bounce (Romany Rover Scout ex a Romantic Vision daughter). The idea was to have a litter from these two, but Bounce proved so outstanding that Raymond Oppenheimer persuaded Winkie to use the great Eng. Am. Ch. Targyt Silver Bob of Langville. She also leased Charity Cyclamen, a Bar Sinister daughter, and mated her to Silver Bob. To date, nearly all of the Banbury stock stems from these two foundation bitches, plus a third – Am. Ch. Woodrow Carrissa (Jacqueminot ex Ch. Woodrow Minx). Carrissa's grand-daughter, Am. Ch. Banbury Beloved of Bedrock, won the Eva Weatherill brood bitch trophy in 1993.

Through her friendship with Raymond and Eva, Winkie imported two important stud dogs – Champions Souperlative Silver Spoon (Sunstar's litter brother) and Souperlative Special of Ormandy (Jacqueminot). The most important home-bred sires have been Chs. Briar, Barnstormer (1986 Silverwood winner), Benson, Battersea and Bellringer, the first Bull Terrier with both American-bred sire and dam (Barnstormer and Belle of

Am. Ch. Banbury Barnstormer, 1984 Silverwood Trophy winner.

Am. Ch. Banbury Battersea of Bedrock.

Banbury) to win the Raymond Oppenheimer stud dog trophy. In 1976, through the joint ownership of the exceptional dam Am. Ch. Banbury Boothia, the Banbury kennel associated itself with Bedrock, owned by John and Mary Remer; Boothia was sired by Sea Boots out of Banbury Bathsheba (Silver Spoon ex a Cyclamen daughter). Since that time, a high percentage of their dogs have been co-bred, though some lines are carried forward with other associates.

Banbury and Bedrock Bull Terriers have achieved an impressive record in the show ring, with far too many big winners to list in this short review. They have figured prominently at Silverwood since its inception, as well as at major specialties, Bounce having won the BTCA national specialty back in 1969. The littermates Chs. Banbury Buttercup and Briar (Silver Bob ex Cyclamen) were winner and runner-up in the second Silverwood in 1971. Banbury-Bedrock has enjoyed many successes in all-breed shows as well. Perhaps their best-known dog was the brindle Am. Ch. Banbury Benson of Bedrock (Special ex Boothia), who was equally successful in specialty and group competition; his wins included Group I at Westminster in 1982. Since then, seven other Banbury-Bedrock Champions – Bendetta (Benson ex Carrissa), Blizzard (Benson), Bluetrain Bentley (a Benson grandson), Blackbean (ex Bendetta), Browning Automatic, Battersea (Batteries Included ex a Bendetta daughter) and Bombshell – have also finished the year as the number one all-breeds Bull Terrier. As an aside, both Winkie and Mary train and handle their dogs superbly. Cheering Mary and her brace of Bull Terriers on to their win at Montgomery County in 1995 was a memorable moment.

The Banbury-Bedrock breeding programme strives to produce dogs which excel in conformation without compromising health, soundness or temperament. Keeping in mind that even the most successful show dog has a long time to live as a pet in someone's household, they emphasise 'liveability' as a key part of their effort. Their focus for the future is to maintain the breed type and soundness they have worked so hard to gain, while breeding for dogs with good temperaments that are symptomatically free of the unhealthy genetic problems that are becoming such a factor today. By testing their stock they will reduce the chances of perpetuating these problems and continue to breed the handsome, sound, loveable dogs for which Banbury-Bedrock is renowned.

BRUMMAGEM

Anna and I purchased our first Bull Terrier from Quita Youatt while living in England – Kearby's Candy Stripe, a black brindle daughter of Ch. Curraneye Independence. Both of us had been involved with pure-bred dogs before we got Candy Stripe 'purely as a pet'. These famous last words, of course, were the prelude to our showing and subsequently breeding Candy Stripe. She was as sound as a bell and wonderfully intelligent, indeed everything a wise and truly grand Bull Terrier should be. Reflecting our growing interest in coloureds, we decided to breed her to the great brindle Ch. Romany River Pirate. Candy Stripe's litter of nine coloureds was, in the words of our mentor 'D' Montague Johnstone, "the best-ever for temperament and character", and this has remained a hallmark of our dogs. From this litter we kept the solid brindle Am. Ch. Brummagem the Brigand, who is behind all of our present dogs.

Subsequently we mated a brindle daughter of the Brigand to Regent Trophy winner Ch. Charlsdon Commander and got Ch. Brummagem Buffoon and a lovely red sister, Sunflower, who, to Monkery Corduroy of Javelin, produced the heavyweight brindle Am. Ch. Bandetta of Brummagem. Another brindle Brigand daughter, Mischief of Brummagem, mated to Jackadandy, gave us the white Am. Ch. Jaquenetta of Brummagem. When we moved to New Mexico in 1979, Jaquenetta and Bandetta were the key youngsters we brought with us.

Am. Ch. Brummagem Spectacular Bid.

Am. Ch. Brummagem Flying Colors.

Jaquenetta proved herself an exceptional dam. From her litter to the tricolour Am. Ch. Beefeater Black Magic came three important bitches – the brindle Ch. Brummagem Genuine Risk, who gained her Championship in a record thirty-eight hours at the Dallas specialty weekend, Am. Ch. Jocko's Almond Bark, dam of the outstanding sire Am. Can. Ch. Jocko's Caesar of Magor, and the unshown Brummagem White Sands, dam of Am. Ch. Brummagem Bacarole. Genuine Risk, in her litter to Am. Ch. Brummagem Mr

151

Chips (The Omen ex a daughter of Bandetta), produced three Champions, including the much underrated brindle Am. Ch. Brummagem Spectacular Bid, sire of the solid red Am. Ch. Brummagem Gold Dust. Bacarole, runner-up in the 1985 Silverwood competition, gave us the brindle Chs. Ragtime and Flying Colors, best coloured male at Silverwood in 1991. Bandetta's line comes down through the brindle Mr Chips. Our most recent specialty winner, the red Am. Ch. Brummagem Sterling's Bonfire, combines both Jaquenetta's and Bandetta's lines, being sired by Caesar out of a daughter of Mr Chips. In 1996, mated to the young German dog Einstein the Joker, Bonfire whelped a litter of five brindle bitches. We have great hopes for two of these puppies – Brummagem Iron Feather and Iron Cameo.

All of our dogs live in the house as part of the family, usually one male with three or four bitches. We breed relatively few litters, aiming for colour, type with soundness and, of course, the best possible temperaments. Our puppies go to pet homes, where hopefully they afford as much joy and companionship as have our own dogs over the past 27 years.

ICENI

Bob and Lynne Myall thank Phyllis Holmes for much of their success since becoming involved in the breed in 1975. It was Phyllis who sold them the great Am. Can. Ch. Monkery's Buckskin (Jackadandy ex Ch. Monkery's Enchantra). Buckskin's half-sister Am. Ch. Monkery's Moon Fairy (Moonride ex Enchantra) also came to them through Phyllis, as later did the Explorer son Am. Ch. Bifray's Magician. Buckskin and Moon Fairy, along with well-thought-out advice and support from Mrs Holmes, led to a philosophy of breeding and an insight into pedigrees which enabled

Am. Can. Ch. Iceni Spellbinder.

the couple to establish the Iceni line. Bob and Lynne look for complementary physical types, usually staying within their own line, but with occasional outcrosses. They make use of colour-to-white and colour-to-colour matings to reduce the incidence of genetic problems. Neither are Bob and Lynne put off by dogs with outstanding virtues if they are accompanied by gross faults, believing that virtue warrants the risk when sensibly used.

This approach has brought them a steady stream of successes, with dogs they have owned taking four BOBs at the BTCA specialties following Silverwood: Am. Can. Ch. Binkstone Buckskin Maggie (Buckskin); Am. Can. Ch. Iceni Micklefell; Am. Ch. Iceni Spellbinder (Magician ex Am. Can. Ch. Pyreril's Milky Way, a Moon Fairy grand-daughter); and Am. Ch. Iceni Taliesin (Caesar ex Spellbinder). Bob and Lynne have also owned three Silverwood runners-up – Buckskin Maggie, the brindle Am. Can. Ch. Bulwark's Iceni Just William (Buckskin), and his brindle son Iceni Micklefell. The brindle Am. Ch. Garalee's Emma Lou O-Faze (Just William ex a Buckskin grand-daughter) was best coloured bitch at Silverwood in 1986. Her brindle daughters by Magician, who gave much in type and quality to his offspring, were reserves in coloured bitches the next two years; in all, Iceni dogs have taken ten reserves at Silverwood. The tail male Iceni line, coming down from Buckskin, Just William and Micklefell, continues four generations on with Am. Ch. Cresy's Iceni Just Magic, reserve coloured dog at Silverwood in 1995, while their bitch line continues with Champions Iceni Isis and Incantation, grand-daughters of their beautiful Spellbinder. Isis took reserve white bitch at Silverwood in 1996 and then BOS to BOB at the accompanying specialty.

Bob and Lynne express concern that the "strong feeling for virtue judging and against fault judging", prevalent when they became involved, has waned, in their view to the detriment of the breed. They think that breeder-judges should have the insight to weigh faults against virtues, and contend that over-emphasis on movement has already moved us towards a Bull Terrier who stands over more ground, has less spring of rib and has a hound-like appearance. The cobby, short-backed Bull Terrier, in their opinion, is becoming conspicuous by its absence. Bob and Lynne want greater focus on the essential breed virtues that have become a hallmark of the dogs coming out of their Iceni kennels, north of Seattle, Washington, over the past 20 years.

JARROGUE

Susan Murphy has been involved with Bull Terriers since 1974 and, after anxiously breeding her first litter from a pet bitch, decided she needed to learn a lot more about the breed to become successful. To this end, she made an annual pilgrimage to the British trophy shows. Next, Susan began a search for some outstanding foundation stock, which came in the guise of Am. Ch. Zodiac Jarrogue Primadonna,

Am. Ch. Jarrogue's Geez Louise, 1991 Silverwood Trophy winner.

from George Schreiber's terrific EyeOpener-Lady Madonna litter, and Am. Ch. Ghabar Midnight Son, a littermate of The Admiral and, of course, an EyeOpener grandson.

Primadonna whelped two key litters. From the first (to Midnight Son, line bred to EyeOpener), came the fabulous Jennifer Jones (1988 Silverwood winner) and Captain Midnight, sire of Brent Ruppell's Am. Ch. Quicksilver Moustache Pete. In the second, Primadonna was outcrossed to Action Newsflash of Booksale (Explorer of Prince Advokat) and produced another Silverwood winner, Geez Louise, as well as O'Gee, sire of Am. Ch. Action the Phantom. In turn, Jennifer Jones mated to Newsflash whelped a litter containing five Champions, including 1995 Silverwood winner Jarrogue's Jim Dandy, Good Golly Ms Molly and Poison Ivy. In an earlier litter to Am. Ch. Action Wise Guy, Jennifer Jones produced two more Champions, Toughguy and Gambit Girl. Next came Geez Louise's turn. Doubling up on Primadonna, Susan sent her to Moustache Pete and was rewarded with the lovely brindle bitch Am. Ch. Jarrogue's For Pete's Sake, runner-up in the 1996 Silverwood trophy.

The three Silverwood trophies that Susan has taken back to her California home confirm how well she has done her homework in learning "a lot more about the breed". Susan's success is even more remarkable given the relatively few litters she has bred; her comment is "I try to go for the gusto on each one." Her philosophy includes breeding only the best of the best, never using a stud dog she has not put her hands on, breeding every litter as if it is the only one the bitch will have, and continuing to learn her lessons well. When selecting a sire, Susan first narrows down the selection for reasons of health and temperament, carefully reviews pedigrees and then concentrates on phenotype. Recognising the importance of line-bred dogs from the great kennels over the years, Susan is concerned that so few are available, with many breeders today jumping from one big winner to the next.

SILMARIL

Veterinarian Dr Carl Pew imported his first Bull Terrier, the brindle Am. Ch. Monkery Sea Boots, from Phyllis Holmes back in 1972. Sea Boots was campaigned with great success and is behind many of the Banbury-Bedrock Champions through his daughter Boothia. In 1980 Carl and wife Gayle moved to Utah and began to actively breed again. They imported the coloured bitch Am. Ch. Always Esme (primarily Aricon breed) in whelp to Ch. Bulivar Battlestar; this mating produced five

Champions and formed the foundation of their kennel. Mated to Cobra Shooting Star, Esme produced the group and specialty winner Am. Ch. Silmaril Snowbird. Other downline matings have produced over twenty Champions, including Wildeagle Silmaril Saki and Wildeagle's Miss Fresca, as well as Silverwood finalists Silmaril Sparrow and Chiltern Dollars and Sense. Silmaril has also been home to a number of imported studs – Am. Ch. Aricon Eye of the Needle, Am. Ch. Aricon Eye Electrify, and Int. Ch. Quest Giancana. Carl and Gayle show their dogs successfully in both the specialty and group rings.

ZODIAC

George Schreiber's first Bull Terrier, Sugarhill Ming the Merciless, acquired from his brother Jerry as a companion in 1973, was not a show dog but did serve to kindle George's interest in breeding. In 1975 he attended the trophy shows in England and secured from Quita Youatt the proven brindle Esses Countess (Ch. Geham Jeroboam). His other foundation bitch, the red Hollyfir's Coppernob (Dog in a Doublet), he imported from Jack and Betty Mildenhall.

Bred to 1973 Silverwood winner Am. Can. Ch. Paupin's Mr Wiggins, Coppernob produced Am. Ch. Ann Dee's Red Adair, an outstanding Bull Terrier as well as a delightful character. George sold Red Adair to Elaine Bernard, who, with her mother Betty Desmond, owns the highly successful Ann Dee kennel, and R. Angus. In 1979 Red Adair made history, becoming the first coloured to win the Silverwood trophy.

Arriving in America in whelp to Sunstar, Countess produced an excellent litter, three of which became Champions, while a fourth, Signature's Sibilant Serpent, George

Am. Ch. Silmaril Sparrow.

Am. Ch. Zodiac Private Eye.

mated to Am. Ch. Abraxas Archibald (Bonaparte), thus replicating the Bonaparte-Sunstar crosses that had proven so successful in England. He was rewarded with the superb-headed Am. Ch. Zodiac Lady Madonna. This wonderful bitch was destined to make a major contribution to the breed in America and to confirm George as one of the country's most talented breeders. To Benson, she produced Am. Ch. Zodiac Star Attraction, who went to Franne Berez as a foundation bitch. Next came Lady Madonna's remarkable litter to EyeOpener, which contained no less than six superb bitches plus the key dog Am. Ch. Zodiac Private Eye, sire of the 1989 and 1990 Silverwood winners. The best of these bitches, Prima Donna, George placed in co-ownership with Susan Murphy. Prima Donna's first litter produced 1988 Silverwood winner Jennifer Jones, giving George as co-breeder his second Silverwood winner, and later the 1991 winner Geez Louise. Interestingly, the EyeOpener-Lady Madonna litter was an outcross, in contrast to the one that produced Red Adair, which was line-bred to Romany dogs.

George is a keen student of the breed. When he started, he read the classic books on Bull Terriers and visited leading breeders both in America and the UK. He recalls being astounded by the quality and quantity of the top dogs at famous English kennels during the 1970s; this set a standard in George's mind, something to aim for. The late Jim Boland, George's mentor, always stressed breed virtues – going for bone and substance, for strong heads with good width and turn and a correct bite, for that typical Bull Terrier expression plus soundness; for all those things that distinguish the breed. In his own breeding programme, George has balanced the type necessary to win in the specialty ring with soundness. He considers an affectionate, outgoing and steady temperament essential in a breed as big and strong as the Bull Terrier.

CANADIAN KENNELS

BULLYROOK
Ken Lock and Gary LaTour's involvement with the breed began in the early 1980s, when they handled Piranha Licorice, a double Harper's Hawkeye grand-daughter belonging to Ken's brother, through to her Championship. On Joan Davidson's advice, Licorice was mated to Can. Ch. Weise Headstrong Huggable Hunk. From the resulting litter, Ken and Gary took two bitches, Bullock's Licorice Allsorts and the red Am. Ch. Bullock's Brown Sugar, three times a Silverwood finalist, as the foundation of their Toronto-based Bullyrook kennels. As an aside, looking for a name with 'bull' in it, they found 'bullyrook' in an archaic dictionary – in Shakespeare's time it meant "good or jolly companion".

With limited line breedings, they were getting quality but losing size and so, again on Joan's advice, they purchased from South Africa Stryel Lovebite, a large bitch with a long sweeping head plus a scissors bite. Meanwhile Ken and Gary had been delighted with a litter from Bullyrook's Babbling Brook, a Licorice daughter, to

155

*Am. Can. Ch.
Bullyrook
Batteries
Included.*

Jocko's Caesar of Magor, and so they sent
Babbling Brook back to him, along with
Lovebite. A bitch puppy from the former
became the foundation bitch for Al and
Dorothy Bassakyros' successful Buldor
kennels, while Lovebite came up with some
top-class males – Am. Ch. Bullyrook's In
XS went to Betty Desmond and Elaine
Bernard (Ann Dee), Cry Havoc to Sandee
Frascone (Sinabar), while Am. Can. Ch.
Batteries Included stayed at Bullyrook.
(Later he too went to Sinabar.) Batteries
Included took BOS at Silverwood in 1991
and was top North American stud dog in
1993. Through these dogs and two of their
sisters, Ken and Gary have linebred to
Caesar with much success. More recently,
they have used some Action dogs; Am.
Can. Ch. Bullyrook Ayre Myles, a
Silverwood finalist the last two years, is so
bred, being sired by Action Top Secret out
of Am. Can. Ch. Bullyrook Vanilla Ice, a
Batteries Included daughter.

With most of their dogs going into family
homes, temperament and character are
number one for Ken and Gary, with quality

a close second. They look forward to
modern techniques helping to detect and
thereby avoid reproducing the breed's long-
time genetic problems

MAGOR
Norma and Gordon Smith have kept their
Magor dogs at the very top of competition
in North America for more than twenty
years. Norma's first bitch came from Eva
Weatherill some 32 years ago. Driven to
learn more about the breed, Norma spent
the winter of 1966/67 working at the
Ormandy kennels (just to learn), a period
when Raymond and Eva were at the height
of their long and extraordinary careers. At
Ormandy, Norma learned much that has
stood Magor in good stead and began a
friendship with Raymond and Eva that
flourished through the years. There Norma
also met Bill Morgan (Maerdy), from
whom she and Gordon imported a number
of their key dogs, notably Am. Can. Ch.
Maerdy Moonstone (River Pirate), sire of
1973 Silverwood winner Am. Can. Ch.
Paupens Mr Wiggins, Am. Can. Ch.
Maerdy Magdalene (Audacity) and
Bancoup Evan's Girl (Maestro).

The first top winner bred at their home in
Thunder Bay, Ontario, was Am. Can. Ch.
Magor The Marquis (Ch. Abraxas Achilles
ex Magdalene), 1976 Silverwood winner.
This great dog laid the foundation for a
fabulous line of stud dogs as well as siring
many wonderful bitches, including 1980
Silverwood winner Magor Mint Julep of
Trebor. The Marquis produced Van Don's
Silver Chancelor, who, to Evan's Girl, sired
Magor Midas Touch, sire to Jocko's
Almond Bark of Jocko's Caesar of Magor.
Silver Chancelor, Midas Touch and Caesar
all became American and Canadian
Champions and were all placed at
Silverwood in their years, but, more
importantly, they made their mark at stud,

LEFT: Am. Can. Ch. Magor Midas Touch.

ABOVE: Am. Ch. Magor Moonshine, 1996 Silverwood Trophy winner, co-owned by the breeders with Allen Lyon.

with many recent winners coming down from Caesar and therefore tracing back to The Marquis.

The winners from Norma and Gordon's kennels are far too numerous to list here. In 1992 Am. Can. Ch. Matinee Idol (Top Gun ex a daughter of Caesar) carried off the Silverwood Trophy, with his sister Maggie Mae runner-up. They won Silverwood again in 1996 with the young Magor Moonshine (Am. Ch. Mere Matador, who has two lines back to Caesar, out of Maggie Mae) and, judging by the puppy photographs, they have another flier in Magor M.V.P., a son of Can. Ch. Magor Turning Point out of Matador's sister. For many years, like Ormandy, Norma and Gordon maintained a kennel of all-white dogs, then, in 1987, they brought out the brindle Champions Juells Augustus of Magor and Magor Simply Mah'valus. These littermates, sired by Caesar, carried off the coloured awards at Silverwood in 1987. Since then they have bred a number of other winning brindles such as Matador and Am. Can. Ch. Magor Miss B'Havin (a

Caesar grand-daughter), BOB at the 1991 BTCA specialty that follows Silverwood. In jest, Norma accuses Anna and I of introducing the 'brown fungus' – better known as brindle – to Magor.

Their philosophy is never to breed for the sake of it, always to be mindful of temperaments (no matter how exceptional a dog's show career it will be short-lived, as the greater part of life is spent as someone's much-loved pet), and always to try to breed from the best (who will produce their share of pets, without breeding from second-rate animals). Norma and Gordon's motto – 'quality not quantity' – has been the consistent theme of a breeding programme which enjoys remarkable and continued success.

RAMBUNCTIOUS
Kay and Lex Marshall bought their first Bull Terrier, Jobrulu Robinia, in 1976. They had great fun with her and bred several litters. Then they imported another Jobrulu bitch, Cleome (Jacqueminot). In 1984, they bred her to Iceni Gallant

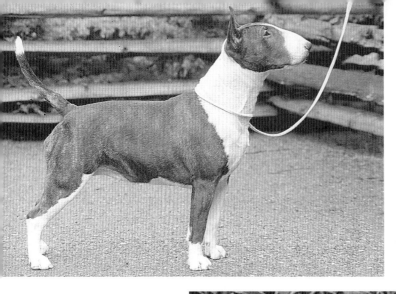

*Am. Can. Ch.
Rambunctious
Riptide.*

*Am. Can. Ch.
Rambunctious
Running Tide*

Phyggen (a Corduroy son), which gave them three top-class Champion bitches – Riptide, Sea Breeze and Spindrift – who are behind all of their Rambunctious dogs. To Am. Ch. Iffinest Local Hero, Sea Breeze produced the famous litter of eleven that included 1986 Silverwood winner Rambunctious Sea Spray, the 1987 reserve coloured dog Readyabout (both were American and Canadian Champions) and Can. Ch. Fair Weather. To Local Hero's litter brother Fastnet, Riptide produced Am. Can. Ch. Running Tide, who, mated to Fair Weather, sired Am. Can. Ch. Rambunctious Casca's Fohnwind, giving a flying start to David and Merna Jarvis'

Casca kennels. In 1991/92, Kay and Lex campaigned the lovely brindle Am. Ch. Spectre's Rambunctious Sea Dog (a Readyabout/Riptide grand-daughter) with great success. At the time of writing they were showing the promising young red dog Rambunctious Casca's Jacktar.

No show is too far from their lovely home on Vancouver Island, from where Kay and Lex set out in their motor home to support specialty shows throughout North America. Their limited breeding programme has focused on sound and healthy animals and has contributed a number of top-class Bull Terriers.

13 THE BULL TERRIER WORLDWIDE

AUSTRALIA

Bull Terriers probably arrived in this vast island continent in the 19th century, though registrations put the date at around 1930. Since then, the breed has gained a strong following, with enthusiastic breeders and exhibitors willing to undertake long journeys by road to reach specialty weekends, which are often judged by top overseas breeders. Annual registrations, though lower than in the late 1980s, are now in the range of 1200 to 1500 dogs. Type and quality have advanced significantly in the past 15 or so years, now ranking with the best in the world. This is a remarkable achievement, given the country's small population (around 18 million) and the paucity of imports resulting from distance, cost and, until recently, the restrictive quarantine laws. It says much for the flair and perseverance of top Australian breeders.

Every state except Tasmania supports a breed club (some have two), most, if not all, of which are affiliated with the National Bull Terrier Council of Australia. Founded in 1947, the BTC (NSW – New South Wales) is the oldest regional club, and its Easter Championship show one of the major attractions of the year. Most of the clubs hold what in America would be called specialty weekends, with a Championship show plus an open show at which breeder-judges from Australia, or often from Britain and America, officiate.

In 1979, the now retired Michael Plane (Xipheres) organised the first Australian Trophy Show, bringing together the best of the breed to compete for trophies donated by Raymond Oppenheimer and Eva Weatherill. The show is staged every two years, rotating between the affiliated clubs. The Ormandy Boxes are awarded to the best Australian-bred dog and bitch, while the Souperlative Boxes go to the best dog and bitch under 18 months.

ORMANDY BOXES WINNERS
1989: Dog: Leitch's Aust. Ch. Westbul Rolling Stone (Westbul Natchez ex Aust. Ch. Westbul Chelsea).
Bitch: Isaacs and Splatt's Nichmari Barbarella (Aust. Ch. Brillywazz Mo Raider ex Nichmari Suzi Q).
1991: Dog: Leitch's Aust. Ch. Westbul Rolling Stone.
Bitch: Isaacs' Aust. Ch. Nichmari Sammy Jo (Aust. Ch. Brillywazz Mo Raider ex

159

Nichmari Suzi Q).
1993: Dog: Hansen's Aust. Ch. Buffington Kicsi Kasper (Aust. Ch. Westbul Rolling Stone ex Westbul Quietsweet).
Bitch: Brown's Aust. Ch. Bargusby Stare Ways (Aust. Ch. Wianna Wine N Women ex Bargusby Lady We All Know).
1995: Dog: Hansen's Aust. Ch. Buffington Kicsi Kasper
Bitch: Martin's Wianna Pinot Noir (Vangelis Driven Thunder ex Wianna Rose).

The National Breed Council was instrumental in adopting and promoting a ROM scheme similar to the American system, though somewhat more straightforward, with two point awards available at any show judged by a specialist judge. The scheme was introduced in 1986, though awards were made back to 1970. During the past 25 years, there have been some 80 ROM winners, placing the award – as intended – on a par with the American ROM and UK Championship. The ROMs are viewed as a valuable aid to assessing pedigrees for quality stock.

At Championship shows, challenge winners are awarded five points plus one point for themselves and every other male (or female) exhibited that day, thereby winning at least six points and up to a maximum of 25; a group winner automatically gets 25 points. To become a Champion requires 100 points and so a number of top Bull Terriers – Nichmari Barbarella and Westbul Citizen Joe are prime examples – gained their ROM certificates but were not campaigned through to their Championships.

IMPORTS

The dearth of imports during the past few years has been more than offset by the intelligent use of those that came in during the late 1970s and early 1980s. The most notable of these were Australian Champions Buzz of Brobar and Barglam Nero of Hollyfir. Buzz, a son of Jackadandy and Brobar Elan, was born in 1977 and imported by the Whitings (Fanghorn). Born just a few months later, Nero was brought over by Morrie Smith (Palooka); he was sired by Ch. Cousin Charlie of Hollyfir out of White Orchid (Maerdy breeding). Buzz and imports from Badlesmere and Booksale made their contributions to the breed in Australia, but these pale in comparison to the impact of Nero. A first-class show dog with 19 BIS and 52 terrier groups wins, Nero also excelled at stud, siring some 37 Champions. This caused Tom Horner to refer to him as "the one that got away". He appears in the pedigrees of virtually all of today's top winners. Steve Isaacs noted that Nero "produced heads and forehand construction never seen before". Even today, on the fourth and fifth lines of the pedigree, his genes are evident. Nero's son Aust. Ch. Kiljarka Kalpa, bred by John and Bev Grace, and Kalpa's son Aust. Ch. Brahma Park Uptown Man, bred by Steve Anslow, were both prominent in progressing the line.

ROLLING STONE

Nero was also integral to the unparalleled successes of Jamie and Shirley Watkiss and their Westbul dogs. Their great Aust. Ch. Westbul Rolling Stone, born in 1988, dominated the breed as a stud dog, producing no less than 20 ROM winners, sons and daughters and grandsons and grand-daughters down the line. He was type, quality and shapeliness personified. Rolling Stone's impact on the breed Down Under can be equated to that of Silver Convention in Europe. Like other Westbul males, he went to a pet home, living 'the

		Aust. Ch. Bulldale Most Noble (Barglam Nero)
	Westbul Natchez	Aust. Ch. Westbul Chelsea
Sire: Westbul Citizen Joe		Zipheres Hellion (Barglam Nero)
	Tamkin Bashful Blonde	Aust. Ch. Bluspec of Badlesmere
Aust. Ch. Westbul Rolling Stone		Aust. Ch. Barglam Nero of Hollyfir
	Aust. Ch. Zipheres Herodias	Charlsdon Bubbles
Dam: Aust. Ch. Westbul Chelsea		Badlesmere Bittern
	Westbul Goldilocks	Xipheres Eliza

life of Reilly' with Vivienne and Sue Leitch. Rolling Stone's pedigree is shown above. This is Jamie's description of how he came about:

"Rolling Stone's heritage contained some of the finest imported UK blood, and his immediate ancestors signalled an impending 'cracker'. We could see the virtues coming together, with Barglam Nero contributing style and unforseen showmanship through his sons Xipheres Herodias and Bulldale Most Noble. Agates Cholmondley gave us neck, depth of brisket and length of foreleg in Xipheres Eliza, who, when put to Badlesmere Bittern, produced Goldilocks, the dam of Chelsea. Another Nero son, Xipheres Hellion, one of the soundest dogs I have seen, was put to Bluspec of Badlesmere, who definitely revised head quality in Australia. This mating resulted in Tamkin Bashful Blonde, a huge bitch with an awesome head. The path was becoming easier: a suggestion from another breeder to put Chelsea to Most Noble gave us Natchez; then Bashful Blonde to Natchez saw the arrival of Westbul Citizen Joe ROM (Spud). Finally, one of Raymond

Oppenheimer's favourite matings – grandson/grand-dam (Spud to Chelsea) – saw Roly arrive, to maintain an unbroken line of six ROMs from Nero down. Jamie considers Citizen Joe the best Bull Terrier they have ever bred."

The Watkisses are a talented and colourful family. Somehow, it came as no surprise to me to discover that Jamie is actually a Londoner by birth. My first meeting with Jamie and Shirley was in Adelaide in 1992. They had driven halfway across the continent, their car damaged by an altercation with a kangaroo en route. However, the journey was worthwhile, as I had no hesitation in awarding their lovely Rolling Stone daughter, Utopia, BIS at the BTC of South Australia Championship show.

OTHER LEADING BREEDERS
On the other coast, the leading breeders are Steve and Judy Isaacs (Nichmari), second only to the Watkisses in number of ROM winners bred. Incidentally, Steve was born in Birmingham, England. Two dedicated and discerning breeders, Steve and Judy have developed a wonderful bitch line, one

Aust. Ch. Nichmari Union Jack.

Aust. Ch. Nichmari Black Jack.

that reminds me of the superb bitches I saw at Eva Weatherill's home in the 1970s. The mating of Aust. Ch. Duncrest Air Daintree, a grand-daughter of Nero and Buzz, to Australian Ch. Brobar Headstrong, a son of Clever Clogs, gave them Nichmari Suzi Q. She in turn they put to Aust. Ch. Brillywazz Mo Raider (a grandson of Kalpa). This produced the lovely brindle Nichmari Barbarella, 1989 Ormandy Box winner. A repeat mating resulted in Aust. Ch. Nichmari Sammy Jo, the 1991 Box winner, who in my estimation is about as good as they come. Barbarella to Rolling Stone produced two outstanding and equally prepotent males, Champions Nichmari Sharpshooter (black brindle) and Union Jack (brindle), who between them have sired six ROM winners to date. Steve and Judy then mated Union Jack to Nichmari Isabella, a Sharpshooter daughter, and got Aust. Ch. Nichmari Black Jack, the top specialty show-winning Bull Terrier bred in Australia. Recently, Steve and Judy mated Black Jack to Sammy Jo and were rewarded with a most promising litter of puppies.

NSW is a stronghold of the breed with, in addition to Nichmari, a number of successful kennels, including Bargusby (Craig Fisher), Vangelis (Sam and Pat Dougan), Wianna (Brent and Linda Martin), Bodalla (Margaret Burgoine) and Bullamakanka (Leon Mayall). Craig Fisher

has bred three ROM Champion bitches, the latest being trophy winner Bargusby Stare Ways, who was sired by Aust. Ch. Wianna Wine N Women (Uptown Man) out of a daughter of Craig's first ROM Champion Bargusby Yangtze. The Dougans have bred two ROM winners, including the successful sire Vangelis Driven Thunder, (almost inevitably) a Rolling Stone son, while Brett and Linda Martin have also chalked up three ROM winners – their most recent being Wianna Pinot Noir (Driven Thunder), whom I put up when judging in Australia.

In Victoria, Vin and Shirley Healand have consistently bred top-winning coloureds, like ROM winners Aust. Ch. Shirvin Young Blood, Aust. Ch. Zulu's Pride (owned by Joe and Lyn Liprino) and Shirvin Grand Deal (ex a daughter of Young Blood). I had the pleasure of awarding both Young Blood and Zulu's Pride their first CCs. Typical of Australian breeding, Young Blood has three lines back to Nero, one of them through Kalpa. Bred and owned by Geoff McCarthy and June Portelli, Aust. Ch. Ziletch Son of Stone (Rolling Stone) is another top-winning dog from Victoria and the sire of Grand Deal. Julie Hansen has put her Buffington affix on the map with successive trophy wins by Kicsi Kasper, who is line-bred to Westbul Chelsea through both his sire Rolling Stone and his dam Westbul Quiet Sweet. David and Diane Cuthbert from South Australia have kept their Maolmhin affix well to the fore, while the leading kennels in Queensland are those of Graham and Patricia Whincoup who recently put a ROM on their Aust. Ch. Melarbro Playboy. The latter is the result of a mother-to-son mating, being by Aust. Ch. Melarbro Dryzzabone out of his own dam Melarbro Heavy Duty (a daughter by artificial insemination of Am. Ch. Action Big Shot).

There is a strong commitment among Australian breeders to taking greater responsibility for the incidence of heritable diseases. The majority of breed clubs are moving towards a health testing scheme, with the NSW club already having passed compulsory testing of breeding stock and puppies sold through members.

NEW ZEALAND

What they lack in numbers New Zealand breeders make up for in enthusiasm and effective use of their Australian and UK imports. There are two Bull Terrier clubs – Auckland in the North Island, formed in 1972, and Canterbury in the South Island, formed in 1980 – each of which hold one Championship show a year, for which they invariably secure the services of overseas judges.

The1990/91 shows were dominated by the progeny of Jeff and Wendy Scofield's British imports Curraneye Ijak (Curraneye Deo Gratius) and Ryaldas Ballad (Ch. Geham Graphite), and by Champions Boltec Private Dancer, Bright Spark and Rio Bravo; all are brindle and white. Rio Bravo in turn sired specialty winner NZ Ch. Pinewood Razamattaz Jazz.

Robert and Debbie Pirika returned from a sojourn in Australia with a number of top-class dogs, including Westbul Xlint (a son

NZ Ch. Tehiwinui Aragorn.

of Westbul Natchez), Tehiwenui Aragorn, Athanasia and Annabel Lee – littermates by Rolling Stone out of their Dorabul Dyne. They swept both 1992 shows, Annabel Lee taking BIS in Christchurch and Xlint BIS in Auckland, a feat he repeated in 1996. Athanasia completed his New Zealand Championship, while his brother Aragorn, owned by Deane and Heidi Holland (Boromir), has been the leading stud dog for the past three years. Aragorn sired both my BIS Boromir Miss Venomous and my reserve BIS Bolio King Cotton at the 1993 Auckland show.

The leading kennels in the South Island continue to be those of Diane and Frank Denson (Catchbul) and Roselin and Terry O'Keefe (Brixton). The Densons own the top-class Natchez son NZ Ch. Orchid Prince Albert, Canterbury BIS winner in both 1988 and 1989. Prince Albert sired Jeff and Wendy Scofield's NZ Ch. Boltec Socialite and, out of Private Dancer, Deanne and Heidi Holland's lovely brindle Thankyou of East, while, to Brixton Watch Out (Ijak), Prince Albert produced Catchbul Splash Gordon, best male at Canterbury in both 1995 and 1996.

The O'Keefes' Brixton dogs have been consistent winners over the years. Their latest flier, NZ Ch. Brixton Face the Music (Aragorn ex Watch Out), took BIS at the 1995 Auckland show and swept both 1996

Canterbury shows. Roselin O'Keefe, together with Chris and Melanie Dalton, imported the outstanding Australian dog Nichmari Guardian Angel (a Rolling Stone grandson), who, to NZ Ch. Brixton High Regards, sired the Daltons' reserve BIS winner NZ Ch. Pinewoods Angels Advakit. The latest import to the Catchbul kennels is Aricon Done by Eye, who has a promising litter on the ground out of Bright Spark.

Back in the North Island, Robert and Debbie Pirika have a promising youngster in Tehiwinui Gandalph, a son of Aragorn out of an Xlint daughter. Deane and Heidi Holland put King Cotton to Thankyou of East and then a bitch from this litter, NZ Ch. Boromir Black Widow, to their new English import Raging Thunder (Kilacabar Rolling Thunder), which has given them a lovely bitch puppy, Boromir White Widow. Visiting judges can look forward to strong entries on both islands as these youngsters mature.

HOLLAND

In 1996 the Dutch Bull Terrier Club celebrated its sixtieth anniversary. The club organizes two major shows each year. In spring there is a Championship show at which the best dog and bitch can each win a double CAC (a dog must win three CACs to become a Dutch Champion, the last one after the age of 27 months). The second show is like the British trophies, with an open show in the morning and then a trophy show at which competitors must have been awarded 'excellent' three times in a row at all-breed Championship shows during the previous year. The club also stages a young dog show for dogs under 12 months of age.

SILVER CONVENTION

Bull Terriers in the Netherlands will always be synonymous with the name of Jacko Bouma, who died in 1995. His involvement with the breed dates back to 1958, with the first litter of Polytelis puppies born some ten years later. Jacko's claim to fame came with his breeding of the legendary Int. Ch. Polytelis Silver Convention and his lovely sister Polytelis Bessie. In the words of Lotte Berg "the Continental Bull Terrier world exploded – wherever Simon (Silver Convention) was shown, he won. And breeders from all over flocked to have their bitches mated to him."

Those breeders who quickly had the foresight to see that here was a dog out of the ordinary got a headstart. He became a terrific stud dog, raising the standard of European Bull Terriers to new heights, siring 35 Champions across three continents and winning the stud dog trophy four times. His influence spread to South Africa and America and then, through his son Am. Ch. Iffinest Local Hero, to the UK. To Jacko goes the entire credit for breeding his dam, Hopelessly Devoted, from two English imports and then having the eye to see that another import Steadfast Thomas was just right for her. The result was Silver Convention, whose pedigree is shown.

Jacko was a grand man, always willing to share his vast knowledge of Bull Terriers with newcomers and long-time breeders alike.

TODAY'S LEADING BREEDERS

During 1995/96, shows in Holland were dominated by John and Yvon van Meel's Kaya From Wishes and Dreams (Gay Bachelor Boy von Donarweiden); she is a Dutch, French, Belgian and International Champion and was best bitch at both the World show in Brussels and the European show in Maastricht. Fred and Karen de Berg's NL Ch. Asphasia vom Kindertreff

Agate's Ottoman of Woolborough

Ch. Hardra's Prince Charming

Ch. Agate's Imperial Silver

Sire: NL (Dutch) Ch. Steadfast Thomas of Hardra

Ch. Souperlative Sunstar of Ormandy

Hardra's Sweetheart

Hardra's Starburst

Int. Ch. Polytelis Silver Convention

Ch. Jobrulu Jacobinia

NL Ch. Jobrulu Anthyllis

Jobrulu Veronica

Dam: Polytelis Hopelessly Devoted

Maerdy Mahmoud

Limelight of Graigville

Graigville Inkey

(Quatermain), a black brindle imported from Germany, was BOS at the club's 1995 Championship show and winner of the Cohen Memorial trophy for best Bull Terrier of the year. Despite the difficulty of winning the terrier group in Holland, the Steins' Didimos Black William (Int. Ch. Mozes Goldisis, a Silver Convention son) has achieved this feat twice. I also want to mention the Champion sisters Quicksilver Jodi and Scarlette Daisy of Serious Desire (Skylark's Noble-Kaiser), bred and owned by A.P. de Wolf-Vissenberg, and Jeannette van Haaften's young Pollyssa's Mannerly Marcus (Quartermain), who won at his first four shows in Germany in 1996.

GERMANY
Long a stronghold of the breed, Germany supports a large and active national Bull Terrier Club, which dates back to 1924. This club – the Deutscher Club für Bullterrier – supports all of the bull and terrier breeds and stages an annual international trophy show (INTRO). Since 1993, a much newer club (GBF) has hosted the Continental European Trophy Show (KETS), at which dogs nominated by various clubs around Europe compete. Winners of the club open shows become Clubsiegers (CSG). Dogs can become club Champions as well as German kennel club (VDH) Champions. Other titles include the Bundessieger (BSG) and Europasieger (ESG), which are awarded to the breed winners at the German Kennel Club's major shows.

LEADING DOGS AND BREEDERS
The current strength of the breed in

Nl. Ch. Quicksilver Jodi of Serious Desire.

Int. Ch. Kaya From Wishes and Dreams.

D. Ch. Brubaker von der Alten Veste.

D. Ch. Egoist von der Alten Veste.

Lux. Ch. Yvonne Royal.

Germany traces back to the arrival of D (Deutscher or German) Ch. Jobrulu Anthyllis, the outstanding son of Jacobinia. Anthyllis was the leading stud dog from 1979 to 1982, siring some 32 litters. He sired the Dutch bitch Polytelis Hopelessly Devoted, dam of the great Silver Convention. Anthyllis' best son was D Ch. Eddy Royal, who unfortunately died young. Ch. Brobar Backchat (Ch. Hollyfir Devil's Disciple) arrived in Germany during this period of dominance by Anthyllis and so his opportunities were limited.

In the mid-1980s, the direct British influence waned as German breeders were attracted to Holland, home of Silver Convention and also of his sire Steadfast Thomas of Hardra. Silver Convention's brindle sister D Ch. Polytelis Bessie was sold to Germany; mated to D Ch. Mercedes Buccaneer (also by Steadfast Thomas), she whelped the famous litter containing the brindle ESG, BSG, CSG, Lux. (Luxembourg) Ch. Explorer of Prince Advokat, plus McArthur and Belinda. Many, perhaps most, German Bull Terriers are now line-bred to Silver Convention and so the challenge today is to breed on without losing the wonderful heads and type with which he stamped his progeny so consistently.

The leading breeder is, without question, Georg Scherzer, whose von der Alten Veste dogs are behind the vast majority of today's winning Bull Terriers in Germany and indeed increasingly in other European countries. Georg put Undine von der Alten Veste (Prince Advokat ex a Backchat daughter) to Silver Convention and got top winner D Ch. Brubaker von der Alten Veste. Mated to the superb-headed Lux. Ch. Yvonne Royal, who is by Silver Convention out of Honey Apolosa (Eddy Royal out of an Anthyllis daughter and thus doubled up on Anthyllis), Brubaker sired D

Int. Ch. Einstein the Joker.

Ch. Merlin von der Alten Veste, who inherited his dam's wonderful head. Georg then mated Merlin to his brindle, Bella Bianca of the French Border (Prince Advokat ex a daughter of the Admiral), and got another winner in D Ch. Quatermain von der Alten Veste. Merlin also sired, out of a Silver Convention daughter, the beautiful Int. Ch. Belphagor's Fairy Queen and, out of a Boco Be Good daughter, the winning young male Zoltan von der Alten Veste.

Yvonne Royal was next mated to Haus Puzzles Choice (Ghabar Greatheart) and from this came D Ch. Union Jack von der Alten Veste. A black brindle dog with a charismatic personality, Union Jack has sired many Champions, including the Alten Veste winners Jumping Jack, Egoist (to Bella Bianca), Nobody is Perfect (to Bonfire Royal, his dam's younger sister), McCoy's Highjacker and Polytelis Red Pollux. Georg is currently taking advantage of a visit to his kennels by the outstanding Norwegian dog Quest Giancana.

Another new bloodline has been made available by Wolfgang and Hermine Bimmerman, who imported from Eric Stanley first Aricon Arum Northern Ruler and then Camquest Theo Sylvander Aricon, both sons of Ch. Aricon One in the Eye. Int. Ch. Theo Sylvander left the UK after taking the CC at Crufts and soon garnered many major wins in Germany, including KETS. Coincidentally, I was delighted to award Theo Sylvander's red son, Ceridwen Gold Coin, his first CC back in the UK in 1996. Having made a promising start to his stud career, Theo Sylvander is poised to become a major force on the German scene.

Spaniard Daniel Meseguer Bernal has been highly successful in Germany with his Int. Ch. Zulog Del Cornijal, a son of D Ch. Double Dutch of Pitmans (Ch. Eyeshiner of Aricon) out of D. Ch. Explorer of Prince Belinda. Zulog carried off the trophies at both KETS and INTRO; his son, Rough Diamond's Hodo, is also an INTRO and a Europasieger winner.

Karin and Rudi Dettmar (Joker) bred their foundation bitch, Liberty's Cholin White (double Silver Convention) to D Ch. Vitus Imperator (a brindle grandson of Silver Convention). From this litter came two Champion daughters, Ambra and Amrai the Joker. A third sister, the red Aika the Joker, was mated to Merlin and produced the sensational brindle Int. Ch. Einstein the Joker – a KETS winner to whom, as a young dog, I awarded BOB at the 1995 Danish specialty show. Einstein's virtues have attracted breeders from many European countries and also from further afield. He has progeny in America, Denmark, Italy, Portugal, Spain and the Netherlands as well, of course, as Germany, where the Dettmars and Georg Scherzer both have promising youngsters sired by him.

In summary, the key bitches in Germany over the past few years have been Yvonne Royal, Polytelis Silver Lightening (McCoy kennels), Bella Bianca of the French Border and Undine von der Alten Veste. On the male side, Georg Scherzer's line has been dominant through Brubaker, Merlin, Union

Jack and Quartermain. It will now be interesting to follow the impact of Theo Sylvander, Quest Giancana, Einstein and Egoist on future generations of German Bull Terriers.

SOUTH AFRICA

Bull Terriers have long been among the most popular dogs in South Africa. Back in the 1980s, registrations stood at about 4000 a year, much higher than in the UK or America. Numbers are now much lower, as they are for other breeds, but, with 1750 puppies in 1994, Bull Terriers remained the second most popular breed. They have done their owners proud in the group and BIS rings, with George Nikitardis' SA (South African) Ch. Foyri Silver Steel of Grechan and Peet and Nonnie Oosthuizen's SA Ch. Hollyfir Poacher's Pocket both winning the Dogmoor Dog of the Year, the South African equivalent of Crufts. The Championship system tends to produce a similar number of Bull Terrier Champions to that in the UK, rather than the much higher number found in America; for example, there were fourteen South African Champions in 1994 and thirteen the following year.

There is a strong supporting infrastructure with twelve breed clubs. The oldest of these, the South African Bull Terrier Club (SABTC), was founded around 1941. In 1975, Raymond Oppenheimer donated the Ormandy Vases (for the best South African-bred dog and bitch under eighteen months of age) and the Ormandy Jugs (for the best over eighteen months). The SABTC hosts an annual show at which these trophies are offered. There are also classes for the best imported dog and bitch. From the winners, the best dog and bitch of the year are selected and finally these two compete for

the title Supreme Bull Terrier of the year.

SUPREME BULL TERRIERS

1990: Molentze's Anwilla's Discoverer of Elmojama (Porthos ex SA Ch. Elmojama Mystique of Anwilla).

1991: Terblanche's SA Ch. Kelavim Kolah (Anto Fortung of Kelavim ex Piketberg Magic Devotion of Kelavim).

1992: Jacobs' Ch. Happy Venture Morning Mist of Noel (Ch. Bonaparte of the French Border at Kingstonia ex Stelron Moccasin Sue of Happy Venture).

1993: Jacobs' Ch. Happy Venture Morning Mist of Noel.

1994: Van Den Bosch's Ch. Jococla Eisenhower (Stryel Roan ex Abenite Woeska of Jococla).

1995: Van Den Bosch's Ch. Jococla Eisenhower.

1996: Evangelides' Ch. Rhinestone Real Magic (Int. Ch. Zulog Del Cornual ex Ch. Rhinestone Rheingold).

IMPORTS

Over the years there has been a steady stream of imported stud dogs from the UK to strengthen the local lines. Typically, they have not been closely related to the available bitches and so most of their litters tended to be outcrosses rather than line-bred. However, with the advent of what Colin Bohler (Kingstonia kennels) calls the Dutch Connection, namely Int. Ch. Polytelis Silver Convention, this changed. Firstly, Franz Stalschmidt went to live in South Africa, bringing with him his bitch Kathy Royal in whelp to Silver Convention. This litter, born in 1983, contained SA Ch. Amy of Keon and a brother, Artline of Delvic, who produced three Champions, including 1986 Ormandy Jug winner Ch. Janfell Poseidonas. Next, Peet and Nonnie Oosthuizen imported Polytelis Silver Birch of Piketberg (a double Silver Convention

SA Ch. Beltone's Big Trouble of Kingstonia.

SA Ch. Rhinestone Real Magic.

grand-daughter), and Gerrit and Elna Dewit brought over the Silver Convention son Polytelis Big Talk of Bonwit. Mated together, these two Polytelis dogs produced Piketberg Magic Devotion of Kelavim, who, to Anto Fortung of Kelavim (a dog going back to older lines like SA Ch. Bruce of Outmore, Souperlative Spyglass and Poacher's Pocket), produced 1991 Supreme Bull Terrier SA Ch. Kelavim Kolah. Big Talk went on to sire five Champions.

SA Ch. Romantic Vision of Imperator of Cramersha (Silver Convention), imported by John and Jackie Galway, was top Bull Terrier in 1986 and also produced Champions Cramerish's Jus Scarlet of Sandawana, owned by Dave and Hilary Harrison, and Cramerish's Jade Magic, owned by Mike Halliday. In the same year, Colin Bohler and Garth Appel (Beltone) sent SA Ch. Riolema Rubygale of Beltone to Holland to Silver Convention, from which mating came SA Ch. Beltone's Que Sera, top bitch in 1988 and 1989 and later brood bitch of the year. Rubygale was sent to Europe again, this time to the German dog Int. Ch. Explorer Prince Advokat, a brindle son of Silver Convention's litter sister. The litter contained the brindle bitch SA Ch. Beltone's Big Trouble of Kingstonia, a top winner in 1989.

Next, Colin Bohler imported SA Ch. Bonaparte of the French Border at Kingstonia, a white son of Prince Advokat and Eng. Ch. Thinato Snow in Summer (The Admiral). With related bitches available, Bonaparte immediately began to make his mark. Besides being the best import and best male in 1991, he was stud dog of the year in 1992 and 1993 and has sired a record sixteen Champions. To Stelron Moccassin Sue of Happy Venture, Bonaparte sired Johann and Matie Jacobs' outstanding SA Ch. Happy Venture Morning Mist of Noel, Supreme Bull Terrier of 1992 and 1993. To Gary Evangelides' imported Dajans Good Hope to Rhinestone (Ch. Aricon One in the Eye ex Ch. Miss Columbus of Dajan), he sired three Champions – Rhinestone Rheingold, Remarkable and Eye Full. To his half-sister Big Trouble, Bonaparte produced Champions Kingstonia Here is Trouble and Tina's Trouble of Beltone. The Evangelides then sent Rheingold to top European winner Int. Ch. Zulog Del Cornual (who is out of Prince Advokat's sister), from which came the lovely SA Ch. Rhinestone Real Magic, bitch of the year in 1995 and Supreme Bull Terrier in 1996.

Meanwhile, Dave and Hilary Harrison imported SA Ch. Dajans St. Nicholas at Sandawana, by Ch. Ghabar Flagship out of Dajans Eyeshiner (a litter sister of Good Hope). St. Nicholas has already made a significant contribution, being stud dog of the year in 1994 and siring ten South African Champions to date. His litter to Que Sera produced no less than four Champions – Beltone Battleship, Silver

SA Ch. Dajans St Nicholas at Sandawana.

SA Ch. Polytelis Frosty Boy of Inkunzi.

Shadow, Haley's Magic of Kingstonia and Beltone's Captain Kariba. To the Harrisons' Bonaparte daughter SA Ch. Sandawana Court Crystill, he sired Sandawana Hoodwink Harry, 1996 dog of the year.

Recent arrivals include Vladimir Skatchkov's Polytelis Flying Dutchman of Dubor and Dave Brennen and Thys Scheeper's SA Ch. Polytelis Frosty Boy of Inkunzi. Dave Harrison and Dave Brennen have eight promising youngsters by Int. Ch. Pollyssa's Terrence out of their Bonaparte daughter, Ch. Inkunzi Lady Vanilla Ice.

BREED MATTERS

In the 1990 Annual, Andre Strydom (Sunduza) voiced his concern about breed progress, or rather lack of it, during the 1980s. He discussed issues such as the variability in size and type and praised "those big, positive, powerful, heavily-boned and masculine dogs" that were by then being put up for BOB – at last, the required type wins! In essence, he was preaching the gospel according to Raymond Oppenheimer, arguing for positive virtues, coupled with good pedigrees and intense quality. He went on to note the faults of the imported Sandawana Souperlative Spyglass with "a bite almost an inch (2 cms) undershot and wry, and loose elbows into the bargain. But didn't he produce some of the greatest bitches (with perfect bites and gliding

movement)...that are behind virtually every winning Bull Terrier in our country today?" Andre's comments were timely because, as Colin Bohler stated recently, "progress has been significant over the past six years with greater depth of line breeding being done. Our top bitches could compete with the best in the world."

Thanks to line breeding, and a focus on virtues in general and the impact of Bonaparte and St. Nicholas in particular, the top Bull Terriers in South Africa are now highly competitive.

SCANDINAVIA
DENMARK

Like Norway, Denmark does not have a Bull Terrier club and so the breed is supported through the Danish Terrier Club (DTK), which uses a points system to determine the top terrier in each breed. About 100 puppies are registered annually. After judging there in 1995, I had the opportunity to visit breeders and owners and was impressed by the way the Danes look after their dogs; typically, they live as pets and are very much part of the family.

Danish-bred dogs have performed well in competitions abroad, though most of these winners are out of imported bitches or sired by foreign-bred males. An exception is Jette and Ulrik Hollensberg's Int. Ch. Firebrand Kim, who was runner-up in white dogs at the INTRO 1992 and winner in Amsterdam in 1994, as well as being top

Int. Ch. Keaton Among Angels.

Int. Ch. Belphegor's Fairy Queen.

Danish male in both 1992 and '93. Kim was bred by Ivy Nygarrd from two Danish-bred Bull Terriers, namely Breslau's Talk of the Town (Ghabar breeding) and her Firebrand Astra, a daughter of Dk. (Danish) Ch. Contango Clown Prince of Hardra and the Swedish import Panzarkrafts Esmeralda. Astra was very much ahead of her time in type, always winning under specialist judges but not under the all-rounders who judge most shows in Denmark.

Top Bull Terrier in Denmark in 1992 and '93 was the outstanding white bitch Int. Ch. Keaton Among Angels, bred and owned by Britta Hast and Carsten Knudsen. Sired by Framajen Gaylord out of Dk. Ch. Grogg Danish Freeborn, she is thus line-bred to Silver Convention. Among her many successes was BOB at KETS 1993. Tragically, she was killed in a shooting incident. Mette and Ole Poulson's Dk. Ch. Keaton Done by Donna, a daughter from Among Angels' only litter (to Aricon Arum Northern Ruler), was best bitch in 1995. Top Bull Terrier in 1994 was Among Angels' younger sister, Dk. Ch. Keaton Belle of the Ball, owned by the Nielsen family, Kirsten, Sannie and Kai (Anzesa), and ably handled by Sannie.

Top Danish breeder Lotte Berg, having owned Bull Terriers since childhood, has pursued a highly successful programme under her Bergalo affix for nearly 20 years. She has bred or owned some 36 national Champions and five international Champions; her dogs have won the Bull Terrier of the Year award seven times. Lotte spent a year at Ormandy – "the best school one could possibly go to" – and then, in 1980, imported Int. Ch. Durena Double Top (Ch. Hardra's Prince Hal ex Ch. Souperlative Spiffing), who opened the door to the Continent for Lotte. Double Top had two litters to Silver Convention that produced six Danish Champions, during which time Lotte became firm friends with the Bouma family. Lotte also bought in Int. Ch. Hau's Approaching Annaliese (Grande Curare ex a Marton's Marauder daughter), who was bred in Denmark by Niels Hau Hansen. This lovely bitch was a winner at the 1994 INTRO and two years later, at the age of seven, was BIS at the Danish Bull Terrier open show. In 1994, Lotte imported the brindle male Dk. Ch. Polytelis Tiger Moth (Polytelis Red Polux ex a Union Jack daughter), who has some promising pups on the ground.

Maintaining her strong bitch line coming down from Double Top, Lotte mated Dk. Ch. Bergalo Double Trouble Angel to Stryker vom Kaiserstuhl (a double Brubaker grandson) and was rewarded with the gorgeous brindle D. Dk. Ch. Bergalo's Tequila Sunrise, who is owned in Germany by Rolf Weidmann. In 1995 Tequila Sunrise won BIS at INTRO and was best bitch at KETS. At Lotte's request she was bred to Polytelis Cross My Heart. With two promising young bitches from this litter – Crystal Clear and Class Act vom Walkenhorst – and three litters on the ground at Bergalo in 1996, we can look forward to more winners from this talented breeder.

The beautiful German-bred Int. Ch. Belphegor's Fairy Queen (Merlin von der Alten Veste ex Polytelis Liberty White) is owned by Marianne Duchwaider (Betterbrand). Fairy Queen was my BIS at INTRO in 1992 and best Danish bitch in 1995; her other titles include WJGSG, DCH , BDSG 94, Dk. Ch. and VDH Ch., which gives an idea of the difficulty of doing justice to Continental awards in short reports such as these. In her only litter, to Union Jack von der Alten Veste, Fairy Queen produced several top-class offspring, including Nitta Andersen and Jacob Bakker's Dk. Ch. Betterbrand the Night Comes Down, top Danish Bull Terrier in 1996. Marianne elected to mate his lovely sister Betterbrand Seven Seas of Rhye, owned by Puk Skov Winge and Per Jorgensen, to Kilacabar Cabin Buoy (now living in Italy with Pierantonio and Laura Guerra), so we can look forward to more winning Betterbrand dogs.

Leading breeders Kim and Bente Bressendorff have kept their Breslau affix well to the fore with Dk. Ch. Breslau's Uncle Jack (Breslau's Explosion ex Breslau's Wonderland), top Bull Terrier in 1995. Uncle Jack is owned by Bitten and Niels Lamp. Kirsten Frandsen's Dk. Ch. Breslau's Wonderland, a daughter of Ivy Nygaard's Dk. Ch. Firebrand Cyros (Quincy Imperator ex Firebrand Astra), was number three Bull Terrier in 1993. Ulla Maindal (Odin) has shown her brindle male Dk. Ch. Odin's Gigolo Is A Gentleman (Jumping Jack von der Alten Veste ex Framajen Josefine, by Merlin) with success. Lizzi and Stig Wolff (Bullington) imported Dk. Ch.

Gay Bachelor Boy von Donarweiden from Germany. Unfortunately he died young, but did sire several good litters; his son Dk. Ch. Binky from Wishes and Dreams lost the 1995 best Bull Terrier competition to Uncle Jack by only one point.

FINLAND

The Finnish Bull Terrier Club (FBTC) was established in 1977 and currently has about 200 members. Bull Terriers live as family pets in Finland – there are no large kennels; about 30-40 puppies are registered annually. Breeders aim for health, good temperament and appearance, in that order, and most dogs are tested for soundness of patellas and hips.

The celebrity spot for Bull Terriers in Finland must go to Esko Kammonen's English import Am. Dk. and Finnish (Fin.) Ch. Hejano Grande Curare (Ghabar Greatheart), who enjoyed tremendous success in all-breed as well as specialty competition, becoming Dog of the Year in 1990. In 1991 he took BIS at the European Winner Show, held for the first time in Helsinki, for Esko and his American co-owner Dr Pat Walters. Sirkku Tuhkanen (Sandinista) used Grand Curare to her imported Fin. Ch. Prettylady of Phidgity (Bercrows Angus Son of Lenster) and was rewarded with Fin. Ch. Sandinista Cicciolina, who was winning best veteran awards in 1996. In her three litters Cicciolina has produced many Champions, including, in her litter to Eirdred's Premier (Ch. Fourheatons the Headonist), Tuija Wegelius' Sandinista Something Else (joint top-winning bitch in 1996) and Sandinista Sugar (a specialty winner); their sister China Blue has whelped seven puppies to Quest Giancana. Sirkku Tuhkanen also imported Fin. Ch. Eirdred's Snow Blossom, a daughter of Ch. Maxdon Hustler at Tiapan.

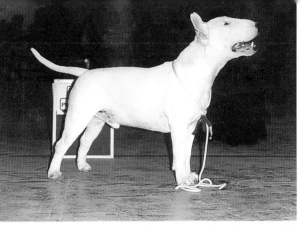

Fin. Ch. Kentauri Yankee Doodle.   *Int. Ch. Hejano Grand Curare.*

Paiva Mantyla (Incredibull) mated her first bitch Fin. Ch. Razorback's Good Grief to Dk. Fin. Ch. Bergalo's Puttin on the Ritz (Grande Curare) via artificial insemination. The only puppy from this mating, Int. Ch. Incredibull Hole in One, took BIS at the FBTC's open show and won the trophy show in 1996. Hole in One has whelped a litter to Esko Kammonen's American import Eaton's Chairman of the Board; two of these pups – Fin. Ch. Incredibull One Iron and his sister One Putt of DJs – have won under breeder-judges. Good Grief was bred by Anne Ericksson (Razorback), who is a long-time patron of the breed and a gifted handler.

Sirkka-Liisa Almgren (Kentauri) has bred Bull Terriers for more than 20 years. In 1988, she brought over chilled semen from Am. Ch. Iffinest Local Hero. The most successful progeny from Local Hero was Fin. Ch. Kentauri Scotch Tartan, a daughter of Kentauri Pohjantytti and top bitch in 1989. Another Local Hero daughter, Silver Agate, mated to Fin. Ch. Eaton's Bosco Be Bad (Grande Curare) produced Fin. Ch. Kentauri Yankee Doodle, the top-winning Bull Terrier in 1996. Sirkka-Liisa has kept two litter sisters of Yankee Doodle to maintain the line.

Albert Muller and Nina Stromholm (Balliol) have campaigned the Finnish Champions Balliol Mac the Knife (Fin. Ch. Quest Magical Savior), BOS at the 1996 trophy show, and General GS Patton

(Balliol General MacArthur) with considerable success. Elina Vanhatalo (Bullskull's), owner of the veteran bitch Fin. Ch. Yungwood Dancing Rosie, has now imported Yungwood Crackerjack (Rolling Thunder). Raimo Virtanen and Sirpa Hopia (Bushman-Rangers) imported Fin. Ch. Coolins Modern Millie, a daughter of Ch. Megavar Moderator, and also, from the UK, some puppies by Turkshead Saracen of Kilacabar. Their Bushman-Rangers Queen Dowager was best puppy in show at the 1995 international show. Anne Landen's Nooakin Arkin Golda (Eirdred's Premier) went BOS at the 1996 international show.

One of the most successful Bull Terriers recently has been the Swedish-bred dog Fin. Ch. Warmasters Christmas Cracker, owned by Arja Lassila. In 1995 Christmas Cracker was BIS at the FBTC's show and also won the trophy show. Since then she has produced a litter to Int. Ch. Camquest Theo Sylvander of Aricon. Nina Lahti and Jari Lahtinen imported the top Australian dog Nichmari Sharpshooter, who took BOB at the 1996 international show. The Norwegian-bred Fin. Ch. Quest Magical Xavier (ex Ghabar Treasure) has many Champion progeny. I had the pleasure of making him best white male at INTRO in 1992, as a young dog, and in 1996 he took BOS at the FBTC's open show. He is owned by Esko Kammonen, Parkkonen and Maattanen.

NORWAY

In terms of Bull Terriers, Norway is a small country, registering only 20 to 30 puppies each year. Numbers are too few to support a club, though there is breed representation in the Norwegian Terrier Club. Fortunately, there are no travel restrictions with neighbouring Sweden, with which Norway shares rabies controls, and so Norwegian dogs can compete there at specialty shows and have done so with considerable success in recent years. These controls are now less restrictive, but still entail a lot of red tape and necessitate planning trips almost six months ahead.

Leading breeder Espen Thygesen has gained an international reputation for the quality of his Quest dogs. He began in the mid-1980s by importing from the UK three daughters of The Admiral: Int. Ch. Ghabar Treasure (ex Ghabar Liberty), Norwegian (N.) Swedish (Swed.) Ch. Blackthorn Princess of Ghabar and Widgery Kathy's Clown. Treasure, of course, has lived up to her name, becoming the veritable goose that laid the golden egg. Her first major bequest came in a litter to the famous Finnish dog, Hejano Grande Curare; the result was Int. Ch. Quest Quiz Queen, who proved equally successful in the show ring and whelping box. In 1990, Quiz Queen was awarded BOS at the Swedish specialty and in 1993 won the Swedish Trophy Show. Thanks to Norway's considerable expertise with artificial insemination, Quiz Queen has whelped two litters with frozen semen. From her first, to Am. Ch. Silmaril Snowbird, came Quest Santa Sangre and Quest Silmarillion Sue, both of whom have had great starts to their show careers, with Sue taking BOS at the 1996 Swedish specialty. Quiz Queen now has a second litter, of three, on the ground, to Am. Ch. Jarrogue's Jim Dandy.

Next, mated to Aricon Sly Eyes (Ch. Aricon One in the Eye), Treasure produced N. Swed. Ch. Quest Giancana, perhaps the most important Norwegian-bred Bull Terrier. Giancana is a top-class show dog and at stud is consistently passing on his superior type and amiable temperament. He has sired 14 Champions to date in Scandinavia. He spent time at the Pews' Silmaril kennel in America and is currently at Georg Scherzer's kennel in Germany for a year in an exchange with Dk. N. Ch. Nobody is Perfect von der Alten Veste. In 1992 Giancana took BOB and best junior, out of some 600 terriers, at the Swedish Terrier Derby and in 1993 he won BIS at the Swedish specialty.

To Pearl (Ch. Swagman of Eirdred ex Widgery Kathy's Clown), Giancana sired four Champions: Rhinestone, Agatha Quest, Diamond Eye and Carat. Rhinestone is a Nordic Champion (by virtue of becoming a Champion in Finland, Norway and Sweden) and has taken BOB at the Norwegian Terrier Club show for the past three years. The breeders of this litter are Espen Thygesen and Lena Sommerfeldt-Ulff.

Other successful imports include Espen Thygesen and Stein Evang's N. Swed. Ch.

LEFT: Int. Ch. Rhinestone.

Photo: Scott.

RIGHT: Int. Ch. Quest Quiz Queen.

Turkshead Duncan of Widgery (Ch. Ghabar Flagship) and Kari Aamodt's Bullyview Party Dress (Bullyview What Ever Next). Duncan is proving successful as a showdog and at stud, while Party Dress is not yet old enough to become a Champion (the minimum age is two years). Kari Aamodt mated her imported Int. Ch. Hollyfir Wild Shamrock (Ch. Jake Hardy Davis of Langville) to Giancana and got two Champions – Keynotes Con Brio and William Tell.

Stein Evang began his kennel av Rootenstock with the outstanding bitch Int. Ch. Quest Fit For Fame (Quest Backstage Phantom ex Widgery Kathy's Clown), who took BIS at the 1995 Swedish specialty. Two Fit for Fame's first litter, to Turkshead Duncan, resulted in two Champions – Egir Eventyraren and Earthcracker av Rootenstock. From her second litter, to Giancana, two puppies – Frederik and Fabi Casimir av Rootenstock – were sent to Holland where both are being shown successfully as youngsters. Both Frederik and his son Grisse Brasse Amigo Mio won BIS at the Dutch BTC Youngdogsday, while Fabi Casimir became World Winner Puppy. A littermate in Norway, Frode av Rootenstock, has won several BOBs and was second best dog at the INTRO show in Germany.

SWEDEN

Four Bull Terriers appeared at the first Svenska Kennelklubben (Swedish KC) back in 1893, but modern interest stems from the importation of Ch. Romany Ringside Critic by Ruth and Olle Hagglund (Panzarkraft) in 1961. Today Sweden boasts an active breed club with about 570 members. Each August, the club holds a major show weekend at which breed-judges from the UK and other countries are invited to officiate. There is a trophy show

Int. Ch. Quincy Imperator.

for Swedish-bred dogs together with an open (specialty) show. In the past, quarantine laws limited overseas entries to Norwegian dogs, but now with lesser restrictions it is hoped that the open shows will attract dogs from other parts of Europe.

The first key Swedish-bred dog was the Hagglunds' solid red Int. Ch. Panzarkrafts Top Hat, with two lines back to Ringside Critic. Other important dogs were Champions Booksale Firebrand (who took BIS at the international show in Helsinki in 1970), Jobrulu Philadelphus and Cockpheasant of Lenster, all imported by Ruth and Olle Hagglund. In 1981, Gunnar Strombert (Warmasters) imported Int. Ch. Falling Snow of Phidgity (a Jackadandy daughter), who produced some excellent stock.

Since then the major influences on Swedish Bull Terriers have been: the Hagglunds' Silver Convention son Int. Ch. Quincy Imperator; Int. Ch. Sonspar Statesman at Upend (Jake Hardy Davies), owned by Ann Christin Granfors (kennel Bowler Hat); Gunnar Strombert's Int. Ch. Wilet The Thing About It Is at Warmaster (Sonspar Inkspot at Wilet); the Hagglunds' black brindle Swed. Ch. Eirdred's Old Jamaca (the Headonist); the Norwegian dog Quest Giancana; and, most recently, the German dog Nobody Is Perfect.

Quincy Imperator, though used very little, sired the lovely Champion sisters

Swed. Ch. Garstangs Mother's Little Helper.

Int. Ch. Bulking's Money Grubber.

Panzarkrafts Swedish Design and Something Special, Anna von Kelsing's Swed. Ch. Whitespooks Grimm (best male 1991 trophy), plus several other Champions. Statesman was popular at stud, siring among others Champions Novens First Lady of White Linen, Warmasters Christmas Cracker and the outstanding Warmasters Yuletide Snowfall. The Thing About It Is has sired a number of Champion bitches, including Siw Linder's Garstangs Mother's Little Helper and the brindle sisters Warmasters Sunshine On Whitespookes and A Rainbow Comes And Goes. Tina Cederstrand has used Old Jamaca with considerable success, producing five Champions under her Bullking affix. Old Jamaca has also sired Champions Special Caribbean Cream and Knucklehead Evolution. Giancana sired both 1995 and 1996 trophy winners, Michael Thompson's Swed. Ch. Sagacious Boffins Shaloderla and Tina Cederstrand's Int. Ch. Bullking's Money Grubber.

Lena Grunden is campaigning her youngsters Bullrup Isaskar Togerhaj and Isebel Tiegeroga, both by Dk. Ch. Polytelis Tiger Moth, with great success. Lisbeth and Lars Eriksson also used Tiger Moth and were rewarded with Topline Buffalo Bill and Annie Get Your Gun. Bodil Granberg is currently winning with Bodils Perfect Maria (Nobody is Perfect) and Bodils Mona Lisa Overdrive, who has Ghabar lines behind her. Ulrika and John Erik Franzen took best dog and bitch puppy at the 1996 open show with Knucklehead Gorgeous George and Graffiti Gal, again by Nobody is Perfect.

TROPHY AND OPEN SHOW WINNERS:
1991 – T: Kelsing's Swed. Ch. Whitespookes Grim (Quincy Imperator).
O: Erlander's Swed. Ch. Warhammer Too Cool To Touch (Penbray's Pied Piper).
1992 – T: Erlander's Swed. Ch. Warhammer Too Cool To Touch.
O: Erlander's Swed. Ch. Warhammer Too Cool To Touch.
1993 – T: Thygesen's Int. Ch. Quest Quiz Queen (Hejano Grandee Curare).
O: Thygesen's Swed. N. Ch. Quest Giancana (Aricon Sly Eyes).
1994 – T: Strombert's Swed. Ch. Warmasters Yuletide Snowfall (Sonspar Statesman).
O: Strombert's Swed. Ch. Warmasters Yuletide Snowfall.
1995 – T: Thompson's Swed. Ch. Sagacious Boffins Shaloderla (Quest Giancana).
O: Evang's Int. Ch. Quest Fit For Fame (Quest Backstage Phantom).
1996 – T: Cederstrand's Int. Ch. Bullking's Money Grubber (Quest Giancana).
O: Thompson's Swed. Ch. Sagacious Boffins Shaloderla.